Beaches of the Big Island

Beaches of the Big Island

John R. K. Clark

A KOLOWALU BOOK
University of Hawaii Press
Honolulu

Photography by
Nelson Makua, Graphic Images Hawaii

Library of Congress Cataloging in Publication Data
Clark, John R. K., 1946–
Beaches of the Big Island.

(A Kolowalu book)
Bibliography: p.
Includes index.
1.   Hawaii Island (Hawaii)—Description and travel—
Guide-books.   2.   Beaches—Hawaii—Hawaii Island—Guide-
books.   3.   Parks—Hawaii—Hawaii Island—Guide-books.
I.   Title.
DU628.H28C53   1985   919.69'1044   85–13971
ISBN 0–8248–0976–9

No nā wāhine o ka moku o Keawe
    i ka wā kahiko ā i keia wā,
Nā mea mālama i ka mēheuheu
    mai nā kupuna mai.

To the women of the Big Island,
    past and present,
The keepers of the island's heritage.

Contents

Maps

Preface

In the feature story of the July 1983 issue of *Honolulu* magazine, Brett Uprichard interviewed a number of Big Island residents representing a wide cross-section of the population and confirmed what he and many other local people have long known: The Big Island is "The Last Hawaiian Frontier," the title of his story. Many Big Island residents see themselves as contemporary pioneers, some electing to live in remote, outlying areas without modern amenities. This same spirit of adventure annually attracts both local and out-of-state visitors, who, although they must live elsewhere, return year after year to experience again in the vast, unspoiled expanses of the Big Island a few days or weeks of wilderness life.

The official name of the Big Island is Hawai'i, but because Hawai'i is also the name of the state, most residents of the Hawaiian Islands avoid confusion by calling Hawai'i Island the Big Island. This widely used common name appears therefore in the title of this book and throughout the text.

The Big Island is a land of great diversity. Its 4,038 square miles, an area greater than that of all the other seven major islands combined, offer something for everyone: It is possible in the morning to ski the snowy summit peaks of Mauna Kea and, in the afternoon of the same day, to go snorkeling in Kealakekua Bay. The island is vulnerable to the action of powerful natural forces that occasionally devastate the land and the works of its people—tsunami, volcanic eruptions, hurricanes, forest fires, droughts, and tropical storms. Two

or more such disasters may even occur simultaneously. In November 1979 a sudden eruption of Kīlauea, a blizzard on Mauna Kea, and a torrential rainstorm all arrived at once. The lava flow closed briefly the Chain of Craters Road in the Hawai'i Volcanoes National Park, deep snow drifts blocked access to the major observatories at the summit of Mauna Kea, and torrential rains caused extensive damage from Ka'u to Kohala and necessitated the evacuation of more than fifty residents of Waipi'o Valley, where raging flood waters destroyed nearly every farm on the floor of the valley. Nonetheless the Big Island continues to attract those self-reliant individualists, people who prefer to live in their own independent way, often in remote areas.

The shoreline of the Big Island is as varied and dynamic as its interior regions. More than 100 black, green, and white sand beaches are scattered along the sea cliffs that constitute the major portion of the island's 361 miles of shoreline. Many of these beaches are not easily accessible for a variety of reasons, including poor access roads, private access roads, and no access roads. Some can be reached only from the ocean or by hiking through rugged back-country terrain. However, it is part of the frontier allure of the Big Island that even on its shoreline there are attractive spots that are still undeveloped and untouched. I explored many remote areas on a 12-foot racing surfboard with a pack strapped to its deck. A friend would drop me at point A and then pick me up a certain number of hours or days later at point B. By using this method I quickly moved in and out of many nearly inaccessible places and covered over 50 miles of shoreline. Although paddling a surfboard alone through unpredictable waters is certainly not for everyone, it was for me an exhilarating and rewarding experience—and helped to make the book possible.

Beaches of the Big Island is a guide to all the beaches on the island of Hawai'i. Like its predecessors, *The Beaches of O'ahu* and *The Beaches of Maui County,* it provides information on beach activities and water safety and, as far as possible, notes on the history or legendary association of every beach. The wide-ranging material in the text was culled from the sources acknowledged in the References, from interviews with the many informants listed in the Acknowledgments, and from my own personal observations at every site. Although the text is a blend of information from all these sources, I assume full responsibility for any errors the reader may encounter. I would like to invite any serious students of Hawaiian history or of beaches in general who wish to discuss any of the material in this book to contact me personally.

Preceding the text is a chart that provides a consolidated description of each beach and the activities and facilities it has to offer. Detailed accounts of the individual beaches, which make up the main body of the text, are accompanied by strip maps pinpointing the exact location of the beaches.

The closing section provides general information on water safety and is intended primarily for people unfamiliar with the ocean and its dangers. Visitors to the Big Island are strongly urged to read this section before entering the ocean anywhere. Water conditions at any beach are subject to extreme change even from one hour to the next, due to variations in tides, winds, and surf. Many beaches also exhibit dramatic variations in appearance through seasonal erosion and accretion of beach sand. *Beaches of the Big Island* points out these changes and many potential dangers.

Acknowledgments

The course of my research for *Beaches of the Big Island* spanned a period of three years and included more than six months living on the island. During this period I interviewed many individuals either personally or by telephone. The information they provided proved invaluable and constitutes an integral part of my descriptions of the historical, physical, and recreational aspects of the beaches. I would like to recognize the following people whose contributions were of major importance:

Francis Aiu, Stella Aiu, Bill Akau, Jr., Emma Ako, Reid Anderson, Virginia Apple, Betty Armitage, Fanny Auhoy, Henry Auwae, Dottie Avisham, Ann Bacon, Nat Bacon, Pat Bacon, Ken Bailey, Peter Baird, Adam Baker, George Balazs, Bob Barnes, Beans Beans, Elizabeth Beck, William Beck, Henry Boshard, Betty Bowman, Craig Bowman, Elizabeth Bowman, Lani Bowman, Pierre Bowman, Mrs. Wright Bowman, Joe Brennan, Chris Brown, Zadoc Brown, Dougie Carr, Bobby Cates, Keith Caldwell, Jean Caldwell, Paul Caldwell, Patty Ching, Val Ching, Jr., Jeff Coakley, Lani Coakley, Lei Collins, Frank Cook, David Cox, Betsy Curtis, Eric Curtis, Agnes Dairo, Roy Damron, Pearl Dinson, Margaret Doody, Bud Doty, Carol Dowsett, Wade Dowsett, Kellen Dunford, Tessa Dye, Del Dykes, Heather Fortner, Virginia Goldstein, Alan Greenwell, John Griffey.

Alice Hapai, Kaniu Hapai, Roger Harris, Pete Hendricks, Beth Hicks, Bobby Hind, Anthony Ho, Bernadette Ho, Bill Hodgins, Tommy Holmes, Floyd Hoopii, Don Hosaka, Yaichiro Hosaka, Lou Huntley, Frank Jahrling, Bill Johnson, Minnie Kaawaloa, Gilbert Kahele, Mona Kahele, Pualani Kaimikaua, Ivar "Little Joe" Kaipo, Harold Kamoku, Pualani Kanahele, Dwayne Kanuha, Red Kanuha, Eugene Kaupiko, Willy Kaupiko, Alapai Ke, Leinaala Keakealani, Marion Kelly, Bill Kikuchi, Cheryl Kurisu, Jay Lambert, Steve Lambert, Les & Zok, Annabel Lindsey, Chris Lothian, Clem Low, Dan Lutkenhouse, Pauline Lutkenhouse, Arthur Lyman, Barbara Lyman, Michael Machida, Aileen MacPherson, George "Airedale" MacPherson, Michael MacPherson, B'Gay Matthews, Mo Matthews, Johnny Medeiros, Billy Moore, Claude Moore, Joe Mossman, Amy Myers, Charles Myers, Dick Myers, Sidney Nakahara, Ben Nary, Just Natural, Jean Nishida, Bob Nishimoto, Mel Nonaka, Junko Nowaki, Roy Ogata, Masa Onuma, Annette Orr, John Orr, Arthur Ortiz, Herman Paakonia, Lillian Paauhau, Muriel Pavao, Richard Penhallow, Thomas Perry, Ilima Piianaia, Norman Piianaia, Lowrey Power, Susan Pua, Jimmy Reid, Jerry Rothstein, Clyde Sasaki, Glen Sato, George Schattauer, Robert Schmidt, Florence Schultz, Barbara Shepard, Jerry Shimoda, Bob Silva, Dane Silva, Alfred Solomon, Tommy Solomon, Wayne Souza, David Sox, Pilipo Springer, Thelma Springer, Bill Sproat, Clyde Sproat, Dale Sproat, Larry Stanley, Howard Takata, Bill Upchurch, Bob Ursal, George Van Giesen, Angeline Victor, Emily Vincent, Mickey Waddoups, Don Walker, Donna Walker, Nakoolani Warrington, Joe Whitney, Jon Willars, George Winsley, Debbie Ziemke.

Finally, I would like to recognize a number of my family and friends who not only served as informants, but who also gave me the encouragement, help, and unfailing support that made the completion of this book possible:

Debbie Abreu, Edean and Preston Barnes, Paul Bartram, Betty Bushnell, Alan "Soupy" Campbell, Jacque Carroll, Alice L. Clark, Camille Clark, Erin Clark, George Clark, Jason Clark, Kristin Clark, Leilee Clark, Jay-nyn Crusat, Piilani Desha, Peter Dungate, Gina Esposito, Ralph Goto, Jean and Norman Greenwell, Dennis Hakes, Jasmine Hakes, Dougie Hooper, Jeanette Howard, Bill Johnson, Pilali and Norman Johnson, Stuart Kiang, John C. Lane, Scott Longstreet, Tim Lui-Kwan, Ross Mace, Kainoa Makua, Nelson Makua, Jean McKean, Marsue McShane, Donald Kilolani Mitchell, Esther "Kiki" Mookini, Kaohu Montgomery, Teddi Mur, Linda Nossler, Diane "Ting" Ortiz-Hakes, Rosalynn Perez, Daryl Picadura, Mike Pierceall, Robbie Rath, Jack Shipley, Carol Silva, Sybil Solis, Bo Tannehill, Jimmy Tannehill, Lynn Tannehill, Punahele Tannehill, Sara Thompson, Miya, Shun, Kim and Ben Tsukazaki, Graley Vasconcellos, Peter Wagner, Irene and Macy Wessel.

xiv

Beaches of the Big Island

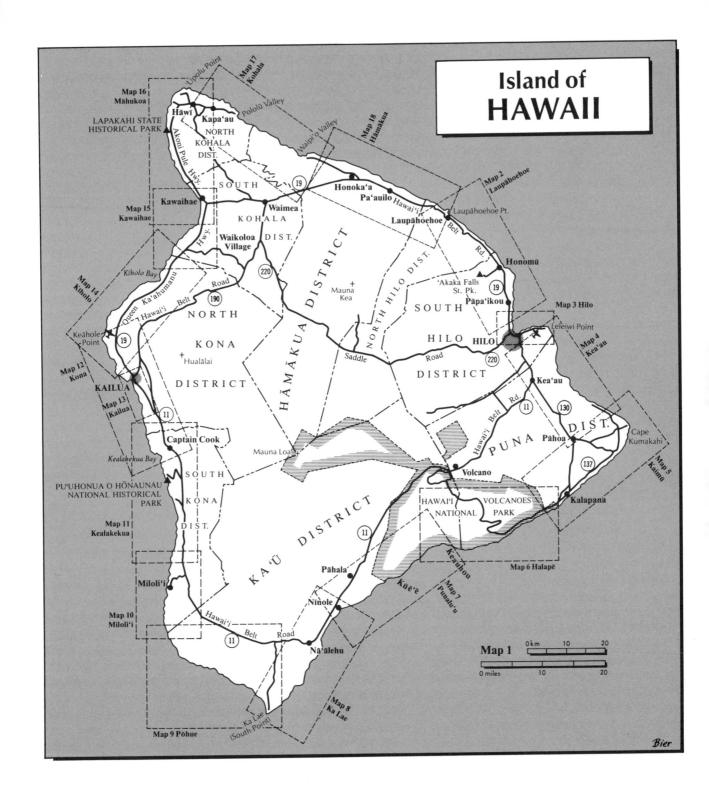

Island of HAWAII

Map 16
Māhukoa

Map 17
Kohala

LAPAKAHI STATE
HISTORICAL PARK

Hāwī

Kapaʻau

NORTH
KOHALA
DIST.

ʻUpolu Point

Pololū Valley

Waipiʻo Valley

Map 18
Hāmākua

Map 2
Laupāhoehoe

Akoni Pule Hwy.

SOUTH

Map 15
Kawaihae

Kawaihae

Honokaʻa

Paʻauilo

Hawaiʻi

Laupāhoehoe

Laupāhoehoe Pt.

KOHALA

Waimea

Belt

Honomū

DIST.

Waikoloa
Village

ʻAkaka Falls
St. Pk.

Rd.

⑲

Kiholo Bay

Road

HĀMĀKUA DISTRICT

Mauna
Kea

NORTH HILO DIST.

SOUTH

HILO

Pāpaʻikou

Map 3 Hilo

Map 14
Kiholo

Queen Kaʻahumanu

⑲

Belt

Hwy.

Hawaiʻi

NORTH

KONA

Hualālai

②②⓪

①⑨⓪

Keāhole
Point

⑲

Map 12
Kona

KAILUA

Map 13
Kailua

DISTRICT

Saddle

Road

HILO

Leleiwi Point

Map 4
Keaʻau

⑫⓪

DISTRICT

Keaʻau

Rd.

⑪

Map 5
Kaimū

Cape
Kumakahi

①③⓪

Captain Cook

Kealakekua Bay

Mauna Loa

PUʻUHONUA O HŌNAUNAU
NATIONAL HISTORICAL
PARK

SOUTH

KONA

DIST.

Map 11
Kealakekua

Miloliʻi

Map 10
Miloliʻi

KAʻŪ DISTRICT

Hawaiʻi

Belt

⑪

Road

Pāhala

Nīnole

Kūēʻe

Map 7
Pumaluʻu

Nāʻālehu

Map 8
Ka Lae

Ka Lae
(South Point)

Map 9 Pōhue

PUNA

Pāhoa

DIST.

①③⑦

Volcano

HAWAIʻI
NATIONAL

VOLCANOES
PARK

Keauhou

Kalapana

Map 6 Halapē

Hawaiʻi Belt

⑪

Map 1

0 km	10	20

0 miles	10	20

Bier

Beaches of the Big Island

	BEACH ACTIVITIES						PUBLIC FACILITIES			BEACH COMPOSITION				ACCESS	
	SWIMMING	SNORKELING	NEARSHORE SCUBA	SURFING	BODY-SURFING	WIND-SURFING	RESTROOMS	FRESH WATER	PARKING	SAND	CINDER	PEBBLES	ROCK	PUBLIC	PRIVATE
1. LAUPĀHOEHOE POINT PARK				X			X	X	X				X	X	
2. HAKALAU	X			X						X				X	
3. KOLEKOLE BEACH PARK	X						X	X	X			X		X	
4. ONOMEA	X	X											X		X
5. HONOLI'I BEACH PARK	X			X			X	X	X	X				X	
6. HILO BAYFRONT PARK	X			X		X			X	X				X	
7. COCONUT ISLAND PARK	X					X	X	X	X				X	X	
8. REEDS BAY PARK	X							X	X	X				X	
9. RADIO BAY													X	X	
10. KEAUKAHA BEACH PARK	X	X		X					X				X	X	
11. ONEKAHAKAHA BEACH PARK	X	X					X	X	X	X				X	
12. JAMES KEALOHA PARK	X	X		X			X	X	X				X	X	
13. LELEIWI BEACH PARK	X	X		X	X		X	X	X	X				X	
14. LEHIA PARK									X				X	X	
15. PĀPA'I	X	X							X	X					X
16. KEA'AU	X	X								X					X
17. HONOLULU LANDING									X				X	X	
18. NĀNĀWALE PARK									X				X	X	
19. KAHUWAI	X								X				X	X	
20. KUMUKAHI									X		X			X	
21. KAPOHO	X	X							X				X	X	
22. ISAAC HALE BEACH PARK	X	X		X	X		X	X	X			X		X	
23. MACKENZIE STATE REC. AREA							X	X	X				X	X	
24. KEHENA	X			X					X	X				X	
25. KAIMŪ BEACH PARK	X			X	X	X			X	X				X	
26. HARRY K. BROWN PARK	X			X	X		X	X	X	X				X	
27. WAHA'ULA							X	X	X					X	
28. 'ĀPUA				X						X				X	
29. KEAUHOU	X	X					X	X		X				X	
30. HALAPĒ	X	X		X			X	X		X				X	
31. KĀLU'E	X						X	X		X				X	
32. KAMEHAME	X										X				X
33. PUNALU'U	X	X		X	X		X	X	X	X				X	
34. NĪNOLE	X								X	X				X	
35. KĀWĀ	X	X		X	X					X				X	
36. WHITTINGTON PARK							X	X	X				X	X	
37. KA'ALU'ALU	X	X		X						X					X
38. GREEN SAND BEACH	X	X			X					X				X	
39. SOUTH POINT PARK								X				X		X	
40. WAI'AHUKINI	X	X		X						X					X
41. KA'ILIKI'I	X	X		X	X							X			X
42. PU'U HOU	X	X		X							X				X
43. PŌHUE	X	X		X	X					X					X
44. ROAD TO THE SEA	X	X	X	X	X	X					X			X	

	BEACH ACTIVITIES						PUBLIC FACILITIES			BEACH COMPOSITION				ACCESS	
	SWIMMING	SNORKELING	NEARSHORE SCUBA	SURFING	BODY-SURFING	WIND-SURFING	RESTROOMS	FRESH WATER	PARKING	SAND	CINDER	PEBBLES	ROCK	PUBLIC	PRIVATE
45. MANUKĀ	X	X	X	X					X	X				X	
46. KAPUʻA	X	X								X					X
47. HONOMALINO	X	X								X					X
48. MILOLIʻI BEACH PARK	X	X	X				X	X	X				X	X	
49. HOʻOKENA BEACH PARK	X	X	X		X		X	X	X	X				X	
50. PUʻUHONUA O HŌNAUNAU	X	X	X	X			X	X	X	X				X	
51. KEʻEI	X	X	X	X	X					X					X
52. NAPŌʻOPOʻO BEACH PARK	X	X	X		X		X	X	X	X				X	
53. KEAUHOU	X	X	X	X			X	X	X			X		X	
54. MĀKOLEʻĀ									X			X		X	
55. KAHALUʻU BEACH PARK	X	X	X	X	X		X	X	X	X				X	
56. WHITE SANDS BEACH PARK	X	X	X		X		X	X	X	X				X	
57. PĀHOEHOE BEACH PARK								X	X				X	X	
58. KAMOA POINT STATE HIST. PARK	X	X	X	X	X				X					X	
59. KAILUA	X	X					X	X	X	X				X	
60. OLD KONA AIRPORT ST. REC. AREA	X	X	X	X	X		X	X	X	X				X	
61. PAPAWAI	X	X								X					X
62. HONOKŌHAU	X	X	X	X				X		X				X	
63. KEĀHOLE	X	X		X	X			X		X				X	
64. MAHAIʻULA	X	X		X	X	X				X					X
65. MAKALAWENA	X	X		X	X	X				X					X
66. MANINIʻŌWALI	X	X			X	X			X	X				X	
67. KŪKIʻO	X	X		X	X	X				X					X
68. KAʻŪPŪLEHU	X	X		X	X	X				X					X
69. KĪHOLO	X	X		X	X	X				X					X
70. KEAWAIKI	X	X		X		X				X					X
71. ʻANAEHOʻOMALU	X	X	X	X	X	X	X	X	X	X					X
72. KALĀHUIPUAʻA	X	X	X	X	X	X	X	X	X	X				X	
73. PUAKŌ	X	X	X	X				X		X				X	
74. WAIALEA	X	X	X	X	X	X		X		X				X	
75. HĀPUNA BEACH ST. REC. AREA	X	X	X		X		X	X	X	X				X	
76. KAUNAʻOA	X	X		X	X	X	X	X	X	X				X	
77. SPENCER BEACH PARK	X	X					X	X	X	X				X	
78. KAWAIHAE	X	X	X	X	X	X	X	X	X	X				X	
79. LAPAKAHI ST. HIST. PARK	X	X	X				X	X	X				X	X	
80. MAHUKONA BEACH PARK	X	X	X				X	X	X				X	X	
81. KAPAʻA PARK	X	X	X				X	X	X				X	X	
82. KAM I BIRTHSITE MEM. to KAPANAIʻA	X	X		X	X				X			X		X	
83. KĒŌKEA BEACH PARK	X	X			X		X	X	X			X		X	
84. POLOLŪ				X	X				X	X				X	
85. HONOKĀNE NUI to HONOPUʻE	X				X					X					X
86. WAIMANU	X			X	X			X		X				X	
87. WAIPIʻO				X	X				X	X				X	

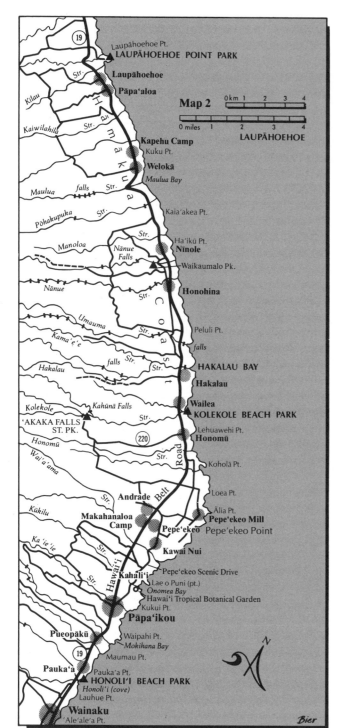

Map 2

0km 1 2 3 4

0 miles 1 2 3 4

LAUPĀHOEHOE

Bier

(1)
Laupāhoehoe Point Park

He akamai loa o Umi i ka heenalu ana, i kona wa e noho ilihune ana ma Laupahoehoe. Ia ia e heenalu ana, heihei iho la laua o Paiea, he kanaka akamai i ka heenalu, no Laupahoehoe. I ko laua wa e heihei ana, hooke loa o Paiea ia Umi i ka papa heenalu, a eha loa ko Umi poohiwi. Nolaila lilo ia i hala no Paiea e make ai ia Umi i ka wa e puni ai o Hawaii ia Umi.

Umi was very skillful in riding the surf, while living a humble life in Laupahoehoe. While surfriding, he had a race with Paiea, a skillful man of Laupahoehoe. In this race Paiea crowded Umi with the surfboard thus injuring Umi's shoulder. Therefore this became an offense for which Umi killed Paiea when Umi came in possession of Hawai'i.

Selections from Fornander's Hawaiian Antiquities and Folk-lore

The peninsula called Laupāhoehoe in the district of North Hilo was formed by a late lava flow from Mauna Kea that descended Laupāhoehoe gulch and entered the sea. As the lava flooded into the ocean, it created a wide, flat point of smooth lava *(pāhoehoe)* shaped like a leaf *(lau).* Hence the name Laupāhoehoe. A Hawaiian legend relates the story of the peninsula's formation in much the same way. Poli'ahu, the beautiful snow goddess of Mauna Kea, loved the deep valleys and high sea cliffs at the foot of her home and often came down the mountain to sport with the Hawaiians who lived along this precipitous reach of shoreline. One day while Poli'ahu was *hōlua* sledding at Laupāhoehoe, she was joined by another beautiful woman, Pele, the goddess of the Kīlauea and Mauna Loa volcanoes. The two were equally skilled in the sport, but Poli'ahu received more attention from the spectators than did Pele. Angered by this favoritism, Pele summoned a fiery eruption and chased Poli'ahu toward the summit of Mauna Kea. But once they reached the higher elevations, Poli'ahu called forth a mantle of snow to battle the molten lava. Aided by freezing winds and a thick cloud cover, Poli'ahu slowly forced Pele back down the mountain until the lava flow finally turned and swept through Laupāhoehoe Gulch into the ocean, creating Laupāhoehoe Peninsula.

4

LAUPĀHOEHOE POINT PARK. The tsunami of April 1, 1946, swept over the Laupāhoehoe Peninsula, reaching heights of more than twenty feet above sea level. The destructive series of waves inundated the elementary school that formerly stood on the point and took the lives of a number of students and teachers. In the aftermath of this terrible tragedy the school was relocated to the top of the sea cliff that is visible beyond the point.

The Hawaiian community at Laupāhoehoe supported both farmers and fishermen. Laupāhoehoe Stream watered taro terraces that were located in and below the gulch, and during periods of calm seas fisherman launched their canoes from the point to fish the surrounding waters. Turtles as well as fish were caught from the canoes with the aid of a special turtle net. Hawaiian linguist and historian Theodore Kelsey described the method as it was told to him by the Reverend Henry B. Nalimu, who was born in 1835 in Pāpaʻaloa, a small community near Laupāhoehoe.

There was a watchman above on the cliff who saw the turtles floating on the surfaces of the sea. And it was his duty to separate and move apart the canoes. At the time that the fish watchman saw the turtle, he signaled with his hand to the two canoes to move. When he opened his arms, they let down the net. The canoe men thrust timbers into the sea splashing water, and the turtle went into the net.

Along the rugged coast from Hilo to Waipiʻo, Laupāhoehoe is the best of the few places where canoes can land safely, so for the Hawaiians the peninsula served as an important transfer point and wayside stop for travelers. Some of Hawaiʻi's great chiefs, for example ʻUmi and Kamehameha I, on occasion spent time in the area, and in later years non-Hawaiian passersby stopped here

5

as well. The Reverend William Ellis recorded the following in his journal in 1823:

Having been informed by our guide that travelling along the coast to the northward would be tedious and difficult, on account of the numerous deep ravines that intersected the whole extent of Hiro and Hamakua, it seemed desirable to take a canoe as far as Laupahoehoe, by which we should avoid some of the most difficult parts of the coast.

After sailing pleasantly for several hours, we approached Laupahoehoe: we had proceeded upwards of twenty miles, and had passed not less than fifty ravines or valleys, but we had not seen a spot where we thought it would be possible to land without being swamped; and although we knew we had arrived at the end of our voyage, we could discover no place by which it seemed safe to approach the shore, as the surf was beating violently, and the wind blowing directly towards the land.

However, when we came within a few yards of the surf, we perceived an opening in the rocks, just wide enough to admit our canoe. Into this our pilots steered with uncommon address and precision; and before we could look around, we found our canoe on a sandy beach, a few yards long, entirely defended by rocks of lava from the rolling surf on the outside.

By the mid-1800s schooners and steamships had almost completely replaced canoes as a means of transportation in Hawaiian waters, but Laupāhoehoe continued to be used as a landing. In his excellent guide *The Island of Hawaii*, Henry Kinney wrote in 1913:

Laupahoehoe (Leaf of Lava) is an extensive village situated at the mouth of a deep gulch, on a flat stretch of land. It has the only landing used for passengers on this side of the island, outside of Hilo. It has a hotel (Rates: $1.00 a day, $10.00 a month). Opposite the hotel, which sells no meals, is a good Chinese restaurant (Dinner $1.00, other meals $.50 each. Longer stays $1.50 a day).

In spite of its importance as a Big Island landing, Laupāhoehoe was relatively unknown to the rest of the Territory of Hawai'i until April 1, 1946. On the morning of that April Fools' Day one of the most destructive tsunami ever to strike the Hawaiian Islands completely overran the low-lying peninsula, obliterating everything in its path and taking thirty-two lives. Many of the victims of the catastrophic inundation were children from Laupāhoehoe School, which at that time was located in the center of the point. Studies undertaken in the aftermath of the tsunami determined that the succession of waves at Laupāhoehoe had reached heights of 30 feet above sea level as they submerged and scoured the point.

One of the few survivors of the tsunami was Marsue McGinnis, a teacher at the school. She had shared a cottage at the very end of the point with three other teachers, Dorothy Drake, Helen Kingseed, and Fay Johnson. About seven o'clock on the morning of April 1, one of their Hawaiian neighbors called them outside to watch the unusual waves. The first was very low and mild, but the following waves built successively higher and receded farther and farther out from the shore. The fifth wave washed into the school yard and deposited a fine array of fish on the grass. The children arriving for class rushed to pick them up, while the teachers returned to their cottage to change. The next wave, however, kept building and building, seemingly without end, and then at last everyone on the point recognized the terrible imminent danger and began to run inland. The four teachers in their cottage bolted for the back door, but it was too late. The massive wave crushed the cottage and collapsed the roof. Helen and Dorothy were lost almost immediately in the swirling water, while Fay and Marsue managed to climb up to the peak of the roof and ride it like a raft. The swiftly receding water carried the roof seaward, but it caught and lodged on the rocks at the edge of the point. Fay and Marsue climbed off and began to make their way inland across the exposed ocean floor, but they had progressed only a few feet when the next wave swept in. Both disappeared underwater, but only Marsue managed to surface. Almost immediately she was pulled down again and slammed violently onto the lava rocks. When she finally surfaced for the third time, she found herself floating past the lighthouse, only the tip of which was visible above the turbulent water. She tried to swim out to sea, afraid that the waves would smash her into the sea cliffs, but she could not, for it felt as though every bone in her body had been broken. Somehow she managed to hold onto pieces of the wreckage that were floating with her in the Kohala-bound current.

Rescue efforts were severely hampered because all the boats and canoes at Laupāhoehoe had been destroyed. But the people who lined the cliffs above the peninsula, seeing the handful of survivors floating offshore, began a desparate, concentrated effort to find a boat. One was finally located in Waimea, but the plantation carpenters at Laupāhoehoe had to rebuild its stern so that the small craft could hold the only motor that had been found.

By the time the boat was finally ready to launch it was late afternoon and the sky was beginning to get dark, but Dr. Leabert Fernandez, the plantation doctor at Laupāhoehoe Hospital, insisted on going out. He was accompanied by three men—the owner of the motor, a skilled diver, and a Hawaiian who knew well the currents and rocks of Laupāhoehoe. They first picked up two boys hanging onto a sodden *lauhala* log. Marsue McGinnis was rescued shortly thereafter. Further search was precluded by darkness and heavy seas; so they had to return to the crowd of anxious families waiting on shore. In the days that followed, only one body was recovered, the skull in fragments, presumably crushed on the jagged shore rocks.

The school was relocated to its present site at the top of the sea cliffs, and a memorial was erected on the former school grounds, which now comprise Laupāhoehoe Point Park. One positive footnote to this tragic story was the marriage of Miss McGinnis and Dr. Fernandez. Marsue's personal account of the events of April 1, 1946, appeared as a First Person Award story in the March 1959 edition of the *Reader's Digest*.

Laupāhoehoe Point Park occupies the outermost portion of the flat-topped Laupāhoehoe Peninsula. Facilities include picnic pavilions, restrooms, showers, a parking area, drinking water, electricity, and a camping site. There is a one-lane boat ramp with paved parking for trailers at the head of a small, protected cove on the windward side of the point. Laupāhoehoe, unprotected as it is on this exposed shoreline, is subject to a continual assault of heavy surf against its rocky border. Although spectacularly beautiful to watch, the surf causes dangerous water conditions throughout the year, precluding almost all in-water activities. The park is visited primarily by shoreline fisherman, picnickers, and campers. Occasionally surfers find waves good enough to ride in the break outside the small pebble beach near the boat ramp.

(2)
Hakalau

North of Honomu the main road passes through the Kolikoli Gulch, the Wailea Village, and Hakalau, the headquarters, landing, and mill of the plantation of that name, the latter lying at the mouth of a very deep and wide gulch, which is reported to have been a robbers' stronghold in ancient days.

The Island of Hawaii
Henry Kinney, 1913

Hakalau Bay is one of the few navigable embayments along this precipitous shoreline, but it is used infrequently, and only by small craft. The small bay and its deep offshore waters are subject throughout the year to heavy surge under normal weather conditions, and hazardous water conditions develop during periods of high surf. At the head of the bay Hakalau Stream empties into the ocean, keeping the inshore waters constantly turbid. A short stretch of black sand beach, comprised primarily of very fine pebbles, edges the bay at the stream mouth. The ocean bottom beyond the beach drops very abruptly to overhead depths, and rip currents commonly run from the bay into the open ocean. The bay is a poor place for swimming, but occasionally there are some excellent surfing opportunities for surfers escaping the crowds at Hilo Bay and Honoli'i. Shoreline fishermen also frequent the bay's rocky points, which are accessible from a number of trails.

Hakalau Bay can be reached by taking the *makai* turnoff from the Hawai'i Belt Road marked "Hakalau" and following it into the gulch beneath the great steel trestle that supports the highway bridge. Also situated on the shoreline of the bay are the ruins of Hakalau Mill, which was destroyed by the tsunami of 1946. The succession of waves that inundated Hakalau in 1946 reached heights of 37 feet above sea level. There are no public facilities at the bay or in the heavily vegetated gulch surrounding it.

(3)
Kolekole Beach Park

Malihini ku'u i ke ana
Kahi wailele o 'Akaka
Wai kau mai la iluna
Lele hunehune mai la i na pali.

Unfamiliar to my sight
Is that certain waterfall of 'Akaka
Water that is set high above,
A delicate spray flying upon the cliffs.

Words and music by Helen Parker
© 1934 by Miller Music, N. Y.

In the long reach of sea cliffs extending from Hilo Bay to Laupāhoehoe, Kolekole Beach Park is the only shoreline park that has the facilities to accommodate large groups of picnickers and swimmers, and so it is often crowded on weekends and holidays throughout the year. Although the ocean offshore is always far too rough and dangerous for swimming, Kolekole Stream that borders the park provides an excellent swimming pool, complete with a small waterfall. The cold stream waters come directly down the gulch from another waterfall, 'Akaka Falls, located approximately 4 miles above the nearby town of Honomū. The spectacular beauty of

KOLEKOLE BEACH PARK. One of the Hilo district's most popular and scenic beach parks, Kolekole is located below a massive highway bridge. The Hawaii Consolidated Railway Company constructed the bridge as part of its Hilo-to-Hamakua line. The structure was converted for use by automobiles during the late 1940s.

8

'Akaka Falls has been the source of inspiration for many poets and song writers, particularly among the Hawaiians, and is one of the Big Island's most famous scenic attractions. The tremendous volume of water that cascades over the falls flows swiftly downstream and meets the ocean at Kolekole Beach Park.

A small rocky beach composed of pebbles and cobblestones at the stream mouth provides only a meager barrier between the ocean and the natural swimming pool in the park. High surf easily washes over the beach, flooding into the pool; the resulting agitation occasionally discourages swimmers. At such times, walking on the rocky beach can be very dangerous. Loose rocks hauled up by the waves can cause painful leg injuries, and the powerful surge can knock waders down and carry them offshore. Swimmers in the stream and divers from the banks should be alert for the submerged boulders that are often almost invisible in the murky water, and they should also avoid the strong currents around the stream mouth where the fresh water flows unobstructed into the ocean.

The black sand beach in the park lies directly beneath a massive highway bridge 100 feet high. The bridge spans the width of the gulch and was formerly used by the Hawaii Consolidated Railway. The tsunami waves of 1946 swept into the gulch at heights of 37 feet above sea level, carried away girders from the middle span of the steel bridge, and left the rails suspended without support. This catastrophe, coupled with destruction to many other sections of the line, put the railroad out of business. The county purchased the bridge, rebuilt it, and incorporated the structure into the Hilo-to-Honoka'a section of the Hawai'i Belt Highway, which was started in 1947.

Kolekole Beach Park's abundance of lush vegetation, including many large trees, and its setting against both stream and ocean combine to make it one of the Big Island's most popular shoreline parks. Many special occasions are celebrated by groups of friends, families, and organizations in the park's five picnic pavilions. The newer of the two large pavilions was named the Epy Yadao Pavilion in 1972 by the Hawai'i County Council, in memory of Elias P. (Epy) Yadao, a former county supervisor. One of his many accomplishments as a community leader and as a member of the county board of supervisors from 1959 until his death in 1966 was to obtain funds for the erection of the building named posthumously in his honor.

Other park facilities include restrooms, paved parking, drinking water, showers, electricity, picnic tables, barbecue grills, a large grassy field, and a camping area. A sign on the Hawai'i Belt Highway marks the turnoff to the park.

(4)
Onomea

This place is grandly situated 600 feet above a deep cove, into which two beautiful gulches of great size run, with heavy cascades, finer than Foyers at its best, and a native village is picturesquely situated between the two. The great white rollers, whiter by contrast with the dark deep water, come into the gulch just where we forded the river, and from the ford a passable road made for hauling sugar ascends to the house.

The plantations in the Hilo district enjoy special advantages, for by turning some of the innumerable mountain streams into flumes the owners can bring a great part of the their cane and all their wood for fuel down to the mills without other expense than the original cost of the woodwork. Mr. A. has 100 mules, but the greater part of their work is ploughing and hauling the kegs of sugar down to the cove, where in favourable weather they are put on board of a schooner for Honolulu.

Six Months in the Sandwich Islands
Isabella L. Bird

During Isabella Bird's visit to the Big Island in 1873, she made a number of excursions to some of the remotest parts of the island. While traveling on horseback from Hilo to Waipi'o, she spent several days as a guest at a sugar plantation. Her lodgings looked down into Onomea Bay, the plantation's port, where the village of Kahali'i was located on a large point of land extending into the bay. Formerly a Hawaiian fishing village, Kahali'i became a shipping terminal for schooners and steamers until the railroad line from Hilo to Pa'auilo was completed. Rail service eliminated the need for large ships to stop at many of the rough-water landings along this preciptious coastline. The Hawaii Consolidated Railway, which began operations in 1899, was put out of business when the tsunami of 1946 severely crippled the entire line. Although some evidence of the former village still remains, the tsunami waves reached heights of 35 feet above sea level in Onomea Bay and scoured the entire area.

Though the village is gone, former residents of Kahali'i still recall some of the old legends of the area's landmarks. One legend tells of the origin of two large rock formations at the head of Onomea Bay that were said to have been a young man and woman known as the lovers of Kahali'i. One day one of the chiefs of the village spotted many canoes with sails heading shoreward in their direction. Fearing an attack, the chiefs and the family elders held a council to determine a course of action and decided to build a reef to prevent a landing on their beaches. Not having the means to complete the task quickly enough, they asked that a young man and a young woman be the guides and protectors of the village by giving their lives. Two willing individuals were found.

That night a decree was sent to all who lived at Kahali'i to remain indoors from sunset to sunrise without making any light or sound, on penalty of death. During the darkest hour of the night steps were heard walking through the village, and then silence prevailed until morning. In the light of the new day, the people moved down to the shoreline where they were amazed to find the lovers gone, and in their place two gigantic rock formations at the entrance to the bay, along with many other smaller rocks strewn about, as if on guard. The chief informed the people that no canoe could pass the treacherous currents swirling around the rocks unless allowed to do so by the guardians. The lovers and their offspring still stand today, sentinels at the head of the bay.

One of the other famous landmarks at the entrance to the bay was Onomea Arch, a sea arch that had been cut by thousands of years of wave action through an old cinder cone remnant. In his book *The Island of Hawaii* Henry Kinney described the village and the arch as they appeared in 1913:

It [the road] passes above the Onomea settlement, one of the more easily accessible typical Hawaiian villages, with grass houses, taro patches, cocoanut, mango and breadfruit trees, canoes, etc. Trails lead down into it on both the north and south side, it being possible to ride down one, and up the other. The north trail continues right up to the railroad station. In the sea makai of the settlement is the kane stone, said to have been placed there by Kane, the Hawaiian creator. The main sight, however, is Onomea Arch, a great natural bridge at the end of the cliff on the north side of the village, which is famous for its beauty and its unique formation.

Located at the north point of the bay, the much photographed scenic attraction collapsed on the morning of May 24, 1956, when the center portion cracked, buckled upward, and then quickly fell in.

In 1978 Dan Lutkenhouse, a retired businessman from San Francisco, and his wife Pauline came to the Big Island to make their home. While scouting locations on the island with realtor Richard Penhallow, they traveled along the 4-mile scenic drive between Honomū and Papa'ikou, which passes Onomea Bay. Immediately taken by the overwhelming beauty of the area, they found that Penhallow himself, during the previous twenty-five years had acquired many small parcels in Onomea, and consolidated them into one large piece of property that he was willing to sell. They purchased it from him and at the same time bought a house and lot several miles away at Honoli'i.

The Lutkenhouses decided that their Onomea property should never be sold or developed and that the bay should always remain as a focal point of natural beauty along the scenic drive. With that end in mind, they created the Hawai'i Tropical Botanical Garden, a nonprofit organization approved by the I.R.S. Here in the gardens are propagated native Hawaiian plants in a natural, informal setting on the tree-covered point where Kahali'i village once stood. The extensive collection of tropical plants includes also palms, bromeliads, gingers, heliconias, and many other exotic trees and fruit trees. Improvements to the area have been limited to maintaining the existing access road to the bay and clearing trails and walkways. The garden opened to the public in August 1984.

Directly above Onomea Bay a colonnade of Alexandra palms lines the scenic drive overlooking the ocean. These magnificent trees were planted between 1912 and 1922 under the direction of Manuel Tavares who for many years was the superintendent of public parks for the Big Island. Tavares, born in the Azores, came to Hawai'i with his parents in 1882 and settled in the village of Honomū. His interest in horticulture led him into the parks department, where in later years as superintendent he did much to improve the beauty of all of the Big Island's parks. The original plantings of shower trees at Kolekole Beach Park as well as the Alexandra palms at Onomea are attributed to his efforts. Native to northern Queensland, Australia, these beautiful palms come from a climate similar to that of windward Hawai'i. There were named in honor of Queen Alexandra, consort of King Edward VII of England. The palms were presented to Alexandra during a trip the royal couple made to Australia to mark the continent's emergence as a part of the British Commonwealth.

The shoreline of Onomea Bay consists of an irregular series of rocky points and coves. Three of the larger coves are headed by pebble and cobblestone beaches, but the rocky shoreline and normally rough water conditions usually preclude most in-water activities. Shoreline fishing is the most popular attraction of the bay.

The smallest cove in the bay borders the northern side of the garden. It was cut by Kūkilu Stream, the only perennial stream in Onomea Bay. The "Living Waters of Kūkilu" is a well-known legend of the area that tells why this particular stream never stops flowing. Long ago a family lived near the cliff of Kahali'i Valley. They were not rich and had few material possessions, but were always friendly and kind. One day a tired old man knocked on their door; so they asked him in, saw to his comfort, and bid him stay until he felt better.

Many days passed and it seemed that the stranger ate so much that there would not be enough food to last another meal, but the family never complained, always seeing to the elder's wants. Finally the time came when the man and his wife, Kauwa and Luahine, had to tell the stranger that they had to leave him to seek food. The stranger said to them, "Go and seek what you will find. May the gods be kind to you as you have been to me. Your love and kindness will always be the biggest blessings to you both."

Luahine and Kauwa and their children traveled far and were always received by strangers with warmth and friendship. They finally passed through Waipi'o where the chief himself saw to their comfort. Then the chief presented them with a war club and said, "I have been waiting for you. I know you have spent many days working to feed my father who has gone to see whom he could help before he returns to the gods. You have served him well. Now you must take this war club and return to Kahali'i."

On returning to their home, they found the stranger almost lifeless, but at their approach he opened his eyes and whispered, "My children, you have returned." "Yes," Kauwa replied, "and we will bring you back to life again so that you may remain many months more." The old man answered, "No, do not keep me long. I have done what I have set out to do, but do this for me that you will remember all of my good deeds. When the spirit has left my body, take me to the spot where the 'ili'ili are small and soft, with their sand as a cushion. Place me beside the stream covered in the tapa that Luahine has made. Then travel to the mountain and find the headwater to the stream. Strike the ground three times. Then return to me and hit the ground where I lie three times also. Nevermore will you need to travel to look for food and water. And there will always be enough to share." So saying, the old man closed his eyes for the last time. Kauwa and Luahine then followed his instructions. That is why Kūkilu Stream has never stopped providing water for the gardens and people of Kahali'i.

Onomea Bay is one of the few places on the coast of the Big Island where red-colored lava is present on the shoreline, and it is particularly conspicuous in the cliff face on the northern side of the bay. Along Kūkilu Stream's course to the sea, its waters cut through a vein of red cinder and transport the eroded material to the head of the cove where it forms the only red sand beach on the island of Hawai'i. The tiny pocket of red sand is fronted by a very shallow, rocky shelf which offers very poor swimming conditions, but a small pond in the stream to the rear of the beach is adequate for children.

No public facilities exist on the shoreline, and there is no convenient public access.

(5)
Honoli'i Beach Park

Pau ku'u aho i na kahawai o Hilo,
He lau ka pu'u, he mano ka ihona
He mano na kahawai o Kula'imano.
He wai o Honoli'i, he pali o Kama'e
He pali no Hilo pali ku.

I lose my breath crossing Hilo region's rivers and ravines,
Countless hills, descents innumerable as I travel.
Kula'imano's gullies and streams.
There's Honoli'i Stream and the cliff called Kama'e,
Single cliff among many in spacious Hilo-of-the-
    standing-cliffs.

Pele and Hi'iaka
Emerson, 1915

The beautiful little river valley of Honoli'i was once the site of a small Hawaiian fishing village; most of the community was concentrated along the borders of Honoli'i Stream between the river mouth and the present highway bridge. A few isolated homes were located farther *mauka* in the valley. The place name Honoli'i is usually translated as "little valley," but Hawaiians from the community say that *hono* in this instance means to sew or patch, as a fishnet, so Honoli'i means a "small weave" or a "little patch."

Fishermen launched their canoes directly into the stream and proceeded either out to sea to fish or down the coast, often into Hilo Bay. The stream estuary also provided a wide variety of seafood, including *'ōpae, wī, limu 'ele'ele, āholehole,* mullet, and *'o'opu.* The *'o'opu nāwao* often grew to a foot long and were considered a great delicacy. One of the common freshwater fishing methods used to catch *'o'opu* was described for Theodore Kelsey in the 1920s by the Reverend Henry B. Nalimu, who was born in Pāpa'aloa in 1883.

Go with the pai, a kind of fishnet. It is a funnel-shaped basket for pond fishing. It is also called a hinai luuluu. It had a mouth above, or else at the side, into which shrimp (opae) was placed for bait. The bait was bundled solidly in a niu, or coconut cloth, then tied solidly in the fishnet. Place a stone in the bottom of the net. Tie the net fast with cord or rope, and take it and let it down in the middle of a deep part of the pond. The surface of the water is deep blue. Use cord of hau bark or of olona, perhaps, or

perhaps wauke. Aholehole, oopu nawao, and anae enter. Let it stay until early morning, then pull it up onto the canoe and go.

During and after heavy rains huge *ulua* swam upcurrent directly into the flooding stream waters in search of anything edible that might be washing down, particularly *'o'opu.* The fishermen then caught the *ulua* with nets and spears, but not without a hard fight. Extremely heavy flooding would completely wash away the pebble-and-sand beach at the mouth of Honoli'i, leaving only boulders on the shoreline, but the sand always returned carried back by the prevailing currents. This cycle gave rise to a well-known epithet, *'ili'ili hele o Honoli'i,* the "traveling sands of Honoli'i." A long-time resident of the area stated that when the beach sand barricaded the river mouth completely, it was a sign of death. Many strange stories are told about the area, especially by fishermen who have been involved in or witnessed unusual incidents and sightings. The *wiliau,* or rip current, at Honoli'i follows a predictable course under ordinary ocean conditions, moving out to sea and then circling into the left point of the bay. Over the years, it has deposited the bodies of many drowning victims each time in almost exactly the same spot.

'Āweu taro, prized for its leaves which are excellent for cooking, grew plentifully in the *mauka* areas, along with *hō'i'o,* a large native fern, the young fronds of which are eaten raw with *'ōpae.* On rare occasions during times of drought, Honoli'i Stream would stop flowing, but a spring which still exists on the Lutkenhouse property, provided a steady source of fresh water. The entire community was self-sufficient, living off the land, the river, and the sea.

During the 1920s and the 1930s, the young people of Honoli'i began leaving the area. Not content with a simple subsistence style of life, they headed for the lights of Hawai'i's port cities.

The old ways were gradually abandoned, and the tragedy is expressed in a story about the *limu 'ele'ele,* a very fine-leafed seaweed that once grew plentifully on the flat rocks around the stream mouth, where the fresh water flows into the ocean. Honoli'i was noted for this *limu,* for in taste, color, and texture it was said to be far superior to that from any other part of the island. The

HONOLI'I BEACH PARK. The surfing breaks at Honoli'i provide some of the most consistently ridable waves for Hilo's surfers. During periods of high surf many spectators line the street above the beach to watch the action. Honoli'i Stream flows into the ocean along the heavily vegetated northern point of the beach.

women of the village harvested the seaweed, but by tradition were prohibited from this activity during their menstrual period. At some time just prior to World War II, however, someone disregarded the restriction, picked the seaweed during her menstrual period, and the famous *limu 'ele'ele* of Honoli'i disappeared, never to return.

The final blow to the community was delivered by the tsunami of 1946, which leveled all of the homes in its path and destroyed the fishing canoes as well. A handful of families rebuilt, but the old ways gave way to the new. In the years that followed most of the Hawaiians moved elsewhere as new owners acquired the land. Today only a few residences are left in the valley.

During the 1960s surfers began finding their way to Honoli'i, hiking down the cliffs from the road above, to ride the waves offshore from the beach. As the traffic across this private property increased, the Bishop Estate, which owned the land, offered to lease the area to the County of Hawaii for development as a public beach park. In October 1969, after the lease arrangements had been completed, a Buddhist groundbreaking ceremony was held to bless the land and chase away any evil spirits. Performing the purification rites was a priest from the Hilo Meisho Mission. The park facilities were completed in 1970.

The beach at Honoli'i is composed primarily of black detrital sand and pebbles that have been eroded from areas *mauka* and transported *makai* by Honoli'i Stream. Liberally mixed in with the sand are tiny quartz-like particles that sparkle in the sun and a considerable amount of well-rounded pieces of beach glass. At the northern end of the beach, where the stream meets the sea, *'ili'ili* dominates and forms a partial barrier between the ocean and a very large pond at the stream mouth. The pond provides an excellent swimming area, especially for the little children, but it is deep and drops off very abruptly. The pond is also popular with throw-net and shoreline fishermen.

The surf at Honoli'i breaks directly offshore of the beach over a bottom strewn with boulders. Rip currents and longshore currents are common and are particularly strong when they combine with the cold waters discharged by Honoli'i Stream. The nearshore ocean bottom drops quickly to overhead depths, and so recreational swimming there is not common. The area is frequented primarily by surfers who ride not only the waves offshore of the beach, but also a break outside the northern point of the bay. Others using the beach are sunbathers and fishermen, and spectators often line the road above the beach to watch the surfing activity directly below. Honoli'i is one of the most popular surfing breaks in the Hilo area.

Honoli'i Beach Park can be reached by turning off the Belt Highway at Nāhala Street in the 'Alae subdivision or by turning *mauka* at Pauka'a and following the old road. Facilities include restrooms, showers, roadside parking, and a paved path from the road down the bluff to the beach. From the time they were built, the park facilities have been the victims of almost constant vandalism; so the plumbing fixtures are often broken or non-operational.

Two small pockets of black sand are located between Honoli'i Beach Park and Hilo Bay. The first lies below the Wainaku Sugar Mill, a very imposing structure with its massive, fortress-like, rock retaining wall. The beach is composed of an interesting variety of materials including boulders, pebbles, black, red, and tan sand grains, olivines, beach glass, driftwood, and other debris. The second small beach along this reach lies below the highway bridge at Pūkīhae and consists primarily of black sand with a sprinkling of olivines and beach glass.

Neither of these beaches offers attractive swimming conditions. Both are exposed to the direct assault of waves from the open ocean and subject to strong currents and periodically high surf.

(6)
Hilo Bayfront Park

If you are so fortunate as to enter the bay on a fine day, you will see a very tropical landscape—a long, pleasant, curved sweep of beach, on which the surf is breaking, and beyond, white houses nestling among cocoa-nut groves, and bread-fruit, pandanus, and other Southern trees, with shops and stores along the beach. Men bathing in the surf, and men and women dashing on horseback over the beach, make up the life of the scene.

Hawaii Nei
Charles Nordhoff, 1873

The sweep of black sand described by Charles Nordhoff, a visitor in 1872, still exists on the shores of Hilo Bay, although the length and width of the beach have diminished considerably since the nineteenth century. The beach formerly stretched from the Wailuku River to the Wailoa River and served the city of Hilo as an unofficial community center. Isabella Bird, who visited the Big Island in 1873, described the leisure activities enjoyed at Hilo's seashore in her narrative *Six Months in the Sandwich Islands*. When she arrived in Hilo Bay on board the steamer *Kīlauea*, "Canoes came off from the shore, dusky swimmers glided through the water, youths, athletes, like the bronzes of the Naples Museum, rode the waves on their surf-boards, brilliantly dressed riders galloped along the sands and came trooping down the bridle-paths from all the vicinity till a many-coloured tropical crowd had assembled at the landing."

In addition to being a recreational center for the town of Hilo, the black sand beach, prior to 1863, was also used as the principal landing for passengers and cargo. Ships anchored offshore in Hilo Bay, and small boats and canoes served as lighters between the ships and the beach. A landing had been constructed on the Wailoa River at Waiakea as early as the 1840s, but Waiakea was considered too far from Hilo town to be convenient for visitors and merchants. In 1863 construction of a wharf at the foot of Waianuenue Avenue made beach landings

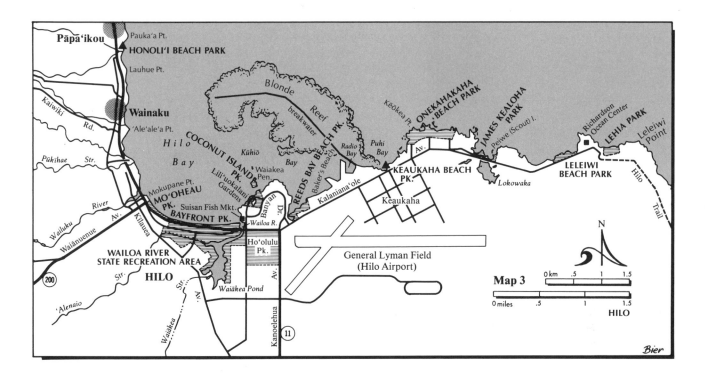

Map 3

0 km   .5   1   1.5

0 miles   .5   1   1.5

HILO

Bier

unnecessary except in periods of high surf or stormy seas. The site served the community until the late 1890s. With the construction of a breakwater at Waiakea in the early 1900s and the already improved ground transportation to the area, Waiakea became the major commercial port for Hilo.

At the turn of the century, when the black sand beach at Hilo extended from the Wailuku River to the Wailoa River, an intermittent stream, the Waiolama, crossed the beach at its center. The Waiolama fed an extensive wetland of taro farms and several fishponds, but its occasional overflow into the ocean presented an obstacle to traffic between Hilo and Waiakea, as it periodically washed out the bayfront road, especially after heavy rains in the *mauka* areas. The final solution to the problem was a recommendation in 1912 by the Department of Public Works to excavate a large canal that would divert Waiolama Stream into the Wailoa River, and then drain and fill the stream and its adjacent wetlands and ponds. The project was begun in 1915 and completed in 1917. Unfortunately, it was directly re-

sponsible for the disappearance of a major portion of the black sand beach at Hilo Bay. Although the contractor had used the excavated material from the canal's construction for some of the wetland fill, the bulk of the 33 acres was filled with sand dredged directly off the beach and pumped inland. The project so completely exhausted the supply of beach sand at the pump's location that by mid-1916 the job came to a halt and was delayed until the winter storms of that year began to transport more sand ashore from the natural reservoirs in the bottom of Hilo Bay.

In 1917, while the Waiolama project was nearing completion, plans were completed for the Ponahawai project—to fill in the taro lands in the adjacent area and on the Hāmākua side of the Waiolama landfill. This project spanned the years 1921 to 1923 and also used fill pumped directly from the beach, further depleting the black sand from the already devastated shoreline. In addition, the Waiolama sand-mining project undermined a section of the Hawaii Consolidated Railway's tracks, which ran along the backshore of the beach. A

15

HILO BAYFRONT PARK. This wide, flat black sand beach once bordered the entire length of Hilo Bay. Extensive erosion during the twentieth century has reduced the beach to half its original size, but it still remains a popular fishing site. During the spring and summer months, the outrigger canoe racing season, many canoe training sessions and regattas are held at the park.

retaining wall, built to shore up the endangered section, destroyed the natural slope of the beach, which in turn stopped the normal accretion of sand, and ultimately resulted in a permanent reduction in the length of the beach. The railroad discontinued service in 1946, and the Bayfront Highway now occupies the former railroad bed. Protection of the highway in the wake of the 1946 tsunami and other inundations reduced the dimensions of the beach to its present size. The Wailuku River, the primary source of the black sand, continues to transport sand particles—eroded volcanic rock fragments—into Hilo Bay, but because of the man-made barriers on the shoreline, the major area of accretion has been severely reduced.

Shoreline construction has not only altered Hilo's famous crescent of black sand, but it has drastically changed the nearshore character of Hilo Bay, destroying productive fishing reefs and a number of important surfing sites. Judging by accounts of nineteenth-century

residents and visitors, the surfing breaks in Hilo Bay offered some of the most spectacular waves and longest rides to be found anywhere in the Hawaiian Islands, but all this was changed too, during the early 1900s with the arrival of trans-Pacific steamships. To protect these deep-draft vessels at the Waiakea end of the bay, construction of a breakwater was undertaken in 1908, and dredging of the existing harbor began in 1913. The final result of these shoreline alterations has been, among many things, a severe reduction in the value of Hilo Bay as a recreation area for diving and surfing. In their exhaustive study *Hilo Bay: A Chronological History*, the most comprehensive and illuminating work produced to date on Hilo Bay, Kelly, Nakamura and Barrère summarize these developments:

The town and port of Hilo grew along with other areas of the islands. The Hilo Railroad Company (later the Hawaii Consolidated Railway), harbor facilities at Hilo

Bay, sugar plantations to the north and south of Hilo town, and a multitude of local industries serving the increasing population of the Hilo area were some of the enterprises into which capital flowed. The bottom line of these commercial enterprises was profits. The characteristics of early Hilo—with people carrying on subsistence agriculture, completely self-sufficient with taro and food gardens providing carbohydrates and fish and other seafoods supplying the protein, beautiful Hilo Bay with unpolluted clear water, people surfing and canoeing, and the beautiful fringing black sand beach—were all sacrificed. The bay was dredged and filled, and hundreds of tons of sugar wastes and millions of gallons of sewage were poured into it, to a point where it was identified as "a menace to public health" in a 1961 research report. As with nearly every other port in the Islands, Hilo was seemingly irrevocably changed, and not everyone would agree that it was for the better.

Hilo Bayfront Park occupies a long, narrow stretch of shoreline between Hilo Bay and the Bayfront Highway. The black sand beach fronting the park begins directly *makai* of the Mo'oheau Park pavilion across the highway. In this area of the bay the narrow ribbon of sand found at the base of the highway revetment is often completely awash at high tide or during periods of high surf. In the direction of the Wailoa River, the beach widens considerably and is backed by Hilo Bayfront Park's large ironwoods and scattered coconut trees. Facilities include a judging tower for canoe races, several canoe storage sheds, several portable toilets, and roadside parking.

The beach here attracts few swimmers because the waters of the bay are generally very murky and also cold due to the continual discharge of fresh water from the rivers. However, in addition to canoe paddling, a wide variety of activities center in the area, including shoreline fishing, picnicking, small craft sailing, windsurfing, and surfing. Surfers in Hilo Bay usually concentrate near the mouth of the Wailuku River where some excellent long rides can still be found during the winter months. Both surfers and fishermen report sighting many sharks, particularly hammerheads, in the bay.

Inland of Hilo Bayfront Park across the highway are three other parks that also attract people to the shoreline of Hilo Bay: Mo'oheau Park, Wailoa River State

Recreation Area, and Ho'olulu Park. Mo'oheau Park, one of the oldest in Hilo, is at the foot of the downtown business district where it offers parking and a large bus terminal. Other facilities include a bandstand, restrooms, and a large athletic field.

The Wailoa River State Recreation Area not only provides a 150-acre expanse of green park on the shoreline of Hilo Bay, but also serves as a tsunami buffer between the city and the open ocean. Hilo is unusually vulnerable to the destructive force of tsunami, which have caused many deaths and millions of dollars of losses in property damage. Following the 1960 disaster in which 61 people were killed, 281 structures were demolished, and 291 more damaged, a redevelopment project called Project Kaiko'o ("rough seas") was initiated to revitalize the town of Hilo. Aware of the vulnerability of Hilo Bay, the planners decided to clear the disaster area and relocate all residents and businesses. Land acquisition and relocation began in 1961 and was completed in 1965. The project also called for the development of an oceanside greenbelt buffer zone of lawns, lagoons, gardens, and recreational facilities which would protect the inland areas by absorbing the impact of future tsunami. The Wailoa River State Recreation Area comprises the heart of the buffer zone. Bordering the inland edge of the 1960 tsunami's high-water mark, a plateau consisting of 40 acres of landfill averaging 26 feet above sea level was created to provide a new commercial center. The plateau houses office buildings, a shopping mall, a hotel, and the County Building and the State Office Building. Hilo is the seat of government and commerce for the Big Island of Hawai'i.

The Wailoa River State Recreation Area consists of a landscaped park along the Wailoa River, a spring-fed estuary into which flow the waters of both the Waiolama Canal and the Waiākea Pond. These waters, as well as Hilo Bay and the Wailuku River, are fisheries management areas that are subject to regulations for both crabbing and fishing. Anyone planning to fish or crab in these areas should check first with the State Division of Fish and Game. In the Wailoa River basin a state small-boat harbor offers for the use of commercial and recreational boaters a two-lane boat ramp and support facilities that include water outlets, parking for trucks and trailers, lighting, and restrooms. Many of the commercial fishermen utilizing the harbor dispose of their catches at nearby Suisan Market, the site of Hilo's famous daily fish auction.

Wailoa Center, a part of the recreation area, offers information services and exhibits the work of local artists and craftsmen. There is also a permanent display of photographs of some of the tsunami which have devastated the Hilo waterfront. Adjacent to the center is the Shinmachi Tsunami Memorial, a monument erected in memory of those who have died during tsunami, especially those of April 1, 1946, and May 23, 1960.

To the east of the Wailoa State Recreation Area, Ho'olulu Park, one of Hilo's major public recreation sites, provides facilities for a wide variety of sports and similar activities. Facilities include baseball fields, basketball courts, tennis courts, an auditorium, an Olympic-sized swimming pool and diving tower, restrooms, and parking. Two of the individual sport complexes within the park are named in honor of men who dedicated their lives to the children of the Big Island. The baseball stadium was named for Walter C. K. Victor, who, for almost his entire adult life until his death in 1975, was a coach or manager of baseball teams and many other organized team sports for young people. In 1970 he received national recognition in a ceremony in Washington, D.C., when the United States Jaycees President's Council on Physical Fitness and Sports honored Victor with an award for his outstanding contributions to sports, over the previous thirty-seven years. The swim stadium, completed in 1973 and initially named Ho'olulu Swim Stadium, was renamed on January 30, 1982, in honor of Charles "Sparky" Kawamoto who was actively involved in competitive swimming on the Big Island for nearly fifty years. From the 1930s to the 1970s, Kawamoto trained thousands of youngsters to be outstanding swimmers. One of his proudest moments as a coach came during the 1952 Olympic Games in Helsinki, Finland, when one of his former swimmers, Yoshinobu Oyakawa, won a gold medal.

In addition to the sports activities that take place in Ho'olulu Park complex, many cultural events are held on the grounds as well. Probably the best known is the annual Merrie Monarch Hula Festival, which honors David Kalākaua who led a resurgence in teaching and performing the hula during his reign as king of the Hawaiian Islands. The idea of such a festival and its name were first suggested in 1963 by Kumu Hula George Naope to Helene Hale, then Hawaii County chairman. The first festival was held in 1964. From modest local beginnings, the Merrie Monarch Hula Festival has become a major event and now draws entries from the entire state and is considered one of the foremost hula competitions in the Hawaiian Islands.

(7)
Coconut Island Park

In the centre [of Hilo Bay], or rather towards the south-east, is a small island connected with the shore by a number of rocks, and covered with cocoa-nut trees. South-west of this small island the native vessels usually anchor, and are thereby sheltered from all winds to the eastward of north-east.

Journal of William Ellis, 1823

Coconut Island today appears much the same to visitors as it did to William Ellis and other early explorers on the Big Island. Although the Hawaiians knew the island as Mokuola, its prominent stand of stately coconut trees soon gave rise to its more common English name. In his journal of the United States Exploring Expedition of 1840–1841, Charles Wilkes, the expedition's commander, recorded Coconut Island as a proper name: "We found the best anchorage on the east side of the bay, where Cocoanut Island and the most eastern point are in range." Apparently by the 1840s the island's still popular English name was already in common usage.

Mokuola, "healing island," was formerly visited by Hawaiians seeking cures for the diseases that afflicted them. Part of the treatment included swimming once around a rock offshore the island under the direction of a *kahuna*. Those who were too ill to make the swim themselves were allowed to name a proxy to do it for them. The fresh spring waters that emerge in the sea water surrounding the island were believed to be endowed with healing properties. An epithet that referred to the special curative powers of the island and its waters was, *'Ane'ane e pae aku i Mokuola,* "You have almost landed at the Isle [of] Life." The saying inferred that someone who had been ill was on the road to recovery. In addition to its distinction as a place of

COCONUT ISLAND PARK. A concrete pedestrian bridge joins Coconut Island to Waiakea Peninsula. The island has long been one of Hilo's most popular shoreline picnicking sites with its spectacular views of the bay, the city, and Mauna Kea in the distance. A diving tower at the outer tip of the island offers children of all ages an exciting recreational diversion.

healing, Mokuola was also recognized as a place of refuge, or *puʻuhonua*, a haven where lawbreakers could find safety and forgiveness.

Directly across Kōwā o Mokuola, the channel between the island and the Waiakea peninsula, was a *luakini* or sacrificial *heiau*. Nothing remains of the structure; the foundation stones were removed in 1861 by Thomas Spencer to construct a boat landing a short distance away, near the mouth of the Wailoa River. However, during the summer of 1925, Theodore Kelsey interviewed several aged informants who accompanied him on a series of trips to Mokuola and the Waiakea area and provided him not only with many of the old place names, but also with this description of the former *heiau*:

The heiau of Kuakaananuu on the land of Maka o Ku was a pyramidal structure of two platforms, the lower about six feet high, the upper about four feet high. A room occupied the central portion. The heiau was used in connection with the puuhonua of Mokuola. The stones were taken by Captain Spencer in the sixties for a boatlanding with the exception of a few that remained by the big kamani tree. The site of the luapau is still marked by two lines of stone buried in the earth about 40 feet mauka of the kamani tree.

The victims were killed by priests who dropped a large oblong stone, held between them, on their chests as they lay bound to the big stone of Maka o Ku. The stone dropped on their chests was Maka o Kui ka lani. After being placed on the lele for a day and a night, the body was laid on Poha Kau, a stone now lying broken in the water a few feet to the left of the present cement landing. The body was then covered with lauhulu during one or two nights of pule, after which it was suspended between the two parts of a double canoe, taken out to sea, and sprinkled with "horse-tails" or ahala. After this the body might be stripped of flesh. The flesh was thrown into the luapau and the bones dried on Kaulainaiwi.

By the turn of the twentieth century, Coconut Island, with its spectacular panoramic view of Mauna Loa and

Mauna Kea, Hilo town and points beyond, and all of Hilo Bay, had developed into one of the Hilo district's most popular picnic areas, a use it still enjoys. Picnickers and sightseers were ferried to the island at first by canoes and later by rowboats, for a nominal fee. In his well-known composition "Hilo March" which was first played by the Royal Hawaiian Band in 1881, Joseph Aea attested to the beauty of Hilo and the *lehua*, the flower of the Big Island.

Hui   *'Ike hou ana i ka nani a'o Hilo*
I ka uluwehiwehi o ka lehua
Lei ho'ohihi hi'i a ka malihini
Mea 'ole i ke kono a ke aloha.

Chorus   Behold again the beauty of Hilo
and the beautiful growth of lehua
Cherished lei worn by visitors
Not indifferent to the call of love.

During World War II, the military took over Coconut Island for use as an exclusive recreation area, an action that angered many local residents. The civilian community regained use of the island in November 1945 and acquired a pontoon bridge, constructed by the army, that joined the peninsula and the island. The bridge was swept away by the tsunami of April 1, 1946. Rowboat service was then re-established, at a fee of 10 cents for adults and 5 cents for children, until a permanent pedestrian bridge was constructed. The new bridge in its turn was destroyed by the tsunami of May 23, 1960, which inundated Hilo Bay and the Waiakea area in particular. The present bridge was build as part of a major restoration project of the island.

Coconut Island still provides Hilo's residents and visitors with a popular shoreline recreation area for strolling, picnicking, fishing, and swimming. Most of the swimming activity takes place around the diving tower, which has survived the devastating tsunami. The tower is a major attraction for youngsters, who leap from its split-level decks into a large inlet that was once known as Kalua'uwao. Near the inlet, in a sheltered cove, is a shallow wading pool for the very young. This pool, formerly known as Kai'au'au a Kāne, occasionally contains some interesting treasures because it traps much of the debris passing by offshore.

Most of the island is a grassy park shaded by coconut trees and a few ironwoods. Facilities include a pavilion with restrooms, picnic tables, benches, and a parking lot adjacent to the grounds of the Hilo Hawaiian Hotel.

Inland of Coconut Island Park on the shoreline of the Waiakea peninsula is Lili'uokalani Gardens, a beautiful, landscaped park named after Hawai'i's last reigning monarch, Queen Lili'uokalani (1838–1917). Landscape architect Kinsaku Nakane of Kyoto University in Japan designed the Yedo-type gardens around Waihonu Pond. The park is reportedly the largest of its kind outside Japan. Like Coconut Island, Lili'uokalani Gardens has survived the onslaughts of tsunami and erosive forces of high seas, and now provides the town of Hilo with a unique setting for weddings and other special events.

(8)
Reeds Bay Park

Reed's Bay is a picturesque inlet, with residences along its shores, a short distance east of Cocoanut Island.

The Island of Hawaii
Henry Kinney, 1913

Reeds Bay, the large natural indentation in the shoreline bordering the eastern edge of the Waiakea peninsula, was named after William H. Reed, a prominent Big Island businessman who died in 1880. Reed's Landing on the western side of the peninsula and Reeds Island in the Wailuku River were also named for him. Reed arrived in the islands during the 1840s and established himself as a contractor specializing in the construction of landings, wharfs, bridges, and occasionally roads. Reed also pursued a variety of other business interests including ranching, coastal trading, and commercial retailing. In 1868 he married Jane Stobie Shipman, the widow of the Reverend William C. Shipman, and thus became the stepfather of her three children: William Herbert Shipman (1854–1943), Oliver Taylor Shipman (1857–1942), and Margaret Clarissa Shipman (1859–1891). Many island residents have long assumed that the bay was named for James Reid, the former harbormaster in Hilo Harbor from 1920 to 1940, but the place name Reeds Bay is found on many maps that predate James Reid's arrival on the Big Island in 1912 to become the head of the stevedores at Hilo Harbor.

The coral rubble and white sand beach comprising the western edge of Reeds Bay is man-made. Coral spoil material from successive dredging operations of the Hilo Harbor basin was deposited there between 1925 and 1930, and the same material was also used to fill a large marsh across Banyan Drive from the park. Waiākea Elementary School was situated on this section of the landfill until the tsunami of 1960 swept through the area. Redevelopment planners relocated the school *mauka* and later approved conversion of the site into a golf course. The landfill comprising Reeds Bay Park, however, has remained almost unchanged.

The park consists of a large, flat, white coral rubble parking lot, with a few scattered trees. There are no facilities, but small boat owners launch their boats across the hard-packed landfill. Sailing craft anchor in the deeper waters offshore. The inner bay affords a calm, shallow, protected place to swim over several small pockets of sand, but most of the recreational swimmers in the area frequent Ice Pond, the large natural pond adjoining the head of Reeds Bay. Formerly called Kanakea, Ice Pond takes its English name from the icy-cold spring waters that constantly rise into the salt water from the bottom of the pond. This cold fresh water is very refreshing for swimmers on hot summer days, but during the winter months only the hardiest swimming enthusiasts venture into these icy waters. Near the inlet to the pond, several low concrete blocks, former supports for the tracks of the Hawaii Consolidated Railway, are used occasionally as jumping platforms. Ice Pond also attracts fishermen who gather a special *limu* used for mullet bait.

Along the shoreline between Reeds Bay and Pier 3 of Hilo Harbor there was once a white sand beach called Bakers Beach. Like the existing beach in Reeds Bay Park, Bakers Beach was also made between 1925 and 1930 by the deposition of coral spoil material dredged from the Hilo Harbor basin. Approximately ten years earlier, about 1915, a prominent Hilo businessman named Adam Baker had selected this then-secluded site to build a palatial three-story beach home. Baker, the son of John Timoteo Baker, the last appointed governor of the Big Island during the time of the Hawaiian monarchy, entertained many celebrities of the day, and his home with its beautiful lawns, rock gardens, and large shade and fruit trees was a famous landmark. When the landfill project was completed, the new beach fronting the Baker residence became known almost immediately as Bakers Beach.

Bakers Beach was an instant attraction to the people of Hilo, who had recently lost most of one of their beloved playgrounds, the famous black sand beach in Hilo Bay. Sand-mining operations during the Waiolama and Ponahawai landfill projects from 1915 to 1923 had all but destroyed the beach and the nearshore sand reservoirs, and so Bakers Beach was a welcome alternative for people of the Hilo district. Though Adam Baker eventually sold his home not long before the outbreak of World War II and later owners used the building to house a series of restaurant and nightclub operations, the area is still known as Bakers Beach.

During the early 1960s, Bakers Beach began showing signs of serious erosion. Because the beach is man-made, no natural process of sand replenishment restores the lost material; the net effect has been a dramatic reduction of the former beach to several large pockets of coral rubble. The ocean eventually will return the shoreline to its natural boundaries. Several public rights-of-way to the beach can be found between the scattered shoreline homes in the area. Few people swim in this part of Hilo Bay, but fishermen frequent the area. It also affords an excellent view of the always-busy shipping activity in Hilo Harbor.

(9)
Radio Bay

Nā pana kēia o Keaukaha
Mai ka palekai a i Leleiwi
Pā mau i ka meheu a nā kūpuna.

Ha'alele aku 'oe i ka palekai
Kahi māka'ika'i e nā selamoku
Lana mālie ke kai 'olu nā lawai'a.

These are the famous places of Keaukaha
From the breakwater all the way to Leleiwi
Resounding to the footsteps of our ancestors.

You leave the breakwater,
The place visited by sailors.
Where the sea lies calm, the fishermen are pleased.

"Nā Pana Kaulana o Keaukaha"
© by Edith Kanaka'ole, 1979

Radio Bay, at the easternmost corner of Hilo Harbor, lies between the breakwater and Pier 1. It is used as a small-boat harbor by small craft and deeper-draft sailboats that cannot be accommodated in the shallower waters of Reeds Bay. The Coast Guard maintains its Big Island headquarters near the loading dock at the head of the bay. The area is used principally by shoreline fishermen, who fish from the shore and from the breakwater, but during the annual outrigger canoe racing season, the bay is a training site for paddlers. A large stand of tall ironwoods occupies the backshore and provides an undeveloped park and parking area for the various visitors to the bay and the breakwater. Surfers occasionally find waves suitable for riding outside the breakwater, and skin divers also spear fish along the massive structure during periods of calm seas.

The extensive fringing reef upon which the Hilo breakwater is built was named Blonde Reef in 1825 in commemoration of a visit by Lord George Anson Byron, cousin of the poet. Byron arrived in Hawai'i aboard the British frigate H.M.S. *Blonde,* which was carrying the bodies of Liholiho (King Kamehameha II) and his wife Kamamalu to Honolulu for burial there. The Hawaiian king and queen had died of measles within six days of each other while on a visit to London. Lord Byron stopped briefly outside Hilo Bay, then proceeded to Maui and O'ahu. He returned to Hilo Bay with Ka'ahumanu, regent of the kingdom, and her entourage on board. On their arrival in June of 1825 Ka'ahumanu declared that Hilo Bay was henceforth to be known as Byron Bay, and from then on the reef that protects the bay has been known as Blonde Reef in honor of the ship that had returned bodies of the royal couple to their homeland.

Construction of the first section of the Hilo breakwater across Blonde Reef began in 1908 and was completed in 1910. Work on the second section was done in 1911, but the third section, which extended the structure to its present length of 10,070 feet, was not finished until November 1929. During this period, Piers 1, 2, and 3 were built along Kūhiō Bay, a natural deep-water gap in the reef. The bay was named in honor of Prince Jonah Kūhiō Kalaniana'ole, Hawai'i's delegate to Congress from 1902 to 1922. In 1914 a deep-water entrance channel was dredged into Kūhiō Bay, and from 1925 to 1930 successive dredging operations expanded the bay to its

present dimensions to form the Hilo Harbor basin. All of this construction made possible the present-day commercial deep-draft harbor and associated terminal and industrial areas, and also resulted in the creation of Radio Bay between the breakwater and Pier 1. The bay was named for the United States Naval Radio Station communication complex that formerly stood immediately inshore. In a presidential executive order dated May 24, 1949, the land set aside for the radio station was restored to the jurisdiction of the Territory of Hawaii, but the name Radio Bay has endured and continues to be the popular designation for this corner of the harbor.

(10)
Keaukaha Beach Park

Huli aku iā Puhi
Kahi pana heiau o ka manō niuhi
'O Kulapae, pae i ke kula.

You turn toward Puhi
The place of the *heiau* of the great shark
At Kulapae, open fields are washed by the sea.

"Nā Pana Kaulana o Keaukaha"
© by Edith Kanaka'ole, 1979

The shoreline community of Keaukaha is one of the oldest Hawaiian Homes Commission settlements in the state, second only to Kalama'ula on the island of Moloka'i. Congress passed the Hawaiian Homes Commission Act in 1920 to provide public lands to be assigned as homesteads to citizens of "not less than one-half part of the blood of the races inhabiting the Hawaiian Islands previous to 1778." Provision was made for a commission to administer the project, and in 1925 the newly formed commission designated the area of Keaukaha to be subdivided into residential lots for Hawaiians and part-Hawaiians. By 1930, more than 200 house lots had been assigned and the population of the area exceeded 1,000.

During its long period as one of the foremost homestead communities in Hawai'i, many individuals from Keaukaha have become prominent in a variety of fields, from sports to civil leadership, but probably the residents' greatest contributions have been in preserving and perpetuating Hawaiian culture. One of the most outstanding exponents of this tradition was Edith Kanaka'ole (1913–1982) whose many accomplishments, awards, and honors testify to her life-long dedication to Hawai'i's people and her love of these islands.

In 1978 in recognition of her expertise in the field of ancient Hawaiian chant and dance, she was awarded the prestigious Nā Hoku Hanohano Award for Best Traditional Hawaiian Album for that year. That album, "Ha'aku'i Pele I Hawai'i," was followed by "Hi'ipoi I ka 'Āina Aloha" (Cherish the beloved land), in which five of the eight songs performed were composed by Aunty Edith. One of these compositions, "Ka Uluwehi o Ke Kai," memorializes her favorite kinds of *limu* and has become a standard item in the repertoire of many local musicians. Another of these compositions, "Nā Pana Kaulana o Keaukaha" (The famous places of Keaukaha), provides a valuable list of shoreline place names previously unrecorded and also reveals Aunty Edith's love for the land and her home. The song ends:

> *Puana ka huaka'i hele loa*
> *Nā pana kaulana o Keaukaha*
> *Mai ka palekai a i Leleiwi*
> *Ho'i a'e ka mana'o i nā kūpuna.*
>
> *Aloha nō ka huaka'i hele i Keaukaha*
> *Nā pana kaulana o Hawai'i.*
>
> Tell the story of the excursion
> To the famous places of Keaukaha
> From the breakwater all the way to Leleiwi
> A remembrance of our ancestors.
>
> Beloved is the journey to Keaukaha
> And the famous places of Hawaii.

Keaukaha Beach Park borders Puhi Bay, a narrow indentation in the shoreline directly *makai* of the intersection of Kalanaiana'ole Avenue and Baker Avenue. The bay takes its name from a former blowhole, a *puhi*, that was located on the western side of the bay fronting the sewage treatment plant. Construction of the outfall from the plant into the ocean completely destroyed the blowhole. Kulapae, the marshy point full of fresh-water springs on the eastern side of the bay, formerly a canoe landing, makes up the greater part of the beach park, but the land is undeveloped and overrun with vegetation. The only visible structure is Hale 'Āina, a pavilion that was used originally as a social hall by the Keaukaha community. At one time a Hawaiian village in this area

catered to Hilo's visitors, but the Hawaiian Homes Commission closed the venture, ruling that such use did not conform with zoning regulations.

Although Keaukaha Beach Park has not been developed as a formal park, many fishermen, swimmers, and picnickers, primarily from the surrounding community, frequent the area. They tend to concentrate near Cold Water Pond, a shallow spring-fed inlet at the head of Puhi Bay that is a popular swimming hole for children. The easily accessible section of the park near the pond offers roadside parking and is commonly known to Keaukaha residents as Front Street, the former name of Kalanaiana'ole Avenue.

(11)
Onekahakaha Beach Park

Hulali aku 'o Keonekahakaha
Kahi huaka'i hele a nā kūpuna
Ma'alo mau 'ia ke kupua honu.

Keonekahakaha's sands glitter
The place frequented by the ancestors
Where the turtle demigod always passes by.

"Nā Pana Kaulana o Keaukaha"
© by Edith Kanaka'ole, 1979

Onekahakaha means "drawing [pictures] sand," but the origin of the place name is now unknown. Besides its Hawaiian name, Onekahakaha was commonly called Machida Beach during the first half of the twentieth century. About 1915, Tomozo Machida obtained a long-term lease on approximately 13 acres of the present beach park. The only access to the natural pocket beach was a trail, so Machida put in a dirt road and then built a two-story beach home. The improvements did not go unnoticed in the community, and soon many of the *kumiai*, the local Japanese social organizations, were requesting use of the premises for annual picnics and other group functions. For a time, the Machida family graciously honored these requests, but after a number of years the burden of maintaining the home and meeting the needs of the *kumiai* and other groups became too heavy. So, in the early 1930s when the territory asked the family if they would relinquish their lease to make way for a public beach park, the family willingly agreed. The house was torn down, but the family name was preserved in Machida Lane, a small road leading to

ONEKAHAKAHA BEACH PARK. The cove of white sand at Onekahakaha, separated from the open sea by a heavy boulder break-water, provides a shallow and current-free swimming area for little children. This feature makes the park an attractive place for family outings and for children's swimming excursions. County lifeguards are on duty throughout the year.

the homes to the rear of the park's main parking lot. The county eventually developed the property as Oneka-hakaha Beach Park and installed public facilities.

During the summer of 1968 county workers began construction of a children's zoo on a one-acre parcel located at the entrance to Onekahakaha Beach Park. The completed project was opened to the public on February 1, 1969, and Mayor Shunichi Kimura presided over the opening ceremonies. In 1973 the small temporary zoo facility was relocated to a permanent 30-acre site in Pana'ewa, next to the racetrack.

Though the zoo is gone, Onekahakaha continues to attract more families with children than any other beach park in the district of Hilo. The park's popularity is due

to a combination of features. Besides lifeguard service provided by the county, there are picnic pavilions, restrooms, showers, and ample parking; but the main attraction is the large shallow, sand-bottomed ocean pool protected by a boulder breakwater. This pool offers one of the safest shoreline swimming areas along this coastline during normal weather conditions and is therefore especially attractive to families with young children. Although occasionally in recent years the sand at the park has been artificially replenished because of erosion, Onekahakaha has always been blessed with a natural pocket of white sand.

A second large ocean pond, north of the first, is not protected by the breakwater and is therefore much less used. This second pond has a deeper, rockier bottom, which harbors a sizable sea urchin population and is subject to much stronger current and water movement, including a persistent rip current that runs seaward from the end of the breakwater.

Over the years, particularly before lifeguard service was provided, Onekahakaha has been the site of many drownings and near-drownings. The offshore currents beyond the breakwater are always strong and during periods of high surf, powerful rip currents can carry swimmers directly into the waves pounding on the rocky shoreline. These conditions have been directly responsible for many fatalities. In spite of the breakwater and a number of retaining walls along the shore, exceptionally high winter surf often floods the park, sweeping through the camping area and into the marsh behind it, discouraging almost all use of the park.

Onekahakaha Beach Park also includes an undeveloped section of shoreline between the park and Kēōkea Point. Although no park facilities are available, a number of large, sand-bottomed tidal pools and inlets indenting the otherwise rocky coast attract many beachgoers, including picnickers, waders, and fishermen. The area has been variously called Kēōkea Point, Lihikai Beach Park, and the Lihikai extension (of Onekahakaha Beach Park). A public right-of-way at the *makai* end of Lihikai Street provides the most popular access to this area.

(12)
James Kealoha Park

Au a'e 'oe e pa mokumoku
'O Peiwe pili me Lokowaka
Kapa'ia 'o "Kealoha Paka," "Mile Ehā."

Kūnou mai 'o Haunai'o
He kahaone hāuliuli
Alu ke pahe'e me ka'ele'ele.

You walk along the seashore and see the islets
This is Peiwe, close to Lokowaka
Called today "Kealoha Park" and "Four Miles."

Haunai'o greets you,
A dark, sandy strip
The *limu pahe'e* and the *limu 'ele'ele*
    are both found here.

"Nā Pana Kaulana o Keaukaha"
© by Edith Kanaka'ole, 1979

James Kealoha Park was named in 1963 in honor of James Kealoha, a former Hawaii County chairman and the first elected lieutenant governor of the State of Hawai'i. Kealoha, the son of a grocer, was born on the Big Island in 1908 and graduated from Hilo High School in 1926. He entered politics in 1934 and held several different offices until 1962, when he was unsuccessful in the gubernatorial primary. The affable, long-time political figure died at the age of 75 on August 24, 1983.

The park is best known to Big Island residents as "4 Miles," a name that dates back to the construction of the Hilo Post Office. After the building was completed, it was designated as the starting point for all road mileage measurements emanating from Hilo. In his 1913 travel guide *The Island of Hawaii*, Henry Kinney wrote, "Beyond the breakwater, which is reached by a continuation of Front Street, the road runs on to a point four miles from the post office, Lokoaka, where there is a fine bay with an island and a pretty lagoon, as well as several extensive fishponds." The distance from the downtown post office building to Kealoha Park is still 4 miles, the distance that became a permanent name for the area. Less widely known today, but also popular at one time, were the names "3 Mile Half" for Onekahakaha Beach Park and "6 Miles" for the end of the road in the present Lehia Park.

James Kealoha Park borders a moderately wide, open bay that affords water enthusiasts a wide variety of recreational opportunities, including swimming, snorkeling, pole fishing, spearfishing, throw-netting, lay-netting, and surfing. The western and central portions of the bay open directly to the deeper waters offshore, and during periods of high surf, a powerful rip current runs seaward through this area. Winter storms not only generate hazardous water conditions, such as rip currents, but also occasionally produce some excellent waves for surfing. Surfers call the break "4 Miles."

In the eastern portion of the bay, Scout Island and a broken barrier of lava form a configuration with Pōhākea Point that makes a large, ponded swimming area which contains several inlets and pockets of white sand. Families with children commonly visit this sheltered area of the beach park where a county lifeguard is stationed. Behind the swimming area a grassy, tree-filled park with one picnic pavilion offers a garden-like setting for picnickers and strollers. Much of this property belonged formerly to the Carlsmith family, and sometimes the area is referred to as Carlsmith Park. The county purchased the land in 1972 and upgraded it in 1975 with tree plantings, landscaping, walkways, and a parking lot.

Scout Island is marked on most maps as Mahikea Island, but long-time area residents state that the correct Hawaiian name is Peiwe. Mahikea is said to have been a small ocean pond nearby in the lee of Pōhākea Point. No trace of it remains, the tsunami of 1946 having greatly altered much of the former shoreline. Scout Island, shortened on its seaward end by the 1946 tsunami, was once a very popular summer camping site among the residents of Keaukaha, as well as with the Big Island's boy scouts. The scouting activity on the island, of course, gave rise to its popular English name. Peiwe, the island's Hawaiian name, is a general name for drupe shells, the snails of which were eaten as commonly as *'opihi, pipipi,* and *leho.* Drupe shells are rather small and thick and are covered with exterior nodules or tubercles; they are distributed throughout the Hawaiian Islands in shallow, rocky areas. Peiwe, or Scout Island, is now part of Kealoha Park.

The shoreline lands of the Waiakea peninsula and Keaukaha contain fourteen fishponds, the largest of which, 60 acres in area, is Lokowaka, located directly across Kalaniana'ole Avenue from James Kealoha Park. Lokowaka is owned by the State of Hawai'i but is under lease to private interests. Renowned island-wide for its excellent mullet, Lokowaka, or "Waka's Pond," was named for Waka, a *kupua* (or demigod) who could assume the form of either a giant lizard or a woman, who dived into the pond to escape the jealous wrath of Pele.

(13)
Leleiwi Beach Park

Alu mai 'o Kaumaui
Wai'olena a 'o Waiuli
'O Puakahinano o Malo.

Kaumaui,
Wai'olena, and Waiuli are next encountered.
Then Puakahinano [where lived] the Malo family.

"Nā Pana Kaulana o Keaukaha"
© by Edith Kanaka'ole, 1979

The irregular shoreline of Leleiwi Beach Park consists of a series of natural ponds, inlets, and coves fronted in part by a handful of small rock islets. Park improvements along Kalaniana'ole Avenue include eight picnic pavilions constructed in 1970 as a joint effort of the Lions Club and the county, as well as showers, restrooms, paved walkways, and several parking lots. The county also provides lifeguard service. Within the eastern portion of the park is the Richardson Ocean Center, an outdoor recreation and interpretive center that was developed cooperatively by the Hawaii County parks department, the University of Hawaii Sea Grant Extension Service, and the state's Department of Planning and Economic Development. The building housing the center, formerly the home of Elsa and George Richardson, was acquired by the county along with the lands surrounding it for use as a park. Richardson Ocean Center not only quarters the Sea Grant program personnel, but also provides a marine education center and display area open to the general public and special interest groups.

Although most beach-goers today know the area surrounding the ocean center simply as Richardson's, many *kama'āina* families still recall that the Richardson estate was also the home of the Malo family. Originally from 'Opihikao in the district of Puna, the first Malo family member to take up residence on the land was Kauikoa'ole, who moved into the area during the late 1800s. Kauikoa'ole's wife bore him two children, a boy and a girl, and he named his son David Malolauliioliloanaipualoha. David shortened his last name to Malo as a result of a night dream—a phenomenon common among family members—in which David was instructed to drop all of the components of his Hawaiian name except Malo for common use. Malo thus became the family name for the generations that followed, and the now widely extended family still acknowledges David as their patriarch.

David Malo and his wife Elena made their home on his father's shoreline property, which they knew as Leleiwi. The first of their seven children, all of whom were born on the land, came in 1901. He was named John David Malo. Each succeeding male child was also given the middle name David, a tradition to which some lines of the family still adhere. Life proceeded peace-

LELEIWI BEACH PARK. A small pocket of black sand borders the retaining wall at Richardson Ocean Center in Leleiwi Beach Park. Sunbathers relax on the wall and on the lawn behind it while snorkelers explore the protected waters offshore. The ocean center, formerly the home of Elsa and George Richardson, is open to the public.

fully for the Malos until 1920 when the entire family was stricken with typhoid fever. Elena, the least severely afflicted of them all, walked to the home of George Richardson on Reeds Bay to seek help.

Richardson, a part-Hawaiian originally from Kohala, regularly fished up and down the Keaukaha coastline in his boat and had become a close friend of David Malo's. When Elena showed up on his doorstep with the terrible news, he immediately put her on board his boat, the fastest means of transportation then available, and returned to the Malo home. There he gathered up the rest of the family and headed for Hilo and the hospital. In spite of these valiant efforts, two of the children died.

After the family returned home to convalesce,

Richardson continued to look in on them and see to their welfare by bringing medicine and other necessities. Malo felt deeply indebted to Richardson, believing that without his help he might have lost his entire family. When he was fully recovered, Malo suggested that Richardson build a home on the Malo property if he wished and that he consider the land as his own. Richardson accepted the offer and in the early 1920s constructed a large house on the property that is now the Richardson Ocean Center. Malo helped design the structure, recommending the large doors at the front and back of the house to provide a corridor for the periodic inundations by high winter surf and tsunami. This plan did actually save the building on a number of occasions when the ocean flooded through the house rather than carrying it away.

By the early 1930s, after both Elena and David Malo had died, the remaining children moved in with their oldest brother, John, who was married and living on homestead land in Keaukaha. At that time George Richardson, his wife Elsa, and their three sons became the sole permanent residents on the estate. After some years, however, the Richardsons moved away and the property eventually became part of Leleiwi Beach Park.

The many aquatic activities for which the beach park is used include swimming, snorkeling, throw-netting, bodyboarding, and surfing. At Kaumaui, where the three westernmost pavilions are located, the shoreline is exposed directly to the open ocean and to strong alongshore currents. Most families with children, therefore, congregate around the protected inlets at Waiʻolena in the center of the park or in the sheltered bay bordering Richardson Ocean Center.

Although its surface water is cold because of profuse fresh water intrusion, the bay is home for a wide variety of fish and other marine life. This feature, combined with shallow, nearly current-free waters in the lee of outer point, have made the bay the most popular snorkeling area on the Hilo side of the island. Beyond the protection of the point, surfers and bodyboarders ride the break they call "Richardson's," where rip currents are common during periods of high surf.

A sea wall fronts much of the bay's shoreline, but a tiny pocket beach at the base of the wall offers an excellent entry and exit point for all in-water activities and a limited area for sunbathing. Sunbathers also utilize an open area of the park behind the sea wall and near the beach.

(14)
Lehia Park

Pā aku nā wāwae ia Lehia
Keonepūpū a ʻo Laʻieikawai
Nā wahine kaulana o Leleiwi.

Then your footsteps touch Lehia,
Keonepūpū and Laʻieikawai,
The famous wives of Leleiwi.

"Nā Pana Kaulana o Keaukaha"
© by Edith Kanakaʻole, 1979

Lehia Park is more popularly known to Big Island residents as Puʻu Maile, the name of a hospital that once occupied the backshore lands of the park. The original Puʻu Maile Home, built in 1912, was a territorial tuberculosis sanitorium serving the entire island. Until 1939 it was located at the site of what is now the old terminal building at Hilo Airport. The sanitorium took its name from a nearby cinder cone approximately 50 feet high. The Hilo Airport, dedicated in February 1928, was enlarged considerably in the 1930s, and during the latter half of the decade Puʻu Maile was leveled to provide fill needed for the new runways. By this time, the wooden buildings of Puʻu Maile Home were run-down and overcrowded, so in April of 1938 construction of a new facility was started at the end of Kalanianaʻole Avenue. When the new concrete buildings were completed in July 1939, the old buildings at the airport were leveled and burned. The new facility was named Puʻu Maile Hospital.

The hospital remained on the shoreline until 1951 when it was relocated once again, this time to the grounds of Hilo Hospital. Although the buildings were razed, the area is still popularly known to many Big Island residents as Puʻu Maile. The only visible reminder of the former hospital is the long, thick concrete sea wall in Lehia Park that once fronted it. A project of the WPA, the wall raised a great deal of controversy during its construction, but many observers credit the 2½-foot-thick structure with saving the hospital and the lives of the 218 patients and 100 employees who were in the facility when the tsunami of April 1, 1946, struck the area. Except for flooding the kitchen with sand and debris, the waves left the building undamaged, and the patients and staff were able to reoccupy the building by April 12.

Although completely undeveloped as a park, Lehia is much used by picnickers, fishermen, and particularly campers, especially during the summer months. Almost all of the other Keaukaha shoreline sites that formerly allowed camping now prohibit this use, so Lehia Park is one of the few sites close to the population center of Hilo where a wilderness shoreline camping experience is possible. There are no facilities, but it is an attractive area covered with ironwood trees, false *kamani, hau, milo, hala,* and *naupaka.* Access is from a dirt road that begins at the intersection of Kalaniana'ole Avenue and Leleiwi Street and ends at Keonepūpū, a large open grassy field at the water's edge. From this area, a trail leads into the lava mounds and depressions that comprise this rocky shoreline and emerges after a short distance at La'ieikawai, a cluster of shallow brackish-water pools near Leleiwi Point. These sand-bottomed pools are popular as swimming holes, especially among children. Fresh water seeping into the pools froms a cold surface layer, while the denser salt water below is warmer and harbors a variety of marine life, intriguing to youthful visitors.

Lehia Park is fronted by low lava cliffs exposed throughout the year to strong alongshore currents and washing waves, so most fishing and gathering activities take place on shore rather than in the ocean. During the winter months, heavy surf at times totally inundates portions of the park, including Keonepūpū, the major camping site, and under these conditions the park is almost unusable.

(15)
Pāpa'i

Aloha nā 'ahahui o nā ali'i,
Nā ali'i mai nā kūpuna mai.
E pa'a i nā 'ōlelo kaulana,
E hele a moe i ke ala.

Hail societies of chieftains,
Chieftains of our ancestors.
Remember the famous saying,
Go and sleep upon the byways.
"Nā Ali'i"
Song by Samuel Kuahiwi

During the early 1780s Kamehameha began his campaign to become the sole ruler of the island of Hawai'i. By 1783 he controlled the district of Kohala, where he had been born and raised, and the district of Kona, which had fallen into his hands after the battle of Moku'ōhai at Ke'ei. Kamehameha then moved against the district of Hilo, but his forces suffered severe losses, and Kamehameha himself barely escaped in a canoe. His army withdrew to the safety of Laupāhoehoe.

Kamehameha was much distressed, not only because of his defeat at Hilo, but because he personally had

failed to kill or capture any of the enemy, leaving the altars of his temple without sacrifices and setting an example he felt unbefitting of a great commander. To salvage his reputation he devised a plan which, if successful, would raise the spirits of his men, harass his enemies, and give him the sacrifices he needed to insure a victory. Early one morning, well before daybreak, Kamehameha quietly left Laupāhoehoe in a canoe with only a few trusted warriors. They included his favorite

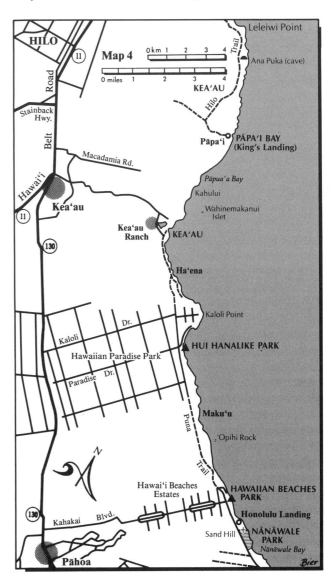

steersman, Kahaku'i. Traveling well out to sea, they quickly made their way along the coast past Hilo into Puna, and as the morning sun cleared the horizon, the canoe sailed into Pāpa'i Bay.

The bay then had a configuration different from the present one. Since that time many sections of the Puna shoreline, including the bay, have been altered dramatically by subsidence during severe volcanic activity. In 1793, however, the bay at Pāpa'i was well protected, with a good entrance channel that allowed canoes to go in and out even in the roughest of seas. Bordering the north edge of the entrance channel was a big *papa,* a wide, flat shelf of rock which abutted both the channel and the shoreline and provided a natural landing against which canoes could easily pull up and discharge passengers and cargo.

When Kamehameha's small raiding party approached the bay, they spotted some of the villagers fishing off the *papa.* As the canoe approached, the villagers recognized the danger and turned to flee. Quickly instructing his friends to remain in the canoe, Kamehameha leaped onto the *papa* and gave pursuit, but as he ran he stepped into a crevice in the lava and his foot caught fast. Seeing his plight, some of the fishermen picked up handfuls of small rocks and threw them at Kamehameha, who tried to protect himself in the same way. Then one of the fishermen, named Ku'iniki, picked up a canoe paddle and broke it over Kamehameha's head. By this time other men from the village had armed themselves and were running to join in the fray. But at last Kamehameha's friends managed to free him, and they all made a hasty retreat back to Laupāhoehoe. After considering the outcome of Kaleleike, "the skirmish" as the incident was later named, and the defeat that had preceded it, Kamehameha concluded that the gods did not favor his battle plans. He retreated to Kohala.

Some years later, after Kamehameha had successfully conquered not only the entire island of Hawai'i, but all the other major islands in the chain with the exception of Kaua'i, he visited the town of Hilo. Members of his retinue, still incensed that a commoner had struck a high chief and had not been punished, rounded up the fishermen who had attacked Kamehameha at Pāpa'i, brought them before the great chief and demanded their execution. At Kaipalaoa on the shores of Hilo Bay, in a house called Kahale'iole'ole, Kamehameha answered the cries for punishment with a pardon in the form of the now legendary decree known as the Law of the Splintered Paddle, or Māmala hoe (often Māmala hoa) Kānāwai:

> *E nā kānaka,*
> *E mālama 'oukou i ke akua*
> *A e mālama ho'i ke kanaka nui a me kanaka iki;*
> *E hele ka 'elemakule, ka luahine, a me ke kama*
> *A moe i ke ala*
> *'A 'ohe mea nāna e ho'opilikia.*
> *Hewa nō. Make.*

> O my people,
> Honor thy god;
> Indeed, respect men great and small
> Where old men, old women, and children go
> and lie down on the roadside,
> Let no man cause harm.
> Disobey, and die.

As ruler of the islands, he chose to forgive rather than to punish; he admitted his fault in attacking innocent bystanders; and he showed his respect for human rights by proclaiming—and enforcing—such a decree. These actions are testimony to Kamehameha's greatness as a leader and demonstrate why he was one of the most revered and beloved rulers in the history of the Hawaiian Islands.

For many years, a lone coconut tree at the bottom of Waiānuenue Avenue in Hilo was pointed out to visitors as the site of Kahale'iole'ole, the house where the decree had been issued. The fishing village of Pāpa'i, which was still inhabited in the 1930s, was given the English name of King's Landing. At Pāpa'i, a *noni* tree that stood near the shoreline was often pointed out to visitors for the scars on its trunk, scars which were said to have been made by the pebbles Kamehameha threw at the fishermen. The incident was also commemorated in many personal names, such as the name of the father of Bernice Pauahi Bishop, Abner Ka'ehu Pākī. His Hawaiian names indicate that the fishermen threw (*pākī*) showers of stones which hit Kamehameha like a shower of sea spray (*ka'ehu*). The name of the village itself,

Pāpaʻi, a name much older than the incident, is usually translated as "crab," but long-time residents of the area say the name refers to another meaning of the word—a simple fisherman's shed or shelter consisting only of four corner posts and a roof.

A narrow crescent of black sand approximately 400 feet in length lines the inner shore of Pāpaʻi Bay. In several places the sand appears to be light green due to the high concentration of olivine grains mixed in with the fine black cinder. A natural barrier of broken lava protects the little bay from the dangerous currents and surf seaward of the rocks, but the bay bottom is very shallow and rocky and harbors a large sea urchin population. The area is therefore probably more appropriate for snorkeling than for recreational swimming, especially considering the wide variety of fish species that inhabit the inner bay. A deterrent to all in-water activities is the tremendous volume of fresh water that enters the ocean here and forms a very cold surface layer. Most of this fresh water flows around the small rock island in the center of the bay and then into the open ocean, drawn seaward by a rip current running through a channel that cuts through the rock barrier. In another smaller surge channel near the eastern point of the bay there is also a dangerous rip current. Swimmers should avoid both areas.

Inland of Pāpaʻi Bay a large grassy field and a large coconut grove are used as picnic and camping grounds. The ruins of the former Hawaiian fishing village are adjacent and easily visible, but the entire area is private property and not open to the general public. There is no convenient public access to this shoreline.

East of Pāpaʻi the rocky shoreline continues all the way to Cape Kumukahi and includes many of the famous ʻopihi grounds of Puna. This long reach of coast, however, is fully exposed to the fury of the open ocean and has accounted for the deaths of many who have unwisely challenged the pounding surf. In addition to ʻopihi pickers, a number of shoreline fishermen have been washed off the rocks and drowned while ulua fishing, another popular sport, from the low sea cliffs. Limu is also harvested from a few areas. On extremely calm days some skin diving from the shore and some scuba diving from boats is possible, but shark sightings are common and divers report the sharks to be unusually aggressive.

(16)
Keaʻau

ʻO Puna:
ʻO Puna paia ʻala i ka hala,
Kea ʻau ʻiliʻili nehe ʻōlelo ike kai.
ʻO Puna ia la e.

And Puna:
Where hala's fragrance blows from Puna's branching
    bower,
And pebbles at Keaʻau whisper to the sea
Puna's forever there.

"He Huakaʻi Kaʻapuni Ma Hawaiʻi"
Traditional Chant

Keaʻau is one of the famous shoreline places in the district of Puna and is often mentioned in songs, chants, and legends. A well-known legend, the legend of ʻIwa, tells the story of a man named Keaʻau who lived in the former Hawaiian fishing village. Keaʻau owned two extraordinary *leho* (cowrie shells, which were highly prized as octopus lures) called Kalokuna. The possesser of these *leho* had only to lower them into the ocean and the octopus would come up the line and climb into the canoe.

The fame of Keaʻau's shells spread around the island, eventually reaching the court of the great chief ʻUmi in Kona. ʻUmi sent messengers to seize the *leho*, and Keaʻau, as a subject of the chief, had no choice but to give them up. Keaʻau then traveled to Oʻahu to seek the services of the thief, ʻIwa, who lived at Mōkapu. Together, they journeyed to Kona where ʻIwa was successful in recovering the shells, and Keaʻau returned with them to Puna.

Another legend of Keaʻau tells of Hopoe, a famous hula dancer of Puna, who taught Hiʻiaka, a sister of Pele, how to dance. Angered and jealous at the attention shown to her youngest sister, Pele turned Hopoe into stone and placed her on the shoreline near Keaʻau in the form of a balancing rock. The earthquake of 1868, however, dislodged the stone from its stand.

One of the first white men to describe Keaʻau (often

shortened in pronunciation to Ke'au) was the missionary William Ellis who walked through Puna in 1823. He wrote in his journal: "Soon after five p.m. we reached Kaau the last village in the division of Puna [heading toward Hilo]. It was extensive and populous, abounding with well-cultivated plantations of taro, sweet potatoes, and sugar cane, and probably owes its fertility to a fine rapid stream of water, which, descending from the mountains, runs through it into the sea."

Some twenty years later, Lt. Charles Wilkes, commander of the U.S. Exploring Expedition of 1840–1841, recorded this interesting information in the narrative of his travel: "Here [at Kea'au] we found a delightful spring of fresh water upon the shore, and within the flow of the tide at high water. It enabled us to enjoy a bath , which we had not had the means of doing for forty days."

On April 2, 1868,an exceptionally strong earthquake that originated near South Point caused a tremendous loss of life and property, especially in Ka'ū and Puna. The abrupt subsidence of the shoreline following the earthquake generated a tsunami that wiped out every fishing village from Kumukahi to Ka Lae. The northern shoreline of the Puna district was not as hard hit, but it too sank, leaving Kea'au with a small protected inlet fronting the village. Sand was eventually deposited in the inlet to form Kea'au Beach.

Inland of the inlet are a spring-fed marsh and pond that are still in use as a fishpond. The pond waters empty into a small stream that bisects Kea'au Beach and flows into the ocean. Near the pond is the century-old residence of the Shipman family. William H. Shipman was born of missionary parents on December 17, 1854, at Lahainaluna on Maui, but early in 1855 his parents moved to Wai'ōhinu in Ka'ū to take the post left vacant in 1849 when the Reverend John D. Paris left for a visit in the United States. They lived there for six years until his father died. His mother then moved with her three children to Hilo where she later married William H. Reed.

After Shipman had graduated from college in Illinois, he returned to Hawai'i and became manager of Kapāpala Ranch, of which his stepfather was part owner. Later he moved to Kapoho, where he took up cattle ranching with Herman Elderts, and, still later, he bought some property at Kea'au for ranching with Elderts and S. M. Damon. Eventually Shipman bought out his two partners and the land has remained with his heirs ever since.

Herbert C. Shipman, the son of William, carried on his father's business interest, but fortunately for Hawai'i and the world, he pursued others of his own. As a young man in his early twenties, he began to breed four rare *nēnē* geese given him by friends in 1918. This species, native only to Hawai'i, was facing extinction at that time; only a very few still survived in the wild. Shipman was successful in his propagation efforts, and for years he maintained the only captive flock in the world.

The tsunami of April 1, 1946, that devastated Hilo and many other areas also took its toll at Kea'au, leaving in its wake eleven dead *nēnē* of Shipman's precious flock of forty-five. In 1949 Shipman sent a pair of his birds to the Severn Wildfowl Trust in England and also gave a pair to the Hawai'i State Division of Fish and Game. Breeding efforts by both the trust and the state have been successful, and the wild bird population has slowly been increased as birds bred in captivity are released. Shipman, however, is personally credited with saving the *nēnē*, the state bird of Hawai'i, from extinction. Following his death in October 1976, the Hawai'i County Council adopted a resolution renaming Kea'au Park as Herbert C. Shipman Park in honor of his service to the state and dedication to the people of Puna.

Kea'au Beach, *makai* of the Shipman estate, is a small pocket of black detrital sand covered with a veneer of white calcareous sand. Most of the beach is river sand that has been carried to the shoreline by a small stream that empties into the inlet. The inshore bottom is sandy and shallow, making the beach safe for wading and swimming, but the water is cold from the heavy discharge of fresh water. The inlet containing the beach is protected from the rough seas offshore by a barrier of low, flat lava and a number of scattered protruding rocks, but a deep stream-cut channel follows the western point past the ruins of the old landing into the open ocean. The water discharged by the stream flows continually through this channel, generating a powerful rip current. The rip current in turn forms an undertow where it meets the incoming surf at the end of the point. Because the conditions that cause the rip current and the undertow are constant, these hazards are always present—an extremely dangerous situation for swimmers. A large "Danger—Undertow" sign is posted conspicuously on the point. There is no convenient public access to the beach or to any of the adjacent shoreline.

The shoreline from Kea'au to Honolulu Landing consists almost entirely of low sea cliffs, with only a few low-lying areas such as those at Hā'ena and Maku'u. Also located along this beach are two large subdivisions, Hawaiian Paradise Park and Hawaiian Beaches Estates. On the shoreline of each subdivision a small public park is located on top of the cliffs. Hui Hanalike Park, named for Hawaiian Paradise Park's lot and homeowners' association, is a 6-acre area situated near the end of Paradise Drive. Hawaiian Beaches Park consists of 3.6 acres at the *makai* end of Kahakai Boulevard. Both of these undeveloped parks are frequented primarily by picnickers, fishermen, and *'opihi* pickers. During the winter months humpback whales often come in very close to the sea cliffs in these areas; on calm nights especially, their noises and splashings can easily be heard.

(17)
Honolulu Landing

After conversing some time [at Kahuwai], we traveled in an inland direction to Honolulu, a small village situated in the midst of a wood, where we arrived just at the setting of the sun. Whilst the kind people at the house where we put up were preparing our supper, we sent and invited the inhabitants of the next village to come and hear the word we had to speak to them. They soon arrived.

We afterwards spent a hour in conversation and prayer with the people of these sequestered villages, who had perhaps never before been visited by foreigners, and then lay down on our mats to rest.

Journal of William Ellis, 1823

Three places in the Hawaiian Islands are named Honolulu, the "protected bay": the capital city of O'ahu, a large bay in Nāhiku on East Maui, and this former village and canoe landing in Puna. The only easily visible landmark at the site, a small, deteriorating building constructed of beach boulders and concrete, was apparently built in the 1920s by the territorial Board of Agriculture and Forestry as an equipment storage shed. The old

Government Road ended at Honolulu and only the *ala hele*, the circle-island shoreline trail, continued on to Kapoho. The village was located among the trees *mauka* of the storage shed, but former residents of the area say that a developer clearing the land for house lots leveled the entire village with a bulldozer, completely obliterating house sites, graves, and other platforms and walls, all of which had been in excellent condition. The only ruins that survive are the interconnecting rock walls located in a depression that also harbors a large dense grove of tall old coconut trees, a common sign of former Hawaiian shoreline habitation sites. The depression is directly *mauka* of the boulder beach and like much of the surrounding land is completely overrun by *hala*, philodendrons, and other dense vegetation.

Prior to the subsidence of the shoreline in 1924, Honolulu was a canoe landing visited periodically by coastal trading vessels to pick up coconut, coffee, and dried *'awa*. Canoes dispatched as lighters were launched over a black sand, olivine, and *'ili'ili* beach and paddled out to service ships anchored in deeper waters. The beach may have been created during the eruption of 1840 that built the sand hills in Nānāwale. In the August 29, 1840, issue of *The Polynesian* the editor reported that "two beaches were thrown up [near Nānāwale] where previously there was nothing but bold rock. The longer is on the north of the hills and about 100 yards in length; the other lies at the farther extremity of the lava and is but a few rods long."

Ships called at Honolulu Landing particularly for *'awa* (*Piper methysticum*), especially the *'awa kau lā'au* of Puna, the "tree-resting *'awa*." These plants grew in the crotches of trees and were believed to be extremely potent. The root of the *'awa* contains a resin that acts as a mild motor depressant. The Hawaiians and other Polynesians used *'awa* as a ceremonial and medicinal drink, but Westerners were most interested in its medicinal properties. Most of the commercially produced roots were trans-shipped to the mainland United States to be rendered into various types of tranquilizers and anesthetics. Between 1846 and 1932 Hawai'i law required a license to sell *'awa*, but the regulation was intended chiefly for revenue-producing purposes and was repealed in 1932.

In April of 1924 a series of violent earthquakes caused

the shoreline at Honolulu Landing to sink and left only boulders in place of the black sand. Shortly after this catastrophe, the few Hawaiians who had been living in the area moved inland or to other parts of the island. Ships stopped calling, but the site continued to be known as Honolulu Landing, its common name today.

Honolulu Landing is a boulder beach bordering the shoreline road, the only place for miles in either direction where the road drops down to sea level. Seaward of the boulders is a large reservoir of black sand, but shoreline geographical features which would promote the accretion of this sand as a beach do not exist here. The low rocky sea cliffs bordering both sides of the boulder beach are very popular both for *ulua* fishing and *'opihi* picking. This coast, however, is very dangerous and many lives have been lost to the heavy surf. Fishermen spending the night at Honolulu Landing report many strange occurrences and sightings, and the area has a wide-spread reputation as a ghostly, mysterious place.

(18)
Nānāwale Park

The width of the lava stream was found to be about three-fourths of a mile. It is said to have passed over the ancient village of Nanavalie, and left upon its site and cultivated grounds a deep layer of rock.

There are three sand hills, which caused me more astonishment, and involved greater difficulties to account for them, than any other phenomenon connected with the eruption. From all accounts, the formation of these took place at the time the lava stream joined the ocean, which must have produced a violent sandstorm, the effects of which are rendered evident for a mile on either side of the stream, by the quantity of sand and gravel that is lodged in the pandanus and other trees.

Narrative of the U.S. Exploring Expedition, 1841
Lt. Charles Wilkes

During May 1840 an eruption occurred along the east rift zone of Kīlauea volcano that sent a lava flow into the ocean, destroying the Hawaiian coastal village of Nānāwale. Lt. Charles Wilkes, commander of the first formal U.S. exploring expedition in Hawai'i, and his party passed through the area about six months later and obtained first-hand accounts of the eruption from the Hawaiian residents of Nānāwale who had only recently lost their entire village to the lava flow. They described how they had remained in their homes until the last moment, hoping that the lava would stop short of their village and spare it, but the flow had continued on into the ocean. As the flow entered the sea, tiny particles of *'a'ā* were blown into the air and piled up on both sides of the flow as littoral cones.

Almost immediately the ocean began to erode the three cones thus formed at the edge of the Nānāwale flow. Some forty years later J. W. Powell in the annual report of the U.S. Geological Survey for 1882–1883, noted: "The sea has in great part demolished one of these cones and has made considerable ravages in the others. In a few years, doubtless, they will all disappear."

The remnants of two of the three cones are part of Nānāwale Park. The Hawaiians called the cones Pu'u One, literally "sand hills," the name still used for the site by former residents of the area. Most fishermen today know the area simply as Sand Hill, the cones providing an important landmark for shoreline and offshore fishermen and for mariners. The *U.S. Coast Pilot*, a publication for mariners, offers this description looking inland from the ocean, "an old lava flow reaches the sea 4 miles NW of Cape Kumukahi and is marked by two black hills, about 50 feet high, lying close together at its seaward end."

Nānāwale means to "just look around." The long, narrow Nānāwale Park borders the old Government Road running from Hawaiian Beaches Estates to Kapoho. A fairly dense grove of ironwood trees fills the entire park, the dominent features of which are the two dark cinder cones at the water's edge. Hikers on the cones should be extremely careful, as the cinder is very loosely compacted and will slide over the moderately high sea cliffs with only the slightest disturbance. The park is undeveloped, offering no facilities, but camping is permitted.

Besides sight-seers and occasional picnickers, fishermen and *'opihi* pickers are the principal visitors in the area. Trails they have worn leading through the underbrush and down the cliffs to the rocky shoreline ledges and points are numerous and most of them easily found. To the east, between Nānāwale and Wa'awa'a, a beach of *pa'alā*, or rounded boulders, called Kīholo was in former times one of the most famous *'opihi* grounds in Puna. By common agreement among the area residents, no commercial harvesting was allowed, so *'opihi* were always available for home consumption. In recent years, however, the tremendous demand for *'opihi* and the high prices it commands in the local markets has caused the well-known Puna grounds such as Kīholo to be heavily picked. As a result, not only has the *'opihi* supply been drastically reduced, but many drownings have occurred in and around Nānāwale Park, where the ocean is almost always rough and waves pound relentlessly against the sea cliffs.

Fishermen, too, have been swept off the rocks to their deaths and many boats crippled by engine or other problems have been lost along this coast, dashed to destruction against the rocky shoreline by the strong currents, waves, and wind. During periods of calm seas some diving is done from boats offshore, but shark sightings are common and the sharks are reported to be much more aggressive than in other areas.

Inland of Nānāwale Park the heavily vegetated land comprises the Nānāwale Forest Reserve, an important nesting area of *'io*, the Hawaiian hawk. Nesting sites have also been reported in the neighboring *mauka* portions of Wa'awa'a, Kahuwai, and Halepua'a. The birds themselves range for miles and are often seen at the shoreline.

(19)
Kahuwai

Our way [from Kapoho] now lay over a very rugged tract of country. Sometimes for a mile or two we were obliged to walk along on the top of a wall four feet high and about three feet wide, formed of fragments of lava that had been collected from the surface of the enclosures which these walls surrounded. We were, however, cheered with a beautiful prospect; for the land, which rose gradually towards the mountains, a few miles to the westward of us, presented an almost enchanting appearance.

The plain was covered with verdure; and as we advanced, a woody eminence, probably some ancient crater, frequently arose from the gently undulated surface, while groups of hills, clothed with trees of various foliage, agreeably diversified the scene.

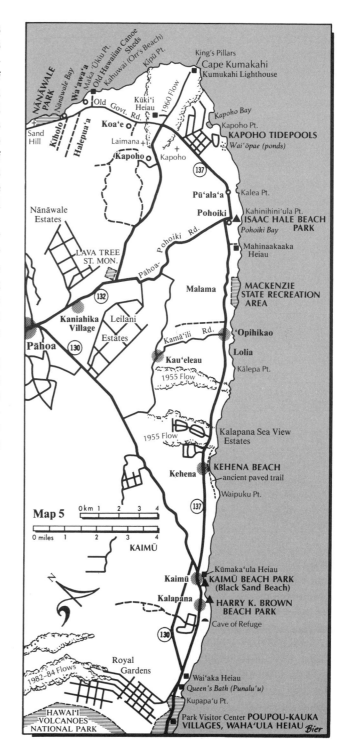

KAHUWAI. This beautiful pocket of black sand formed in 1960 shortly after the end of the Kapoho eruption. The Kapoho lava flow entered the ocean immediately east of Kahuwai and is visible as a narrow point on the horizon. Steam explosions from the interaction of the molten lava and the ocean created the black sand. The prevailing ocean currents then transported the sand along the low sea cliffs and deposited it on the shoreline at Kahuwai.

The shore, which was about a mile to the eastward of us was occasionally lined with the spiral pandanus, the waving cocoanut grove, or the clustering huts of the natives.

At half past four we reached Kahuwai, where we sat down and took some refreshment, while Makoa was engaged in bringing the people of the place together. About one hundred and fifty assembled around the door, and were addressed.

Journal of William Ellis, 1823

The very violent volcanic activity at Kīlauea volcano in April 1924 was accompanied by several days of rare explosion earthquakes that rocked the district of Puna. The earth buckled and shifted in many places, huge cracks appeared, and at Kahuwai the shoreline dropped at least several feet—and probably more, according to former residents of Koa‘e village. The earth movement also robbed Kahuwai of a small black sand beach, leaving only boulders in its wake.

In January 1960 a volcanic eruption broke out in a sugar cane field half a mile northwest of Kapoho village. By the time the lava stopped flowing, approximately one month later, the entire village of Kapoho was destroyed, the shoreline on either side of Cape Kumukahi was extended seaward, nearly a half mile in some places, adding approximately half a square mile of new land to the island of Hawai‘i. The flow did not come close to Kahuwai, but it provided the ancient settlement with a brand new black sand beach. The ocean began immediately to attack the flow of 1960 and between October and December of the same year the longshore currents and the surf carried enough black cinder ashore to make a new beach.

Soon after the new beach had formed, an annual visi-

36

tor to the Puna district, John Orr, happened to hike through the area. Coming upon the beach at the historic village, he felt it would make an excellent site for his home. He negotiated a long-term lease with the landowner and built a house on the bluff above the beach in 1963. Although Orr's lease is for only 5 acres, which include his home and his access road, he is the official caretaker for the remainder of the parcel, some 195 additional acres. Because he has been for so long associated with the area, most Big Island residents now know Kahuwai as Orr's Beach.

Orr has spent much time and effort clearing and keeping open fourteen sites of historic and archaeologic interest, including five canoe sheds, a large canoe-building shed, an elevated trail, and various stone platforms, one of which that may have been a *heiau*. Visitors are welcome to tour the area on their own, and Orr himself conducts tours for organized groups. Kahuwai appears to have been not only a center for canoe building, but a residence of *ali'i* as well. Fresh water flows among the rocks at the west end of the beach, the last vestige of a spring that was called Waikahuwai. Offshore, beyond the east end of the beach is a small sea stack. Known as Ke'apele, the rock once served as a *pōhaku piko*, a sacred place for depositing umbilical cords. According to some informants the rock was named for a white alga called ke'apele that sometimes forms at certain times of the year.

Orr's Beach is a small, steep pocket of black cinder sand tucked into the rugged Puna shoreline between two low sea cliffs. The beach is completely exposed to the open ocean and drops very abruptly to overhead depths. Strong alongshore currents prevail throughout the year, and high winds or high surf generate a pounding shorebreak with a powerful undertow and rip currents. Several drownings and many near-drownings have occurred here, John Orr himself having accomplished a number of daring rescues at the risk of his own life. With no electric or telephone lines to the area, professional rescue assistance can be obtained only by driving to a telephone. Recreational swimming is at best a marginally safe activity, possible on only the calmest of days during the summer. In addition to the beachgoers at Orr's Beach, shoreline fishermen and *'opihi* pickers frequent the bordering sea cliffs.

Non-human visitors to the beach include hawksbill turtles that have successfully nested in the volcanic sand, and during the winter months humpback whales range close to shore where they are easily seen and heard. Access to Orr's Beach is over a half-mile-long dirt road that winds through the *hau* jungle. The turnoff from the old Government Road is between two large mango trees located 1.5 miles from the end of the paved road from Kapoho.

(20)
Kumukahi

E 'ike mai 'oukou.
Nā mokupuni a pau,
Mai Ka hikina i Kumukahi
I ka welona i Lehua,
Keia hae kalaunu,
Kapalili nei i ka makani.

Behold, everyone and all.
Let all islands
From the sunrise at Kumukahi
To the sun's rest at Lehua
Gaze upon this royal flag
Fluttering in the breeze.
"Ke Ali'i Milimili"
Traditional song

Kumukahi, "first beginning," is the easternmost point on the Big Island and therefore the easternmost point in the Hawaiian Islands. A famous place name in Hawaiian songs and chants, Kumukahi also appears in legends as the name of several legendary persons who either stopped, lived, or died in the area; appropriately it is also the name of the easterly wind. Massive Cape Kumukahi, pointing directly into the rising sun, is one of the Big Island's most prominent shoreline features. Kumukahi is in the heart of the Puna district, where the threat of damage or destruction from volcanic activity has always been accepted as a part of life. References to Pele are numerous in epithets and sayings referring to Puna. For example:

Lohi'au Puna i ke akua wahine.
Weliweli 'ino Puna i ke akua wahine.
Ke lauahi maila 'o Pele ia Puna.

Puna is set back because of the goddess.
Puna is terrified of the goddess.
Pele is pouring lava out on Puna (a saying for anger).

Pele continues to ravage the district of Puna with eruptions in Kīlauea caldera and along its southwest and east rift zones. The east rift of Kīlauea extends 28 miles to Cape Kumukahi and at least 70 miles beyond on the ocean floor. The rift zone has been the source of many of the island's severe earthquakes and lava flows in historic times. Macdonald, Abbott, and Peterson in *Volcanoes in the Sea* offer this description of the 1924 activity in Puna:

> In April a great swarm of earthquakes commenced on the east rift zone of Kilauea. At first the quakes came from centers near the caldera, but the points of origin shifted farther and farther east, indicating a progressive opening of the rift zone. At Kapoho . . . about 200 earthquakes were felt on April 22 and 23, and there must have been many hundreds more, too small to be felt. Some of the quakes were violent. They were accompanied by cracking open of the ground. . . . It was reported that some cracks opened to a width of several feet, and then closed again.
>
> . . . About half a mile inland from Koaʻe [village], near the old quarry which supplied rock for the Hilo breakwater, the railroad tracks were bent downward 8 feet. Along the coast just north of Cape Kumukahi the ground sank 14 feet, allowing the ocean to flood inland nearly half a mile. The waves soon built a bar of gravel across the mouth of the flooded area, leaving a brackish pond, fed by ground water, that received the formal name, Ipoho Lagoon, though it was generally known locally as Higashi's Fishpond. Until 1959 the stumps of coconut trees could still be seen standing in the water around the head of the pond.

Lorrin A. Thurston, publisher of *The Honolulu Advertiser* at the time, visited Puna in May of 1924 to survey the damage; he also noted coconut trees 10 to 12 feet deep in water at Kapele, a bay near Kumukahi. Shoreline subsidence occurred to a lesser but not less dramatic extent to the north at Kahuwai, Waʻawaʻa, Honolulu, and Makuʻu—canoe landings where all of the black sand beaches disappeared with the change in shoreline.

Pele did not further rearrange eastern Puna's coastal features until January of 1960 when molten lava broke out in a sugar cane field half a mile northwest of Kapoho village. When the eruption ended, about one month later, a cinder cone 350 feet high stood around the vents, the village of Kapoho was completely destroyed, much of Koaʻe village was leveled, and several beach homes at Waiakaʻea Bay were buried.

On the shoreline the new lava flow stretched from Koaʻe to the Kapoho Beach lots, having pushed seaward in places nearly half a mile from the former shoreline, and added approximately half a square mile of land to the island of Hawaiʻi. All of these sites disappeared: Kipu, a sea cliff seaward of Koaʻe where sea birds, including *koaʻe* nested; Kaʻohe where *hala* leaves were gathered for weaving; Kapele, a small bay with small sand pockets that was used as a canoe landing and fishing area for mullet and turtles; Ipoho, the large fishpond created by the 1924 subsidence; and Waiakaʻea, the narrow bay on the southern side of the lighthouse. The Kumukahi lighthouse barely escaped destruction; the lava flow that threatened it came to a stop literally just a few feet away. Also spared near the lighthouse were a number of stone cairns that are known as the King's Pillars.

Where *ʻaʻā* lava enters the sea, water penetrating the hot central part of the flow causes steam explosions that throw out drops of liquid lava. When these drops contact the air or water, they chill into sand-sized particles of volcano glass, drift with the ocean's current, and accumulate to form Hawaiʻi's most common variety of black sand beaches. After the end of the Kapoho flow of 1960, the entire 3 miles of new shoreline was fronted by a continuous black sand beach, but the ocean soon began to cut it away. The normal wave assault on Kumukahi is devastating, and so the new accumulations of unprotected sand were soon moved to other places. Much of the material was simply thrown up onto the top of the new flow where it formed a series of hanging beaches or storm beaches. The rest of the sand collected elsewhere along the shoreline, as at Kahuwai to the north, where an entirely new beach developed.

Although the production of black sand ended when the lava stopped flowing, other beach materials are still continually created by the erosive force of waves pounding against the exposed edge of the flow. The waves constantly break rocks loose as they assault the land and eventually deposit well-rounded boulders, cobbles, and pebbles on shore. The boulders and cobbles, commonly used in former times as stepping stones on shoreline trails across the *ʻaʻā* flows, are known as *paʻalā*, the stuff of boulder beaches. The pebble-sized rock fragments, or *ʻiliʻili*, which served a wide variety of uses from hula implements to flooring material, accumulate to form another common type of beach often called a black sand beach.

Lava flows on the Big Island in post-contact times have provided materials for many new black sand beaches in both North and South Kona, Kaʻū, and Puna, but the district of Puna has seen more beaches appear and disappear than has any other. Subject to submergences of the shoreline, lava flows, and the relentless attack of the ocean, Puna has probably the most dynamically transitional coastline in the Hawaiian Islands. One of the best and most accessible places to observe the results of the interplay of these forces is Cape Kumukahi.

The shoreline at Kumukahi is most easily reached by following the cinder road to the lighthouse. From this point very rough roads bulldozed through the *ʻaʻā* lead either south to Kapoho Bay or north toward Kahuwai. Numerous black sand storm beaches, all of them tinted green with olivines, rest on top of the low sea cliffs. No shade or protection from the elements is to be found anywhere in this hot, desolate area. Offshore waters are deep and currents are strong, precluding recreational swimming or diving, but the storm beaches attract shoreline fishermen and nude sunbathers. The rough terrain is also used as an unofficial track for off-the-road motorcycles and four-wheel-drive vehicles.

(21)
Kapoho

But though lava crawled to its very base, the lighthouse itself remained unscathed. Lava filled Waiakaea Bay, and advanced into the edge of the settlement along the beach, destroying several houses; but most of the beach houses remained intact.

Volcanoes in the Sea
Macdonald and Abbott, 1970

To many island residents, the name Kapoho often brings to mind destructive volcanic activity. The entire Puna district has always been beset by earthquakes and lava flows, but to date, during this century only the Kapoho area has suffered severe property losses. The very active east rift zone of Kīlauea volcano runs from Kīlauea caldera straight through the Kapoho area to Cape Kumukahi.

On February 28, 1955, lava fountains burst out near the Pāhoa-Pohoiki Road. Within a few days the activity shifted east toward Kapoho, and on March 3, the village of Kapoho seemed doomed. Fortunately the flow missed the main section of town, although it did overrun fifteen houses in its march toward the sea. In January of 1960, however, Pele returned to Kapoho and totally destroyed not only the remaining portion of Kapoho, but the neighboring village of Koaʻe and a number of beach homes at Waiakaʻea Bay. The volcanic activity centered just to the northwest of Kapoho village, and when it finally ceased after twenty-three days, 3 miles of new shoreline and half a square mile of new land had been added around Cape Kumukahi. This particular eruption is noteworthy also because walls were constructed in an attempt to reduce the spreading of the lava flows. In *Volcanoes in the Sea* Macdonald and Abbott offer this descriptive critique:

> The walls, about 20 to 30 feet high, consisted of loose rock fragments and soil pushed up by bulldozers. . . . Altogether about 3 miles of walls were built.
>
> The degree to which the walls succeeded in their purpose is a matter of controversy. Some people, including some of our professional colleagues, claim that they failed. . . . Although there is no way to prove it, it is our opinion that the walls prevented additional southward flooding of lava which would have destroyed not only the lighthouse, but most or all of the remaining beach houses as well. Thus, we believe that, although to some extent they did fail, the walls served a real purpose. And no one can deny what is perhaps the greatest dividend of all: a great deal of information was gained on how such walls behave, and how they should be built when they are again needed.

Makai of the former village of Kapoho is Kapoho Bay, the backshore of which is lined with beach homes

KAPOHO TIDEPOOLS. The shoreline of Kapoho Bay consists of an extensive assemblage of interconnecting tidepools. Many of the pools are large and deep enough to accommodate swimmers and snorkelers. The area is popular with residents of both the Hilo and Puna districts.

of the Kapoho Beach Lots and Vacationland. The homes are situated atop a low lava flow that in many places is barely above sea level and is pitted with numerous salt-water-filled depressions. (Kapoho means, appropriately, "the depression.") Many of the larger pools are now backyard fishponds and swimming holes. In the middle of the bay fronting Vacationland an extensive interconnected assemblage of these huge tidal ponds comprise the most popular snorkeling area in the district of Puna. In the outer pools near the reef, where the ocean has considerably fragmented the lava and penetrates more freely, a wide variety of sea life is found, including fish, shellfish, crabs, and sea cucum-

bers. Picnicking and swimming are also popular, especially around the inner pools that are always calm, clear, and protected, even when the ocean outside the reef is rough. Swimmers and snorkelers who venture farther out should stay well inshore of the surf line, where strong rip currents and very powerful longshore currents are common. Fishermen frequent the tidal pools and report excellent *ulua* fishing at the edge of the reef when it is approachable during periods of calm seas. At these times some diving from boats occurs offshore.

The Kapoho tide pools are most easily reached by following Vacationland Drive to the ocean. There are no facilities of any kind for the general public. Visitors should remember that the entire area is bare lava, most it rough and sharp. No sand is to be found anywhere along the shoreline. The strip of white bordering the eastern point of the bay is actually a small stretch of coral rubble. Visitors should also be aware that the backshore of the entire bay is a very low-lying area and is therefore subject to extensive flooding from the ocean during storms and periods of high surf. This is the reason why most of the homes near the ocean have been built well above the ground.

Beyond the tide pools, toward Kapoho Point, a large fishpond congested with mangrove and *hau* occupies the inner portion of the bay. The pond provides a wetland habitat for various species of birds but is not used for raising or stocking fish.

(22)
Isaac Hale Beach Park

A good road leads to Pohoiki, once the site of a coffee mill and a prosperous village, but now almost deserted.

The Island of Hawaii
Henry Kinney, 1913

Isaac Hale Beach Park borders the eastern point of Pohoiki Bay, a small indentation in an otherwise fairly straight and rocky shoreline. The bay is the site of a one-lane boat ramp, the only boat ramp serving the entire district of Puna. The ramp and its breakwater adjoin the beach park, which by virtue of its location serves as a support facility for the recreational and commercial boating traffic attracted by the ramp. Facilities at the park include a pavilion, restrooms, picnic tables, and a camping area, but the small two-acre park is often very congested, especially during the summer months, with sight-seers, picnickers, shoreline fishermen, campers, surfers, boaters, and of course, all their cars, trucks, and trailers.

Prior to its development as a port for the Puna district beginning in the 1870s, Pohoiki served the surrounding Hawaiian communities as a canoe landing. Chester Lyman, who passed through the area in 1846, described "fine groves of coconut trees and the situation of a hamlet on an inlet of the sea." Few changes occurred in the community until the arrival of Robert Rycroft, an Englishman who moved to Pohoiki in 1877.

Rycroft initiated a wide variety of commercial activities that included purchasing and shipping 'awa, cattle ranching, milling hardwoods, manufacturing guava jelly and jam, and raising and grinding coffee. Rycroft built a coffee mill at Pohoiki in the early 1890s, a large two-story building with concrete walls that is still standing in the dense vegetation inland of Isaac Hale Beach Park. Other structures around the bay included a courthouse-jail, a sawmill, a church, a boat house, and several shops and homes. Rycroft's commercial activities required adequate landing facilities, so he maintained a wharf at the site of the present boat ramp. Lighters transported incoming goods and outgoing products to and from the ships waiting offshore. By 1899, however, Rycroft had divested himself of all his Pohoiki interests and moved back to Honolulu, where he established a soda works on what is now Rycroft Street. He died in 1909.

The turn of the century marked the end of Rycroft's era at Pohoiki, but also the beginning of the Puna Sugar Company, which was started at Kapoho. The company made extensive use of the Pohoiki landing to bring in their seed cane and later all the materials used in the construction of the plantation camps. As the Puna Sugar Company began to expand, it sought to acquire the best arable acreage in the area. One particularly good parcel of farmland the company wanted belonged to a Hawaiian family with the Hawaiian name Hale. In a land exchange in which both parties retained ownership of their respective newly acquired properties, the Hale family moved to the shoreline of Pohoiki Bay, where today their descendents are the only permanent residents of the area. Isaac Hale Beach Park was named in 1951 in honor of a member of the family killed in the Korean War.

By 1940 the wharf at Pohoiki had been abandoned as a commercial stop, but the bay was still used as a canoe landing by local fishermen. During the 1950s, boating traffic from outside the district began to increase substantially as commercial and recreational fishermen began buying smaller boats that could be easily trailered to any part of the island. Today the boat ramp is used extensively, especially by commercial fishermen who frequent the excellent fishing grounds offshore.

Other popular activities in the bay include surfing,

bodyboarding and swimming. Surfers ride the generally small waves in the center of the bay where there is often a rip current, and swimmers usually congregate around the boat ramp. A black sand beach composed of pebbles and cobblestones lines the inner shoreline of the bay, but most swimmers and surfers use the boat ramp as an entry and exit point. Inland of the beach, hidden in lush vegetation, Pohoiki Warm Springs provides a unique place to rinse off. The pool of volcanically-warmed fresh water rests in a lava sink and is a popular natural attraction for visitors to the area. Warm water also seeps into Pohoiki Bay from the bay floor.

(23)
MacKenzie State Recreation Area

Tribute was paid to the memory of Ranger A. J. W. MacKenzie of the Department of Agriculture and Forestry last week when a monument to him was dedicated at Malama, Puna, Hawaii. Members of the family who took part in the ceremony included Mrs. MacKenzie, Mrs. Roland Smith, Mrs. Paul Tate, and Gordon MacKenzie. Mr. MacKenzie was killed in an accident last year.

Honolulu Star Bulletin
April 4, 1939

MacKenzie State Recreation Area was named in 1939 to honor Albert J. W. MacKenzie, who had been a forest ranger for twenty-one years until his death on June 28, 1938. A quiet, gentle man of great physical strength and infinite strength of character, MacKenzie was completely at home in all of the Big Island's forests and possessed an infallible sense of direction, giving him the unique ability to hike safely in and out of places generally considered to be inaccessible. MacKenzie worked extensively in the Puna and Kaʻū districts replanting burned-over areas, and he also planted many windbreaks on both Mauna Kea and Mauna Loa. As part of one of his shoreline projects he planted ironwoods along the rocky sea cliffs in the land section called Malama, the land now bears his name.

MacKenzie's ancestral origins were in the MacKenzie Highlands of Scotland, but his family had sailed to North America and settled in Nova Scotia. Like many other restless boys of the time, the young MacKenzie went to sea, arriving in Hawaiʻi in the 1890s as a young man of sixteen years. He made his way to the Big Island where he became a stage driver for the old Volcano Stables, not only taking tourists and the mail to Kīlauea volcano, but also serving as a guide on the upper slopes of Mauna Loa. During this time he met and married Catherine Lee, the daughter of Peter Lee, manager of the Volcano House. They lived at their ranch, called Anuhea, at the 29-mile marker along the Hilo-to-Volcano road. Here, all of their ten children were born.

On October 1, 1917, MacKenzie became a forest ranger with the territorial Department of Agriculture and Forestry, a position he held for the rest of his life. One day in 1938, while inspecting a project site above Waiʻōhinu, he was killed in an automobile accident. In 1939 a monument was dedicated to him at Malama in Puna, and the park in which the monument is located was subsequently called MacKenzie State Park. A second monument, a stone drinking fountain, was placed in the park by family members to honor the memory of MacKenzie's wife, Catherine, after her death in 1952.

In 1981 Michael McPherson, MacKenzie's grandson and one of Hawaiʻi's finest contemporary writers, published a poem entitled "Malama," a literary memorial to his grandfather. The poem, interwoven throughout with McPherson's powerful imagery, is also an incisive examination of Malama's past and present and the links between them. Here is its first section.

Malama

On the Puna coast, near the easternmost tip of the island Hawaii, in a grove of tall ironwoods planted early in this century stands a lava and mortar marker, similar in shape and height to older, mortarless markers found on trails which cross the flanks of Kilauea Volcano, and bearing this inscription:

MACKENZIE PARK
IN MEMORY OF
FOREST RANGER A.J.W. MACKENZIE
OCTOBER 1, 1917–JUNE 28, 1938

1

What angry ghosts are these
that roam the salt washed
honeycomb of corridors
through the belly of the earth,
fingering outward and down for miles
from the sea to the heart of the mountain?
Who can sleep in this grove

in the broken night, a windy
cacaphony of flutes and drums,
and grinding of stones deep in the belly,
the ground trembling
as the heartbeat shifts,
and chants of the procession
as they mark again the passing of their king—
is it any wonder then
that the campers
often in their haste
leave food and gear behind?
And from where comes
this orange glowing light
somewhere upward and ahead, around
the endlessly rounded corner in the corridor
of the dream?

The ranger slept here, long ago.
Alone he rode the two days down
from his home at Kilauea. He planted trees
in the days, trees which frame the king's highway,
labor of prisoners in late Hawaiian times,
and at night he lay alone by his fire
and listening to the stories on the wind
and rumblings in the earth's belly
he was content, and slept
dreaming the warm belly of the woman
in the orange glow
from the heart of the black mountain.

© 1981 by Michael McPherson

MacKenzie State Recreation Area is a long narrow 13-acre beach park situated between Highway 137 and a long reach of low sea cliffs. The entire park is heavily forested with ironwoods, the needles of which completely blanket the ground, allowing little else to grow besides a few scattered patches of *naupaka, hala,* and *hau.* A conspicuous sign erected near the park entrance marks a portion of the so-called King's Highway, a former Hawaiian trail. Facilities in the park include one pavilion, restrooms, picnic tables, and a camping area.

Over the years MacKenzie State Recreation Area has been the site of many drownings and near-drownings, most of them of fishermen who have been swept off the rocky ledges along the park's shoreline. These ledges provide excellent fishing platforms, but at the same time are subject to the ravages of high surf. Veteran fishermen at the park suggest that drownings can be prevented if a person swept off the rocks can stay offshore,

swimming and floating, and wait for help rather than try to scramble back up the cliffs in the pounding surf. Currents running toward the open sea are generally short-lived and are unlikely to carry victims very far. Longshore currents that prevail throughout most of the year drift parallel to the shoreline in the direction of the tradewinds. MacKenzie State Recreation Area is also well known as a place of eerie sounds and strange sights after dark, not the least of which are the "night marchers," processions of the spirits of ancient Hawaiians.

(24)
Kehena

After traveling a mile and a half along the shore, we came to Kehena, a populous village; the people seemed, from the number of their canoes, nets, etc., to be much engaged in fishing. Their contrivance for launching and landing their canoes, was curious and singular.

Journal of William Ellis, 1823

The Reverend William Ellis observed the *paepaewaʻa,* the canoe ladder, that seems to have been developed in Puna specifically for negotiating an outrigger canoe over the low sea cliffs comprising most of the district's shoreline. These ladders or ramps were lashed onto rocky inclines, and the canoes were launched and landed over them, a risky operation demanding a great deal of knowledge and skill.

Fishermen or travelers landing in a canoe today would have a much easier time because Kehena now has a black sand beach. This beach, however, did not exist before 1955. In March and May of that year massive lava flows poured down the *mauka* slopes and cascaded into the ocean. The ensuing steam explosions threw out vast quantities of glassy sand-sized ash, which immediately began accumulating on shore downcurrent of the flow, creating Kehena Beach. Once the eruption ended, the ocean tapered the beach to its present dimensions, but did not erode it completely away. The new point of land made by the flow provides a barrier that allows permanent sand accretion—although Pele challenged this permanence in 1975.

On Saturday, November 29, 1975, two sharp earthquakes severely jolted the Big Island, generating a tsunami that took the lives of two people at Halapē and caused over four million dollars in property damage as

KEHENA. This long, narrow black sand beach was formed in 1955. The tip of the lava flow that created the sand, now a rocky point of land, borders the eastern end of the beach. In 1979 the beach dropped nearly three feet after a severe earthquake shook the Puna district. The concrete stairs that led to the beach collapsed and sheered off halfway down the sea cliff.

well as dramatic shoreline subsidence in the districts of Puna and Ka'ū. At Kehena, the beach sank almost 3 feet, collapsing the former concrete stairs which now hang more than 10 feet above sea level. But the sand held its ground.

The resiliency of the beach proved to be the good fortune of an errant automobile driver. On May 14, 1981, a man alone in his car accidently drove it over the sheer sea cliff above Kehena Beach. The incident was witnessed by a young girl from the neighborhood who was taking an afternoon walk along the beach with her younger brother. She reported that the car suddenly flew over the cliff from the parking lot above and landed upside down in the sand. She and her brother immediately summoned help, and within a short time the driver was extricated and sent off to the hospital, alive. If the car had landed on rocks instead of sand, the outcome might have been different.

Kehena Beach is divided into two pockets of sand by a small rocky ridge that inclines *makai* from the low sea cliffs. An easily negotiable footpath descends the ridge from the viewpoint parking lot at the top of the cliffs. The remains of the former stairway that led down to the beach are suspended above the pocket of sand to the

KAIMŪ BEACH PARK. Kaimū Beach is probably the most famous and most photographed of all the Big Island's black sand beaches. Severe erosion has been a problem here for many years, threatening not only the beach but the beautiful coconut grove that surrounds it.

west of the ridge. The surf here commonly covers the entire beach, surging into the base of the sea cliffs; so most people choose the smaller patch of sand to the east of the ridge, where the range of the waves is not a problem. Ironwoods and coconut trees grow on the backshore—a nice little grove that provides shade in an area that can get extremely hot.

During most normal ocean conditions the beach is safe for swimming, but this shoreline is directly exposed to the open ocean and is often subject to heavy surf. Occasionally bodysurfers attempt to ride Kehena's shorebreak, but the break is not considered to be partic-

ularly good nor is it a very safe bodysurfing site. The drop to overhead depths at the water's edge is very abrupt, a beach feature that commonly causes undertows. Heavy surf generates not only undertows, but powerful rip currents and longshore currents as well. There have been many rescues and near-drownings at this beach. Heavy surf also rolls pebbles and cobblestones around in the shorebreak, which may cause painful leg injuries to people wading in and out of the water.

The beach is easily accessible from the Kehena lookout. There are no facilities except for the small parking area at the lookout. Besides swimmers and bodysurfers,

45

Kehena attracts shoreline fishermen, but its accessibility and seclusion have also made it a very popular "complete suntanning" beach among the Big Island's nudists.

(25)
Kaimū Beach Park

'Auhea 'o ka lani la?
Aia i ka he'e nalu,
He'e ana i ka lala la,
Ho'i ana i ka muku.

A ka nalu o Ho'eu la,
E uho'i a'e kaua,
A pae a'e a i Kaimū la,
Ho'omu nā kānaka.

The royal chief, where is he?
There, surfing.
On the long wave, sliding out to sea,
On the long wave, sliding out to sea,
On the short wave, returning.

On the Ho'eu surf,
We both return,
And land at Kaimū,
Where the natives gather.

" 'Auhea 'o Ka Lani La?"
Traditional chant honoring
Alexander Lunalilo

The black sand beach at Kaimū and the adjoining coconut grove are among the Big Island's most famous and most photographed scenic attractions. The beach formed about 1750 when a lava flow from the east rift zone of Kīlauea entered the ocean approximately half a mile to the northeast of the former Hawaiian fishing village of Kaimū. As the molten lava poured into the sea water, the resulting steam explosions produced a tremendous volume of black volcanic sand which subsequently washed onshore to form the beach. Over the years, however, the beach has gradually become smaller, a result primarily of the erosive force of the ocean. This phenomenon of black sand beaches appearing and disappearing, so common to the districts of both Puna and Ka'ū, has probably been witnessed more frequently on the Big Island than any other place in the world.

Volcanic activity dealt the beach an additional blow on November 29, 1975. A very severe earthquake, centered inland of Kamoamoa under Kīlauea's south flank, caused a major subsidence of the shoreline at Kaimū, dropping the ocean floor almost 3 feet. The land movement not only further reduced the size of the already diminishing beach, but it exposed the famous coconut grove to the erosive force of the ocean. Many of the tall old trees have been undermined, causing them to topple into the foreshore.

The beach at Kaimū is not safe for swimming. It is unprotected from the open ocean and usually has a hard-hitting shorebreak. The foreshore of the beach is steep and drops very abruptly to overhead depths at the water's edge. During periods of heavy surf, the force and size of the shorebreak increase and generate powerful rip currents. Island residents enter the water to windsurf, paddle canoes, or to surf, but rarely to swim. A county lifeguard tower is manned regularly, however, because of the great numbers of tourists who visit the beach, most of them completely unaware of the dangers. The beach experiences some seasonal erosion during the rougher winter months, exposing more boulders than are ordinarily seen at the eastern end of the beach.

In former times Kaimū was the most famous surfing area in Puna, and large crowds often gathered to watch the riders. The name Kaimū means "gathering [at the] sea [to watch surfing]." Although surfers still ride the breaks offshore of the beach and outside the eastern point of the bay, subsidence in more recent times has apparently altered the ocean bottom enough to affect the waves, making them break much more poorly than before. As a result, most of the surfing activity now takes place to the south at Kalapana Beach fronting Harry K. Brown Park.

Kaimū Beach Park, often mistakenly called Kalapana Beach, borders Highway 137, the main road through the tiny present-day village of Kaimū. There are no facilities for park users other than the lifeguard tower and roadside parking. Lonowai, the small fresh water pool on the *mauka* side of the highway, serves as the traditional bath to rinse off the salt water. The coconut and *hala* grove that covers the backshore provides an undeveloped park for picnickers and sunbathers. Shoreline fishermen report excellent success in the bay, particularly at the eastern end of the beach where a section of the old road remains. A number of 100-pound-plus *ulua* have been caught in this area. Signs are posted at the beach prohibiting the removal of the black sand, a common practice of visitors seeking souvenirs. Taking sand for any reason will only exhaust more quickly the already diminishing sand reservoir.

(26)
Harry K. Brown Park

Huli aku nānā ia Kalapana,
Alo ana Kaimū i ka 'iu'iu.

Here we turn aside to view Kalapana
With a glimpse of far-off Kaimū.

"Ka Pū'ali Inu Wai a Mī Kakina"
Traditional song

The district of Puna's most popular beach park was named in 1953 for Harry Kaina Brown, a former Hawai'i County auditor. Before then it was known as either Kalapana Park or Wai'ākōlea Park. The beautiful black sand beach fronting the park is Kalapana Beach, a name that for many years has been mistakenly applied to Kaimū Beach, another black sand beach less than a mile away.

Formerly a Hawaiian fishing village, Kalapana today is a small thriving residential community that has grown up around its noted beach. In the sandy backshore of the beach stands a shallow, stagnant pond, the remnant of Wai'ākōlea Pond, once one of the most famous landmarks in the district. In times past the beautiful freshwater pond provided an idyllic setting for bathers, especially those returning from surfing in the challenging waves at Kaimū. In the traditional song " 'Auhea 'o ka Lani La?" (Where is the royal chief?) composed in honor of King William Charles Lunalilo (1835–1874), two verses make direct references to these pastimes:

A ka nalu o Hō'eu la	On the Hō'eu surf
E uho'i a'e kāua	We both return
A pae a'e a i Kaimū la	And land at Kaimū
Ho'omū nā kānaka.	Where the natives gather.
'Au'au i ka wai la,	We bathe in the water
A'o Wai'ākōlea,	Of Wai'ākōlea,
Lu'u aku a ea maila	We plunge and surface,
Kānaenae o ka lani.	A eulogy for the royal one.

In 1883 Queen Emma (1836–1885), the widow of Kamehameha IV, spent a week vacationing at Wai'ākōlea Pond, which then opened directly into the ocean. At the time of her death in 1885, a severe storm shifted the sand dunes, closing the channel into the pond and sealing it inland. Native residents of the area interpreted this event as an act of the gods to commemorate the death of their beloved queen. Years later, when the popular natural swimming pool became part of the public beach park, a low rock retaining wall was constructed around its perimeter and a large drainpipe was installed to reconnect the pond waters and the ocean. Then, on November 29, 1975, a powerful earthquake generated a local tsunami and caused the shoreline to drop approximately 3 feet. This violent disturbance broke the drainpipe into several sections, severing its connection with the pond and allowing the surf to keep it plugged with sand. Tons of sand also filled the once large pool, reducing it to a fraction of its former size. Its stagnant waters no longer attract swimmers.

Harry K. Brown Park includes a part of the old Kalapana village, a *heiau*, and a number of historic stones from various parts of the district of Puna. These stones were moved to the park in 1934 by A. R. Hall as part of a WPA reconstruction project. Hall and his wife Annie believed that these historically important objects were in danger from vandals and artifact hunters if left in their original locations. With the concurrence of Samuel Spencer, the Big Island county chairman, the stones were gathered and placed in the park, known then as Wai'ākōlea Park. Hall and his crew also erected a Hawaiian thatched house and marked the stones with small signs describing their history and importance. All the signs have long since disappeared. In a newspaper interview in 1950, Hall's wife once again explained how the collection had arrived in Kalapana and gave a brief description of each one. The stones included a large, round grinding stone; Pohaku Naki'iki'i Kanaka, four slab-like stones in a line and, opposite them, four lower square stones from Kahuwai; Makanoni, a fish god from Kula near Kumukahi; Ku'ula and Hinalele, two fish gods from Kolele below Pāhoa; the Bell Stone or Honolulu Stone from Honolulu Landing; a large maika stone; and the Nānāwale Stone from Nānāwale. Although some of the smaller stones have disappeared, a

HARRY BROWN BEACH PARK. Kalapana Beach, another of the Puna district's famous black sand beaches, fronts the beach park. A large drainpipe once ran from a pond behind the beach to the ocean. In 1979 the pipeline collapsed and broke apart when a severe earthquake jolted the area. Portions of the drainpipe and the concrete blocks that supported it are still visible in the surf.

number of the larger ones can still be found in the park today.

Harry K. Brown Park is Puna District's most popular park for sunbathing, swimming, and surfing. Although the ocean fronting the long black sand beach is often too rough and hazardous for non-swimmers and children, many mothers bring their little ones to the southwestern end of Kalapana Beach, usually to swim in the large pond at the site of the former canoe landing. The Kalapana canoe landing, formally known as Kalapana State Wayside Park, is just beyond the historic painted church, Star of the Sea, and formerly consisted of a stone ramp over which canoes from the village were launched and landed. The shoreline subsidence that occurred in 1975 erased the former landmark and left a portion of the nearby coconut grove partially submerged in a new tidal pond. A natural rock barrier protects the shallow pond from the open ocean, offering a safe, sandy swimming pool for children.

Offshore from Harry K. Brown Park is the surfing

spot that the Big Island surfing community knows as Drainpipes. This break attracts riders from all over the island, particularly from Hilo, because of its excellent and occasionally big surf. Some of the biggest rideable waves seen in the latter half of this century occurred on Saturday, June 19, 1982, when a tremendous swell from the east struck the Hawaiian Islands generating waves at Drainpipes that ranged from 15 to 20 feet. In 1977 Big Island surfers organized a surfing contest at Kalapana that has evolved into an annual event.

During periods of high surf, a very powerful rip current runs along the shoreline from the broken drainpipe at the water's edge and into the waves offshore. County lifeguards stationed at Kalapana Beach have rescued many swimmers caught in this current, which caused a number of drownings over the years before lifeguards were assigned to the beach. Although local residents bodysurf and bodyboard around the drainpipe without

mishap, visitors unfamiliar with the beach should completely avoid this potentially dangerous area. Facilities in Harry K. Brown Park, located directly across the road from Kalapana Beach, include pavilions, restrooms, parking, drinking water, showers, and picnic and camping areas.

Midway between Harry K. Brown Park and the Hawai'i Volcanoes National Park visitor center at Waha'ula is the Queen's Bath, a popular swimming hole. Shaded by large mango trees and surrounded by vegetation, this pool of cold, slightly brackish water once provided the women of the neighborhood with a pleasant place for washing clothes and bathing. Longtime residents of the area know the pool as Punalu'u and say that the name Queen's Bath originated during World War II from the soldiers who were stationed in the district of Puna.

Hawai'i Volcanoes National Park

Hawai'i Volcanoes National Park covers more than 200,000 acres of land on the shield volcanoes of Mauna Loa and Kīlauea. Preserved for their geologic, volcanic, biologic, and historic interest, the park lands also provide a refuge for native plants and birds, including many endangered species.

The first national park in the Hawaiian Island (and the eleventh in the nation), called Hawai'i National Park, was dedicated in 1916. It included not only Mauna Loa and Kīlauea volcanoes, but Haleakalā on the island of Maui as well. The awkward geographical split of the single park ended in 1961 with the creation of Hawai'i Volcanoes National Park on the Big Island and Haleakalā National Park on Maui, the state's second and the nation's thirty-first national park.

The coastal section of the park is nearly 30 miles long and includes all the beaches and sites from Waha'ula to Kalu'e. It offers many opportunities for sight-seeing, picnicking, hiking, and camping in easily accessible areas, such as Waha'ula and Kamoamoa, and in remote wilderness areas such as Keauhou, Halapē, and Kalu'e. All hikers and campers planning overnight stays are required to register at park headquarters at the Kīlauea

Visitor Center—and this is a must. In the event of any life-threatening situations such as advancing lava flows, earthquakes, or tsunami, it is vital that the park rangers or rescue personnel be able to locate and account for everyone in the wilderness areas. Fishermen should also be aware that exclusive fishing and seafood-gathering rights have been granted to native Hawaiian residents of Kalapana and their guests in the area from the eastern park boundary to the fence line halfway between Keauhou and Halapē. Check at either visitor center—Waha'ula or Kīlauea—for additional information. The following five sites are all located within the park limits: Waha'ula, 'Āpua, Keauhou, Halapē, and Kalu'e.

(27)
Waha'ula

At noon we passed through Pulana, where we saw a large heiau called Wahaula, Red Mouth, or Red-feather Mouth, built by Kamehameha, and dedicated to Tairi, his war-god. Human sacrifices, we were informed, were occasionally offered here.

Journal of William Ellis, 1823

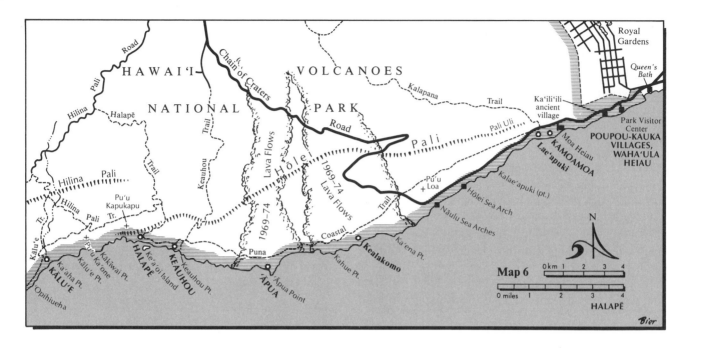

The construction of Wahaʻula, a *luakini*-type *heiau* (where human sacrifices were offered), is attributed to Paʻao, a powerful priest from Tahiti who is said also to have build Moʻokini Heiau in Kohala. In later years, Kamehameha I used Wahaʻula and dedicated the temple to his war god Kūkāʻilimoku. With the collapse of the Hawaiian religion in 1819, almost all of the *heiau* in Hawaiʻi were abandoned, but tradition died hard at Wahaʻula, the last major temple in the islands to be actively used. The partially reconstructed temple is located on a low rise directly behind the Wahaʻula Visitor Center, and is well worth a visit.

The visitor center marks the coastal entrance to Hawaiʻi Volcanoes National Park and is located on the Chain of Craters Road. In addition to parking, drinking water, and restrooms, the center offers an information desk, an exhibit of events in Hawaiian history, a trail with markers identifying historic sites and native Hawaiian plants, and a shoreline walk along the low sea cliffs. The rocky coastal terrain, combined with pounding surf, deep water, and strong longshore currents precludes all in-water activities.

Two miles west of the Wahaʻula Visitor Center are the ruins of the Hawaiian fishing village Kamoamoa which was almost completely destroyed by a tsunami in 1868. The site is now an excellent area for picnicking and camping, well shaded with trees and shrubs. A parking area, restrooms, and drinking water are also available. The entire Kamoamoa shoreline is one of low lava sea cliffs that are completely exposed to the open ocean. With no safe entry and exit points, deep water directly offshore, strong longshore currents, and pounding surf, recreational swimming is extremely hazardous. Fishing restrictions apply to this section of the park's shoreline, and interested fishermen should inquire at the visitor center for details. Essentially, only residents of Kalapana and their guests are permitted to fish the part of the coast extending roughly from Wahaʻula to Keauhou.

(28)
ʻĀpua

Ua uahi Puna i ka ʻolokaʻa pōhaku,
I ka huna paʻa ia e ka wahine.

Nānahu ahi ka papa Oluea
Momoku ahi Puna hala i ʻĀpua,
Uluʻā ka nahele me ka lāʻau.

50

Puna smokes mid the bowling of rocks,
Wood and rock heaped about in confusion
  by the goddess
The plain Oluea's one bed of live coals;
Puna is trewn with fire clean to 'Āpua,
Thickets and tall trees ablazing.

"Mele No Ka Hula Ala'apapa"
Unwritten Literature of Hawaii
Nathaniel Emerson

In 1868 a short-lived eruption occurred at Kīlauea during an extended eruption of Mauna Loa, one of the rare occasions of simultaneous eruptions of both volcanoes. Swarms of earth tremors accompanied the volcanic activity for almost a week, culminating in a tremendous earthquake on April 2, the severest in Hawai'i's recorded history. The earthquake caused widespread damage on the Big Island and was felt as far away as Kaua'i. In the district of Ka'ū, every European-style building collapsed, and in Wood Valley, where heavy March rains had saturated the soil, the violent agitation generated a massive mud flow that buried a village killing all thirty-one inhabitants and 500 domestic animals. Landslides were triggered as far away as Honopu'e Valley in Kohala, while rockfalls near Hilo killed two people.

On the southeastern side of the island, large sections of shoreline sank abruptly, in some areas as much as 7 feet, and the resulting tsunami destroyed all the coastal villages from Kapoho to Honu'apo. In addition to the tremendous loss of property from the widespread inundation, forty-six lives were lost in the waves, which reached heights of 50 feet about sea level. King Kamehameha V personally helped to organize and distribute a relief fund for the victims, a fund which amounted to several thousand dollars within a month of the disaster.

The fishing village of 'Āpua was completely swept away and was never again rebuilt or inhabited. Some of the survivors moved *mauka* to Pānau, where they worked harvesting *pulu*, the soft "wool" from the base of treeferns' frond stalks. The bundled *pulu* was shipped out of Keauhou to the United States, Canada, or Australia where it was used as stuffing for mattresses and pillows. Most of the 'Āpua residents, however, moved to the neighboring shoreline villages of Kalapana and Kaimū where many of their descendants still live.

During the 1920s and 1930s, many large goat drives passed through the 'Āpua area on their to Punalu'u or Kalapana. Goats had been introduced into the Hawaiian Islands late in the eighteenth century. Released under the protection of a royal *kapu*, they multiplied rapidly and were soon wreaking widespread havoc by denuding the land of vegetation. Of the resulting problems the most important was serious soil erosion. When Hawai'i National Park was created in 1916 with a mandate to preserve all of the natural features within its boundaries, there was great concern over the destructiveness of the large goat population. Therefore, park officials sanctioned eradication efforts by civilians. These efforts took the form of large-scale goat drives.

Most of the drives were organized in Kalapana where more than thirty *paniolo* were recruited, primarily from the villages of Punalu'u, Kalapana, and Kaimū. These cowboys brought their own horses and gear, but they were rewarded with $5.00 a day for three days, all their meals, and a huge party after it was all over.

On the first day the *paniolo* fanned out in a long line across some part of the Ka'ū Desert. Riding roughly parallel to the coast, they headed *makai* for 'Āpua Point. As the goats saw the riders coming, they would run ahead, but the cowboys always stayed at least half a mile behind lest the goats should spook and bolt. By the end of the day the hot, tired goats were easily herded into 'Āpua Point and a wire fence that had already been placed flat on the ground across the width of the point was quickly raised. Smaller herds were penned several miles to the east of 'Āpua in a large rock wall enclosure that is still standing. On the second and third days the goats were so thirsty and tired that they were herded almost as easily as domesticated animals to the Kalapana area where they were slaughtered—some 500 to 5,000 goats in each drive.

The hides were salted, dried, bundled into bales of 100, and shipped to California, an export activity that had actually begun about 1885. During the 1920s the hides brought wholesale about 50 cents each. Besides providing some extra income for both the organizers and the *paniolo*, the drives provided adventure and excitement for the people of this part of Puna. Many older residents of the area still recall these roundups and the parties that followed them.

In 1969 a series of intermittent eruptions began along Kīlauea's east rift zone. By 1973 a new mountain, Mauna Ulu, had been built. Lava from the erupting vents covered several miles of the Chain of Craters Road and flowed over Hōlei Pali onto the flatlands behind 'Āpua Point. The lava that entered the ocean to the east of the point produced a large amount of black sand, and several small beaches appeared in the lee of the point, as well as a number of storm beaches on the sea cliffs on the windward side. The leeward beaches were very short-lived, however, for on November 29, 1975, an extremely violent earthquake, centered inland of Kamoamoa to the east, caused portions of 'Āpua's shoreline to drop almost 6 feet. The beaches disappeared and 'Āpua Point itself was considerably shortened. But soon sand again began to accumulate and new beaches have been formed.

On the leeward, or western, side of 'Āpua Point a storm beach of black sand and boulders backs a low rocky shelf lining the water's edge. No easy entry and exit points exist over the shelf, which is usually awash with surf. Offshore the water is deep, with strong currents running out to sea. In line with the end of the point and directly out from the beach is a deep-water surfing break that generally breaks only on a big swell. Some surfers call it Trains because both a left and a right slide originate from a single peak, breaking with such speed that they resemble trains moving in opposite directions, the flying spray simulating trailing smoke. Because of the difficult logistical problems involved in getting a surfboard to the area and the dangerous water conditions, the break is rarely ridden. Other than hikers passing through on the Puna Coast Trail, 'Āpua is visited primarily by shoreline fishermen whose camping sites are located near the beach. Visitors wishing to fish, however, should check first at one of the visitor centers (at Waha'ula or Kīlauea) because fishing at 'Āpua is limited to residents of Kalapana and their guests. The restrictions apply to the portion of the park roughly from Waha'ula to Keauhou.

'Āpua is a rocky, barren, windswept place with little natural shelter and no man-made facilities. Vegetation consists primarily of *naupaka, pōhuehue,* and some young coconut trees. Brackish water can be found in several lava cracks, but it is difficult to locate without very specific instructions or guidance from someone who has already visited the sites. Pu'uloa on the Chain of Craters Road is the nearest departure point for 'Āpua, but the hike is 6.6 miles one-way across lava fields that radiate intense mid-day heat. Even casual hikers should be well prepared with sturdy shoes, hats or visors, and plenty of water. For the visitor who does make the journey to 'Āpua, the view inland from the tip of the point is a spectacular panorama of the entire Hilina Pali fault system. A short distance southwest of 'Āpua lies the boundary between the districts of Puna and Ka'ū.

(29)
Keauhou

Keauhou is but a low finger reaching out to sea and provides a somewhat protected anchorage to the lee. There are a few houses, many native shacks with stone walls and grass or palm-thatched roofs. Here a Mr. King keeps the pulu-shipping business.

Journal of a Pioneer Builder
Boone Morrison, 1977

Keauhou, "the new era" or "the new current," was once the site of a Hawaiian fishing village that was almost totally destroyed in the tsunami of 1868. Part of the original village was rebuilt and several western-style buildings added, all of which constituted a base of operations for a *pulu* business. *Pulu,* the soft wool from the frond stalks of the tree fern, was collected, dried, baled, and hauled to Keauhou. Small carts drawn by mules transported the bales over a long narrow road down the *pali* to the landing where the *pulu* was exported to the United States, Canada, and Australia, where it was used for mattress, pillow, and upholstery stuffing.

The business venture was organized by Julius Richardson, George Jones, and George Kaina; the three had also acquired the Volcano House hotel on the edge of Kīlauea caldera. In 1877 the business partners decided to expand their hotel operation by replacing the thatched-roofed inn built in 1866 with a modern, entirely wooden building. All of the tools, equipment, and supplies used in the construction were landed at Keauhou and transported 18 miles over the *pulu* wagon track to Kīlauea.

Almost a century later, when Keauhou had long since

been deserted, the area was devastated by an earthquake and tsunami. On November 29, 1975, an extremely severe earthquake, centered inland of Kamoamoa, caused a major subsidence of the shoreline in sections of Puna and Ka'ū. At Keauhou the beach disappeared, a brackish-water well was submerged, and a thicket of *kiawe* trees was swept away as the shoreline dropped more than 10 feet. The tsunami that immediately followed rose highest along the low shoreline in the Keauhou-Halapē area, reaching heights of 30 feet above sea level. Coconut trees generally remained standing, but *kiawe* trees were completely uprooted and carried inland along with huge boulders and other debris.

The shoreline at Keauhou is today divided into two inlets by a low rocky point. Small tidal pools and pockets of black sand line the foreshore of both inlets, but shallow, rocky bottoms make for poor swimming conditions. However, snorkeling is good in the inshore areas, where one finds a wide variety of fish and many sea urchins. A number of decaying tree stumps, both above and under water show the approximate pre-1975 shoreline. Seaward of the inlets, the deep water, the strong currents, and the gusty offshore winds combine to render any in-water activities extremely hazardous. Shoreline fishing is limited to residents of Kalapana or their guests. Further information on this restriction can be obtained from the visitor centers at Waha'ula and Kīlauea.

Facilities provided by the National Park Service include one three-walled, roofed coastal shelter, a rain-catchment tank that provides drinking water, and a rock-walled outhouse. Keauhou can be reached only by hiking down the *pali* 8.0 miles on the Keauhou Trail or 8.8 miles on the Halapē Trail; or 9.7 miles along the seacoast on the Puna Coast Trail. None of these hikes should be undertaken by anyone unless properly equipped with gear and clothing necessary for wilderness hiking. All overnight campers must register at the Kīlauea Visitor Center.

(30)
Halapē

I Halapē aku nei paha. "Maybe at Halapē."
Gourds growing here [on the ground at Halapē] were completely buried by shifting winds; . . . hence the say-

ing, said when things were not found. Also said of drunks, with *pē* in this case meaning "soaked."

Place Names of Hawai'i
Pukui, Elbert, and Mookini, 1974

Halapē, "crushed missing," was once the site of a small Hawaiian fishing outpost that was destroyed in the tsunami of 1868. The habitation sites were never rebuilt, but the area continued to be used as a water stop for fishermen and travelers following the coastal trail between Puna and Ka'ū. During the twentieth century Halapē became a popular destination for back-country *ulua* fishermen and *'opihi* pickers but was visited by few nonresidents. Beginning in the 1960s, the National Park Service has provided the coastal district of Hawai'i Volcanoes National Park with a well-marked and well-maintained trail system, shelters, water-catchment tanks, and outhouses, making the rugged shoreline areas much more accessible and therefore more frequently visited. In spite of these improvements, hikers must still be alert to the dangers of recurring natural disasters.

On the Thanksgiving weekend of 1975, thirty-two hikers were camped at Halapē, including a group of six boy scouts from Hilo's Troop 77 with four adult leaders, a large group of fishermen who had come down the trail on horseback, and several other campers. At 3:36 A.M., on that Saturday, November 29, a sharp earthquake (5.7 on the Richter scale) awakened all of the campers at Halapē. It touched off rock slides from Pu'u Kapukapu, the hill standing 100 feet high inland of the beach. The tremors and dust settled quickly, and so the campers settled down too. A little over an hour later, at 4:48 A.M., the most severe earthquake yet to occur in Hawai'i in this century struck the island (7.2 on the Richter scale). The shoreline at Halapē shook so violently that everyone attempting to stand was thrown to the ground. In the darkness, they heard again a deafening roar from Pu'u Kapukapu where numerous rock slides thundered down the *makai* cliff face. The entire sky filled with dust as thick as talcum powder, and a number of campers observed "earthquake lights," intense flashes of bluish white light that result from distortions of the atmosphere.

The violent ground movement was accompanied by

HALAPĒ. On November 26, 1975, an extremely severe earthquake jolted Halapē, causing the shoreline to subside and generating a local tsunami that swept through a popular wilderness campsite. Two campers were killed. Today only the topless, decaying tree trunks of the former coconut grove mark the original shoreline. A new pocket beach of white sand has formed inland of the old grove.

a very sudden sinking of the shoreline, which caused a locally generated tsunami. The first of five waves of the tsunami struck Halapē within 30 seconds after the ground shaking had diminished. Two people were killed—one of the adults with the boy scouts was swept into a deep rocky crevice behind the beach where he was found dead, and one of the fishermen was carried out to sea, his body never recovered. Miraculously, no other people were lost, although nineteen were injured in the boiling churning water that picked up and tossed about everything in its path: people, horses, boulders, trees, and debris.

The worst of the tsunami was over 10 minutes after it had begun. In the early morning light the survivors saw the entire coconut grove almost completely submerged in the ocean and several of the fishermen's horses drowned where they had been tied. The campers, of course, were unaware of an eruption that broke out in Kīlauea caldera about one-half hour after the earthquake and continued intermittently until almost midnight of the same day. A helicopter airlifted all survivors out of the devastated area.

Although the epicenter of the great earthquake was located inland of Kamoamoa, the maximum measured subsidence, over 10 feet, occurred in the Keauhou-to-Halapē section of shoreline. At Halapē, the former beach and coconut grove were entirely submerged. By mid-December 1975, however, a new and larger sand

54

beach had already formed. Ke'a'oi Island, the islet directly offshore, which is part of the Hawai'i State Seabird Sanctuary, was reduced to approximately one-third its former size, and a shallow reef that formerly connected the eastern point of the beach and the island disappeared entirely.

Halapē Beach, on the windward side of Pu'u Kapukapu, is a beautiful little cove of white sand speckled with bits of black lava. It offers safe, protected inshore swimming. The ocean bottom is sandy and has a gentle slope to the deeper areas offshore. Directly in front of the beach in the center of the cove stand the shorn, decaying tree trunks of the former coconut grove. These stark reminders of the 1975 earthquake and tsunami provide partial protection for swimmers in an area of breaking waves that are occasionally good enough for surfing and bodysurfing. Between the cove and Ke'a'oi Island, a powerful longshore current runs toward Kalu'e, and so swimmers, snorkelers, and divers all should be extremely cautious about venturing into deeper waters. Pole fishermen report excellent catches of *pāpio* and *ulua* all along the Halapē shoreline. Several brackish-water surface ponds and a number of brackish-water wells in the lava cracks are located behind the beach.

The southern side of Halapē Beach is bordered by a rocky point. On the leeward side of the point, a small, sand-bottomed inlet in the rocks contains a tiny white sand beach, offering a pleasant spot to get out of the wind and an excellent place for younger children to swim.

Facilities at Halapē provided and maintained by the National Park Service include a three-walled, roofed shelter, a water-catchment tank that provides drinking water, a barbecue pit, and an outhouse. Use of the shelter is on a first-come, first-served basis. All overnight visitors must register at the Kīlauea Visitor Center before hiking to Halapē or any of the other popular destinations in the Hawai'i Volcanoes National Park coastal district. In the event of an eruption, a tsunami, or any other catastrophic event, it is imperative that the rescue personnel be able to account for and locate everyone in the field.

The 7.2-mile trail to Halapē from Kīpuka Nēnē is a continuous descent to the ocean, negotiating two small

pali and one big one on its way down to the beach. After the first few miles through a sparse *'ōhi'a* forest the trail emerges into open country offering no protection from the hot sun. Hikers should be well prepared with the means of adequate protection from all the elements, including occasionally cold winds and rain. It is best to plan on spending at least one night at Halapē, and not try to complete the 7.2-mile uphill return trip all in one day.

Halapē and the next shoreline site to the south, Kalu'e, are separated by high sea cliffs. Midway between the two, below Pu'u Kaone, a lava point juts into the ocean. A small, crescent-shaped black sand beach lies in the lee of the point. There is no access by land to this remote site.

(31)
Kālu'e

The Hilina Pali has a maximum height of 1,500 feet. Westward it becomes lower and then disappears beneath recent lava flows from the southwest rift zone.

Volcanoes in the Sea
Macdonald and Abbott, 1970

Kālu'e, "hanging loose," is one of the three shoreline camping sites in the coastal district of the Hawai'i Volcanoes National Park that is equipped with facilities and drinking water. One three-walled, roofed shelter, a water-catchment tank, and an outhouse, are located on the southwestern side of a wide, flat point of *pāhoehoe*. Below the shelter the ocean has broken into the seaward edge of the point to form a small inlet bordered by a beach of black sand tinted with a little red cinder and some fine bits of white coral. A large field of *pōhuehue* behind the beach provides a refreshing splash of green in an area otherwise barren of vegetation. The only other obvious signs of life on the shore are occasional sea birds, such as *'ūlili, kōlea,* and *'akekeke.*

Black sand and scattered boulders cover the bottom of the inlet. It is pleasant to cool off in the shallow water, but there is little opportunity for recreational swimming. Surf surges over the low rocks into the seaward side of the inlet, and swimmers and waders should avoid this dangerous area. Beyond the point, the ocean is extremely dangerous, with deep water, strong along-

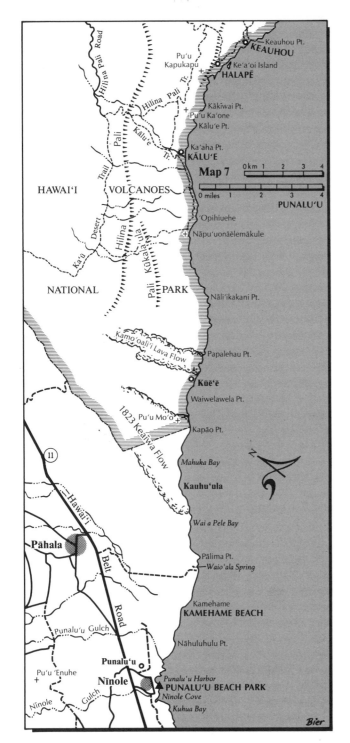

shore currents, pounding surf, and no safe entry or exit points. Shoreline fishermen and 'opihi pickers should be particularly careful along the edge of the point in the splash zone, where not only are the waves dangerous, but many of the boulders are covered with *kauna'oa* mollusks; these tube worms, if stepped on, can cause severe puncture wounds and cuts.

Kālu'e can be reached by hiking 3.8 miles down the face of Hilina Pali and over the flatlands sloping to the ocean. Overnight visitors must register at the Kīlauea Visitor Center before proceeding into this or any other of the back-country areas of the park. In the event of an eruption, tsunami, or any other catastrophic event, rescue personnel must be able to account for and locate everyone in the field. The earthquake that was responsible for the devastation in the Keauhou-to-Halapē area also caused the shoreline at Kālu'e to drop more than 10 feet, considerably altering the shape of the point and nearly closing the access to a brackish-water well in a lava crack. The tsunami that followed the earthquake also inundated the entire point at Kālu'e, but fortunately no one was camping there on that particular night.

(32)
Kamehame

Huhului'i ka hulu o nā manu
I ka ua kakahiaka,
Akaka wale no kau mai ka ohu,
Ohuohu Punalu'u i ka wai hū o Kauila,

I ka ho'owali 'ana pau ia
E ke kai o Kamehame,
'A'ohe wahi hemahema o ka pali o Pohina,
Kahiko 'ia nei e ka ohu o Wai'ōhinu.

Tousled are the feathers of the birds
In the morning rain,
Clearly one can see through the mist,
Punalu'u is decked out in the swelling
    waters of Kauila,
Completely stirred up
By the sea of Kamehame, (but)
The cliff of Pohina lacks nothing.
Clothed in the mist of Wai'ōhinu.

    Untitled *mele*
    Recorded by Mary Kawena Pukui, 1943

KAMEHAME. The picturesque but remote beach at the base of Kamehame cinder cone is located between Hawai'i Volcanoes National Park and the village of Punalu'u. Fishermen from Ka'ū use the eroding hill as a landmark to triangulate the locations of their deep-sea fishing grounds. A shoreline trail from Punalu'u passes through the area.

Kamehame, "the *hame* tree," is the name of a littoral cone located on the shoreline directly below the plantation town of Pāhala. Behind the cone are the ruins of former habitation sites, and in front of it is a pocket beach of black cinder sand tinted green with olivines. Kamehame Beach extends only the width of the cone, while the surrounding shoreline for miles in either direction consists of low sea cliffs. The continuous assault of the ocean against the loosely compacted cinder hill has given it a triangular shape and formed a beach at its base. The beach is steep with a very abrupt drop to overhead depths at the water's edge, and incoming surf often generates a strong undertow and powerful rip currents. High surf sweeps the entire beach, often washes up the face of the hill, and also seasonally erodes sec-

tions of the beach down to the underlying boulders. A small rocky shelf like a small island lies just off the beach. Because most of its mass is submerged or awash, it offers little protection for the beach. Rip currents run out into the open ocean on either side of the island, depending on the direction of the swell.

The littoral cone at Kamehame was once a famous landmark for travelers coming down the coast from Puna to Ka'ū by land or sea, for the village and landing at Punalu'u were just ahead. Local fisherman still use the hill as a mark for their *ko'a*, or offshore fishing grounds. The top of the hill, the site of a triangulation station, affords a spectacular view inland from Hilina Pali to Ka Lae.

Kamehame is a remote, undeveloped, wilderness area

57

with no facilities or shade. Fresh water seeps into several lava cracks, but the sources are difficult to locate without explicit directions. Fresh water also seeps out at the ocean floor. There is no convenient public access to this windy section of shoreline; it is visited primarily by 'opihi pickers and pole fishermen.

(33)
Punalu'u

Aloha Punalu'u, i ka 'ehukai,
Ke kai kokolo a'o Pu'umoa.

Me ka wai kaulana a'o Punalu'u,
Ka wai punapuna a'o Kauwila.

He u'i nā moku, ae kau mai nei,
Kaulana kou inoa i ka po'opa'a.

Mai poina iā Kōloa, ae kou inoa,
Ka home hānau o ka 'ili'ili.

Ho'i aku wau iā Nīnole,
I ka wai hu'ihu'i mai ke kuahiwi.

Ha'ina 'ia mai ana ka puana,
Aloha Punalu'u i ka 'ehukai.

Aloha Punalu'u in the mist of the sea spray,
With the creeping waves of Pu'umoa.

With the famous spring of Punalu'u
The fountaining spring of Kauwila.

Beautiful are the tiny rock islands, sitting on the reef.
Famous for the *po'opa'a* [fish].

Don't forget Kōloa, your name
The home and birthplace of the pebbles.

I return from Nīnole,
The cool water from the mountains.

Tell the refrain again,
Aloha Punalu'u in the mist of the sea spray.

"Punalu'u"
George K. Iopa, 1922

Although there are many black sand beaches on the island of Hawai'i, probably the two most famous are Kaimū in the district of Puna and Punalu'u in the district of Ka'ū. Both of these beautiful beaches have suffered severe sand losses from erosion by the ocean. One of the earliest recorded disasters to alter the beach at

Punalu'u occurred on April 2, 1868, when a tremendous tsunami leveled every shoreline village from Kumukahi to South Point. The tsunami resulted from widespread shoreline subsidence in both Puna and Ka'ū that was caused initially by a violent earthquake. Reaching heights of 50 feet above sea level, the waves swept in over the tops of the coconut trees, demolishing everything in their path. Forty-six people were killed—a surprisingly low figure considering the vast extent of the area inundated. Portions of two letters written by the Reverend Titus Coan in 1868 describe the catastrophe:

> The great shock [the earthquake] has prostrated the stone church at Punaluu and all the houses for six or eight miles along the coast, and a tidal wave came in, some twenty feet high, sweeping off the wreck of all. Thus in a few moments that shore was desolated, and all it substance destroyed.

> The sand beach at Punaluu was swept out to sea by the receding waves, and the beautiful pond of cold water filled with the ocean and apparently blotted out forever. At length, however, the sea brought back her spoils and formed another sand barrier, more than 100 feet within the old line, leaving a few pools of water inside, and protecting them from the ocean surges. But the great, deep, cool and beautiful fish-pond is not there in its normal state.

The Hawaiians rebuilt their village at Punalu'u, replanted the coconut grove (one of the few in Ka'ū), replaced their nets and canoes, and resumed their offshore fishing, living again as they had for generations past. But the complexion of the entire district was destined for further change. During the 1860s, sugar cane was planted as a commercial venture at Pāhala. The enterprise prospered, and by the 1880s, there were in Ka'ū four plantations with mills, half a dozen without mills, and a score of individual sugar planters raising cane on various-sized acreages. The village at Punalu'u grew to become the port town of the district as bimonthly stops by interisland coastal steamers replaced intermittent visits by sailing ships and canoes. A pier was built to expedite the movement of cargo and passengers, both ferried to shore by lighters. Eventually the town boasted several stores, a hotel, a jail, a warehouse,

PUNALU‘U BEACH PARK. A family of fishermen tries their luck atop the ruins of the former Punalu‘u Landing. Prior to the development of adequate roads from Hilo to Punalu‘u, the village was an important shipping point in the district of Ka‘u. Pu‘u ‘Enuhe, the flat-topped hill visible above the trees, is a remnant of the Nīnole volcano which ceased activity over 100,000 years ago.

a stagecoach line linking it with Pāhala and Honu‘apo, and telephone service.

During this period Punalu‘u also became a regular stop for tourists on their way to visit the volcano. It took ten long hours to traverse the 32-mile rutted dirt road from Hilo to Kīlauea by horse-drawn carriage, so the somewhat shorter distance and traveling time from Punalu‘u was often more attractive to visitors. In 1880 the Pāhala Plantation built a 5½-mile railroad track from the mill to the landing. This line was used to freight the bagged sugar down the hill and haul the tourists up. From Pāhala to Kīlauea the tourists rode in a stagecoach or carriage, the entire one-way trip taking about seven hours. The visitor traffic through Punalu‘u was considerably reduced after 1893 when a new macadamized road from Hilo to the Volcano House became

the favored route. The railroad, however, continued to operate until the 1930s.

Punalu‘u was eventually abandoned as a commercial shipping point when automobiles appeared and good roads were built to link the distant parts of the Big Island to the deep-water port at Hilo. By the 1940s, large trucks moving on improved roads hauled raw sugar in bulk—an arrangement much more attractive financially to the plantations than shipping it in bags. The buildings at the landing were torn down and the wreckage removed. Only the concrete foundations and walls and the pier were left. After the 1941 attack on Pearl Harbor army personnel dynamited the high-standing concrete walls, easily visible from the ocean, and stationed troops at the pier for the duration of World War II to ensure that it could not be used as a landing by the enemy. Then in April 1946, the worst tsunami in Hawai'i's recorded history wrecked the army's temporary facilities at the landing. Today only the concrete warehouse foundations remain.

The village at Punalu'u prior to the tsunami of 1946 still supported a sizable population who worked for such employers as James W. Glover, Ltd., Pāhala Plantation, Kapāpala Ranch, Hawai'i County, and the U.S.E.D. (United States Engineering Department). Many of the residents also fished the productive grounds offshore for *'ōpelu, 'ehu, 'ōpakapaka, kalikali,* and *'ula'ula.* Canoe sheds, canoes, and nets lined the backshore of the black sand beach. The large spring-fed pond to the rear of the beach, now landscaped with bridges and walkways, fronted a luxurious home for the plantation administrators. Residents of the area referred to the house at The Haole House and the pond as Nānaku Pond because it was overgrown with *nānaku,* or bulrushes. To the west of Nānaku Pond was another, smaller, spring-fed pond called Kauwila where the women of Punalu'u did their washing on flat laundry stones that had been carefully selected and then placed at the edge of the pond. Each family in the village had its own exclusive stone and washing area. After the washing was completed and the clothes were draped on a nearby stone wall to dry, the women bathed and relaxed with a swim in the pond. This pond no longer exists for the tsunami of 1946 leveled the sand dunes that had surrounded Kauwila and buried it. Residents in those days obtained their drinking water from *punawai* in their yards that had been made by digging down to fresh water underground. In former times some Hawaiians obtained fresh water by diving into the ocean with calabashes, which they filled with spring water bubbling up from the ocean bottom. This method is described in *Native Planters in Old Hawaii* by Handy and Handy:

> At Punalu'u in Ka'u on Hawaii men dived in the bay at some distance from the shore for their fresh water, taking down water bottles, stoppered with a finger. When they reached the chill fresh water welling up from a spring at the bottom of the bay, they removed the stoppers so that the water bottles filled. "This was how the people of Punalu'u obtained their drinking water." Punalu'u

means "diving spring." Mrs. [Mary Kawena] Pukui says there are many other places where drinking water was obtained in this way.

The black cinder sand beach at Punalu'u is situated at the head of a small bay formed by two rocky points. Atop the northeastern point, Kahiolo, are the ruins of a large *heiau* and a huge, flat-topped sacrificial stone that apparently played a part in the *heiau* rituals. A small storm beach of black sand called Keone'ele'ele lies to the east of the *heiau* at the head of a rocky cove.

The southwestern point of the bay, Pu'umoa, is the site of Punalu'u Beach Park, a county park complete with parking, showers, restrooms, picnic pavilions, drinking water, electricity, and camping sites. Punalu'u Beach, a moderately long, black sand beach backed by low dunes, lies between Kahiolo and Pu'umoa points. Lava bedrock is exposed at the water's edge from Pu'umoa to the center of the beach, so swimmers usually concentrate at the more appealing northeastern end of the beach. A small, one-lane boat ramp is also located at this end of the bay next to the ruins of the landing pier. Swimmers and snorkelers should be extremely cautions about venturing beyond the boat ramp because a very powerful rip current constantly runs out the boat channel bordering the northeastern point of the bay. During periods of high surf, this fast-flowing rip current converges with an even stronger longshore current outside the bay, a very hazardous combination for any swimmer. From the boat channel to Pu'umoa, a line of *moku,* lava boulders, form an irregular natural breakwater that partially protects the end of the beach near Pu'umoa Point. Occasionally some surfers and bodysurfers ride the small inshore waves near the point, but caution must be exercised here as well, because the water movement is always toward the channel and into the *wiliau,* the rip current.

As is the case with almost every other black sand beach on the Big Island, the source of the sand at Punalu'u was an *'a'ā* flow entering the sea, and so the supply ended when the flow stopped. The existing volume of sand on the beach, therefore, can only remain stable or decrease, unless another lava flow should happen to reach the ocean nearby and upcurrent. Fortunately for

Punalu'u, under normal conditions, the beach has enough protection to remain fairly stable, but even so, much sand has been lost as the cumulative result of sand-mining, storms, shoreline subsidence, and especially tsunamis. In 1868, 1960, and 1975 tsunami waves scoured the shoreline, swept away huge volumes of black sand, and leveled the former sand dunes. Posted signs warn all visitors to this popular destination not to remove any of the black sand and further deplete this already finite resource.

Inland of Punalu'u Beach Park, atop a high hill overlooking the ocean, is historic Hokuloa Church with its graveyard. Two plaques behind the altar note that the existing structure was completed on April 20, 1957, by the Congregational Christian Churches of Hawai'i and that it is a memorial chapel for Henry Opukahaia (1792–1818), the Hawaiian youth whose zeal and sad story were in part responsible for the arrival of the first Christian missionaries in Hawai'i in 1820. The first chapel, a wooden structure that had fallen into serious disrepair, was demolished, but the chapel bell was removed and erected next to the existing structure.

About five miles inland of Punalu'u stands a massive hill, Pu'u 'Enuhe, one of several large flat-topped hills in the area. These hills are actually remnants of the ancient Nīnole volcano which ceased activity over 100,000 years ago. Stream erosion cut deeply into the Nīnole shield, forming a series of large valleys separated by flat-topped ridges, but the valleys have been almost completely filled by more recent flows of the present Mauna Kea volcano, leaving only the tops of some of the ridges still showing.

Hawaiian legend, however, tells a much different story of the origin of Pu'u 'Enuhe, "caterpillar hill." A beautiful girl of Punalu'u married a handsome young stranger who was secretly a *kupua*, or supernatural being. This *kupua* could assume the shape of a man or that of a cutworm, a caterpillar, and he spent his nights as a worm eating sweet potato leaves. During the day he did nothing to provide food for his wife. Her distressed father advised her to tie a string to her husband's toe while he slept so that she could find out where he went at night. The *kupua*, however, discovered the trick, and avenged himself by attacking all of the sweet potato

patches in the vicinity. The people finally appealed to the god Kāne, who killed the offender and cut him up into little pieces, the size of today's cutworms. Residents of Ka'ū still tell this traditional story and point out Pu'u 'Enuhe, the home of the *kupua*, which so closely resembles a gigantic caterpillar.

The inshore waters from Punalu'u to Nīnole have long been a popular fishing area with both pole and throw-net fishermen who find there a wide variety of reef fish. Some of the more-frequented spots are still known by their older names: Pu'umoa, Wailaumakai, Laupapa'ōhua, and Kōloa. One Sunday in September 1980, an unusual set of circumstances on this shoreline culminated in a new song about Punalu'u. Samual Pua, a fisherman from Pāhala, decided to go fishing at Punalu'u and asked his wife Susan to accompany him. As she began to pack the things they would use at the beach, she also picked up her 'ukulele, something she had never done before on a fishing trip. Her husband hesitated because according to fishing tradition, a fisherman with an 'ukulele does not have his mind on the ocean and will not catch any fish. But Susan had a strong feeling that the instrument should accompany them, and so she brought it.

At the beach Samuel first went diving for *wana*, and then took his throw-net out on the rocks. Susan picked up the 'ukulele, sat down at Laupapa'ōhua, and began to sing some of the hula songs to which her daughter dances. Part way through one song she suddenly heard herself singing unfamiliar Hawaiian words to a different tune. Frightened and confused, she stopped singing immediately, but again she had a strong feeling, this time that she should continue. She did, and in a short time five verses came to her.

Susan's song mentions three old Punalu'u place names that she didn't recognize, but her good friend Jeanette Howard who runs the gift shop at the beach and who has lived in Punalu'u most of her life, identified the places for her and also translated the song into English. This is her song:

Mai poina, mai poina,	Don't forget, don't forget,
Ka nani a'o Punalu'u	The beauty of Punalu'u,
He beauty maoli nō.	Its everlasting beauty.

Pu'umoa, Pu'umoa	Pu'umoa, Pu'umoa,
Ke kai hāwanawana,	The whispering sea,
He beauty maoli nō.	Its everlasting beauty.
Kauwila, Kauwila	Kauwila, Kauwila,
Ka wai onaona,	The sweet water,
He beauty maoli nō.	Its everlasting beauty.
Hānau ia, hānau ia,	Laboring, laboring,
'Ili'ili hānau keia,	These pebbles are born,
Kanani a'o Kōloa.	The beauty of Kōloa.
Ha'ina, mai poina	Tell the refrain, don't forget
Ka nani a'o Punalu'u	The beauty of Punalu'u
He beauty maoli nō.	Its everlasting beauty.

Probably the most famous place name associated with Punalu'u is Kōloa, the home of the *'ili'ili hānau*, the "birth pebbles" mentioned in both George Iopa's and Susan Pua's songs. The first Western description of these tiny water-worn stones, which cover a small beach between Punalu'u and Nīnole, was written by the Reverend William Ellis who passed through the area in 1823:

> The interest attaching to them is derived from the curious belief still held by many natives with whom I have conversed that they are of different sexes and beget offspring which increase in size and in turn beget others of their kind. The males are of a smooth surface without noticeable indentations or pits. The females have these little pits in which their young are developed and in due time separate from their mothers to begin independent existence.

In September 1971, a columnist for the *Hawaii Tribune Herald* offered an alternate explanation of the birthing process. The *'ili'ili hānau*, she said, are conglomerate stones, which form when *pāhoehoe* flows down a dry watercourse or over a pebble beach at low tide while the upper layer of the beach is dry. The molten lava envelopes the little pebbles, but does not remelt them because they are cool. In this way the lava became "impregnated." As the ocean erodes the new lava flow, new water-worn stones are deposited on the beach, some of which contain the older, smaller stones. Eventually, the outer layers of the conglomerate stones is worn away, releasing the older, smaller stones—the moment of birth. An informant who once witnessed the event claimed that water had seeped into the cavity of the conglomerate stone and had, from the heat of the sun, turned to steam, forcing the smaller, captive stone out with considerable force. Others had just dropped out quietly.

Whatever their origin, few of the *'ili'ili hānau* remain on the beach at Kōloa. Before sand-mining was prohibited, private contractors and various county agencies hauled away not only the beach sand at Punalu'u, but the beach pebbles at Kōloa as well. In addition, the great tsunami of this century have further depleted the already dwindling supply of beach material.

(34)
Nīnole

I have just been told of an incident that occurred at Ninole during the inundation of that place. At the time of the shock on Thursday [April 2, 1868], a man named Holoua, and his wife, ran out of the house and started for the hills above, but remembering the money he had in the house, the man left his wife and returned to bring it away. Just as he had entered the house the sea broke on the shore, and, enveloping the building, first washed it several yards inland, and then, as the wave receded, swept it off to sea, with him in it. Being a powerful man, and one of the most expert swimmers in that region, he succeeded in wrenching off a board or a rafter, and with this as a papa hoo-nalu [surfboard], he boldly struck out for the shore, and landed safely with the return wave. When we consider the prodigious height of the breaker on which he rode to the shore [50, perhaps 60 feet] the feat seems almost incredible, were it not that he is now alive to attest to it, as well as the people on the hillside who saw him.

Hawaiian Gazette, April 29, 1868

The tsunami of 1868 destroyed all the shoreline homes at Nīnole, but residents soon rebuilt their homes, as in the past, near the brackish water fishpond at the shoreline. Nīnole Pond, famous for its mullet, received its fresh water from extremely productive springs called Pūhau. Pū is short for *puna* and *hau* means icy, so the name meant "icy-cold springs." The name Pūhau was also occasionally used to identify the entire pond. To the east of Pūhau another, much smaller pond is fed by a

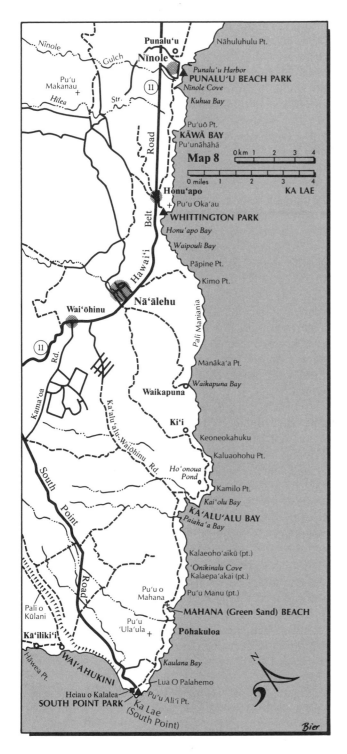

Map 8

0 km 1 2 3 4

0 miles 1 2 3 4

KA LAE

spring known as Kauale, once said to be a female spring that complemented the male spring of Pūhau.

By the 1800s, commercial sugar cane production was booming in the district of Kaʻū, and in order to meet the heavy demand for manual labor, the plantations brought in workers from all over the world. With the sudden upsurge in population, came a new and steady market for fresh fish, especially among the restaurants that catered to Oriental customers. The mullet harvested at Nīnole Pond were soon finding their way into restaurant kitchens from Pāhala to Nāʻālehu, but often the demands of the large plantation populations far exceeded the production capacities not only of Nīnole, but of other ponds in the district as well.

In addition to its traditional use as a fishpond for mullet, Nīnole Pond served as the local swimming hole for kids from both Nīnole and Punaluʻu, especially during the summer months when the children were out of school. The young boys often tried to spear the big mullet that hid back in the bulrushes, but were usually unsuccessful. Diving underwater into the icy spring waters of Pūhau proved to be almost unbearable, and even a swim in the pond usually lasted no more than ten or fifteen minutes.

During the twentieth century, high storm surf and a number of severe tsunami totally destroyed the pond walls, but the springs at Pūhau continued to flow until the winter of 1979. During that winter and then again in the winter of 1980, extremely heavy rains caused flash flooding down the intermittent stream that empties into the pond. Tons and tons of soil and boulders washed onto the shoreline, completely burying Pūhau and much of Nīnole Pond. Lands *mauka* of the shoreline had been cleared for agricultural and resort purposes, leaving great expanses of soil denuded of vegetation and subject to rapid erosion. A small landscaped park, Nīnole Cove, now occupies the backshore of the former spring-fed pond. Although Pūhau disappeared under the layers of rocks and mud, Kauale to the east continues to flow as do still a number of other tiny springs along the water's edge from Punaluʻu to Nīnole.

During the early 1970s, Hawaiiana Investment Company, the Kaʻū development subsidiary of C. Brewer and Co., started construction of the Seamountain Resort complex, which includes a restaurant behind the black sand beach at Punaluʻu, several retail shops, a condominium unit, and a golf course with a clubhouse. The resort takes its name from the Lōʻihi Seamount, an active submarine volcano that someday, many thousands of years from now, may emerge as another Hawaiian island. Located approximately 20 miles offshore of this section of the district of Kaʻū, the summit of the seamount now lies about 3,000 feet below the surface of the ocean. Lōʻihi's status as an active submarine volcano, which had been suspected since 1952, was confirmed conclusively from dredge samples and underwater photographs taken in 1980.

Nīnole Cove, a small public beach park that was developed along with the resort complex, is located directly below the parking lot of the Seamountain Golf Course. A small inlet from the ocean and several small ponds in the lava rock are shallow and protected, thus attractive primarily to children. Several pockets of black sand also offer some small beach areas for easy entry and exits at the inlet and ponds. The otherwise rocky shoreline, high surf, and the dangerous currents preclude all swimming in the open ocean, but pole fishermen report some good catches taken from these rough waters. Above the park on the top of the ʻaʻā flow that extends into the ocean, hikers can locate the remains of Kaʻieʻie Heiau. Nīnole Cove has no facilities, but public showers and restrooms are available just down the road at Punaluʻu Beach Park.

(35)
Kāwā

I kekahi la nae, hiki maikai iho la ka nalu o Maliu a me Kapaelauhala, olioli iho la ke keiki haehae poko o Naalehu, ka heenalu lala o Kawa.

One day when the waves of Maliu and Kapaelauhala were rolling in magnificiently, the cut-worm tearing son of Naalehu resolved to show the skill he had got through practice [in surfing] on the bent wave of Kawa.

"Ka Moolelo o Kamehameha I"
S.M. Kamakau, 1867

In February 1867, the Hawaiian newspaper *Kūʻokoʻa* printed a story written by historian Samuel Kamakau about Nuʻuanupaʻahu, a chief of Kaʻū. Nuʻuanupaʻahu had journeyed to the district of Kohala where Kala-

niʻōpuʻu, high chief of the island, was relaxing with other chiefs and members of his court. Kalaniʻōpuʻu, suspicious that the chief of Kaʻū was conspiring to usurp his power, decided to kill him. Kalaniʻōpuʻu and his chiefs, knowing Nuʻuanupaʻahu to be an excellent surfer, agreed they would take him surfing at Kauhola in Halaʻula where they knew he would be attacked and killed by sharks. Nuʻuanupaʻahu, however, battled his way successfully through the sharks, earning the admiration of both chiefs and commoners, who watched him fight his way to shore. Later he died of his wounds at Pololū, where he was buried.

In the story Kamakau describes Nuʻuanupaʻahu as "the cut-worm tearing son of Nāʻālehu," a direct reference to the famous legend of Puʻu ʻEnuhe, the large caterpillar-shaped hill inland of Punaluʻu, and also notes that the Kaʻū chief gained his skill in surfing from riding waves at Kāwā. In former times, Kaʻū boasted three famous surfing breaks, Punaluʻu, Paiahaʻa, and Kāwā. The waves at Kāwā are still surfed regularly, but present-day surfers know the break as Windmills, named for the small windmill onshore in a cattle pasture. Most other visitors to the area are shoreline fishermen.

No one has lived permanently on the beach at Kāwā since the tsunami of 1868 wiped out the former fishing community, but the beach is still a popular fishing and camping spot, and a surfing site. When Punaluʻu supported a large plantation population, young boys during the summer months often walked the trail paved with water-worn beach stones that crossed the ʻaʻā flow between Nīnole and Kāwā. They would camp near the once-famous fishpond Kaʻalaiki and go spearfishing offshore if the ocean was calm. In the pastures inland, they found *pāhoehoe* mounds surrounded by soil that the Hawaiians before them had used for planting. Here the boys occasionally located the so-called Hawaiian pineapples that some people believe to be native to the islands. There were two varieties, the Halakea and the Halaʻula, neither grown commercially. The fruits were very small—about the size of a fist—and very sweet; they matured at the end of long stems.

In February 1977 a very important legal question concerning public access to Kāwā was addressed in a class action suit filed by several individuals and the Sportsman's Club of Ka'ū. The private owner of the extensive expanse of low-lying pastureland behind Kāwā Bay had denied all access to the shoreline across his property. The plaintiffs alleged that they had a legal right to cross the defendant's land without fear of prosecution for trespass and to use the beach and the adjoining shoreline, primarily for fishing and surfing. One of their basic contentions was that they had inherent rights through ancient Hawaiian tradition, custom, practice, and usage, which entitled them to unobstructed access to the beach.

After a week-long jury-waived trial, the Third Circuit Court on October 14, 1980, awarded the plaintiffs four easements: to Ka'alaiki fishpond, to Ke'ekū Heiau near Kāwā Bay, and to Kāwā Bay. By ruling in favor of the plaintiffs Judge Ernest Kubota upheld the public's traditional rights of access to the shoreline, a landmark decision for the Big Island, where many miles of shoreline backed by private property are not conveniently accessible to the general public.

Many landowners did not share the enthusiasm of the fishermen, surfers, and hikers over the court's ruling because uncontrolled public access through private property has over the years resulted in many problems. When the public utilizes easements and rights-of-way, they often do not behave in a responsible manner; this was the principal concern of the private landowners, many of whom are cattle ranchers. Problems in the past have included gates left open to allow pasture animals to escape, attacks on pasture animals by pet dogs, vandalism of ranch buildings and equipment, illegal hunting and fishing, and littering. These issues need to be jointly addressed and resolved by all parties concerned in all similar access situations to insure the protection of everyone's rights.

The eastern edge of Kāwā Bay is a massive *'a'ā* flow, upon which sit the ruins of Ke'ekū Heiau. The *heiau* offers a commanding view of the shoreline and points *mauka*, including Pu'u Makanau, the huge flat-topped hill located almost directly inland. A black sand beach sprinkled with olivines rims the head of the bay, appearing green in sections where the olivine concentration is high. The northeastern end of the beach consists primarily of *'ili'ili* and *pa'alā* (water worn pebbles and cobblestones) and fronts a small brackish spring-fed pond,

that marks the seaward end of intermittent Hīlea Stream. Driftwood and wind-blown *'ōpala* (trash, rubbish) litter most of the southwestern end of the beach.

Large, relatively shallow sand deposits cover most of the inshore areas of the bay, over which shorebreak-type surf breaks almost constantly, driven by prevailing trade winds that blow nearly directly onshore. A rip current usually runs toward the northeastern end of the beach where it converges with the brackish water escaping the pond and flows out to sea along the northeastern point of the bay. In the open ocean, strong longshore currents usually pull toward Honu'apo. Sometimes an offshore wind produces excellent surfing conditions, and occasionally, when the ocean is calm, conditions are fine for diving, but divers should always be alert for stong currents and sharks, both of which are common in the area.

Beyond Kāwā Bay toward Honu'apo are several small ponds and inlets and a large number of springs. The entire reach of shoreline from Punalu'u to Honu'apo was once famous for the many springs that well up not only along the shore but also from the ocean bottom. Many migratory birds such as *kōlea* and the shorebirds *'ulili* and *'akekeke* share this area with the fishermen and surfers. While one of the pedestrian rights-of-way from the highway has been roughly marked, persons seeking to visit Kāwā Bay should check with local Ka'ū residents for details of this access.

(36)
Whittington Park

The same wave that swept away Punalu'u, also destroyed the villages of Ninole, Kawa and Honuapo. Not a house remains to mark the site of these places, except at Honuapo, where a small "hale halawai," on the brow of the hill, above the village, still stood on Friday last. The large cocoanut grove at Honuapo, was washed away, as well as that at Punalu'u. A part of the pig pali at Honuapo, on the road to Waiohinu, had tumbled into the sea, and people coming from thence are now obliged to take the mountain road through Hiilea-uka.

Letter published in the *Hawaiian Gazette*, April 29, 1868

After the tsunami of 1868 swept through the lowlands at Honu'apo, none of the Hawaiians who had lived there returned to rebuild, but in the Honu'apo fishpond mullet continued to flourish—a fish for which it was famous as were the neighboring ponds at Ka'alaiki, Nīnole, and Punalu'u. Fresh fish was in great demand at the restaurants and markets serving the large plantation populations in Wai'ōhinu, Nā'ālehu, and Hīlea.

Sugar cane, first planted commercially in Ka'ū in the 1860s, had become the basis of a major industry in the district by the 1880s. Until then, Wai'ōhinu and its distant port Ka'alu'alu had been the principal town and landing in the district of Ka'ū, but as the plantations spread and mills were built at Nā'ālehu, Hīlea, and Honu'apo, the sugar planters moved their shipping operations to a much more convenient and central site at Honu'apo.

Honu'apo Bay was deepened in the 1870s and a wharf was completed in 1883, allowing lighters to transport passengers and cargo safely between steamships anchored offshore and the wharf. The road that had tumbled into the sea during the earthquake and tsunami of 1868 was realigned; it was described as follows in a U.S. Geological Survey report published in 1884: "A good road leads from Waiohinu to Honuapo, the distance being about five miles. Through about two-thirds of the distance it runs along the terrace, at a of 600 to 800 feet above the sea, and at length winds down the hillside to the beach at Honuapo. As we descend the hill we have upon our right a vertical cliff formed by the waves driven against it by the trade-wind."

By 1890 the Hutchinson Sugar Plantation had a railroad in operation over this same steep grade, connecting Honu'apo and Nā'ālehu. On occasion, the cutworms associated with the famous legend of Pu'u 'Enuhe, "caterpillar hill," swarmed over the rails during their periodic attacks on the sugar cane, making the rails so slippery that, even if the tracks were covered with sand, the locomotives could not climb the grade. Most of the harvested cane was flumed to the railroad and then hauled by locomotive to the mills. A second railroad line ran from Hīlea to Honu'apo, and a spur led to the wharf. With the new landing, the improved roads, and a servicable railroad line Honu'apo became a busy industrial port, with several large warehouses and other associated structures in addition to the mill just inland.

Like almost all of the major landings around the island, Honu'apo gradually fell into disuse during the 1940s, as the use of large trucks on improved roads made hauling raw sugar in bulk much more economical for the plantation than shipping it in bags, as before. Then the devastating tsunami of 1946 severely battered the wharf, and it was simply abandoned and left to pounding waves of ensuing tsunami, hurricanes, and ordinary storms. Today it is little more than a ruin.

The grounds that once accommodated the former landing and the other port facilities were converted into a public beach park by the plantation and various local civic clubs, and then turned over to the County of Hawai'i to administer. In 1948 the park was named Whittington Park in honor of Richard Henry Whittington, one of the early-twentieth-century residents of Ka'ū.

Whittington was born in California in 1885 and came to Hawai'i as a teenager. He first lived with his father, a former sea captain, at Kalāheo on Kaua'i, but soon moved to Nā'ālehu to work on the sugar plantation. There he met and married his Hawaiian wife, Kalei, and eventually they settled in Wai'ōhinu, where for years the family owned and operated a soda works. Whittington also worked for the county as a road supervisor in the district of Ka'ū and was very well liked by all Hawaiian crews who worked for him. A highly esteemed and beloved resident of Ka'ū, he built a home on the hillside just above the park that now bears his name and lived there until his death in 1945.

Whittington Park consists of a grassy field with a coconut grove, three picnic pavilions, picnic tables, restrooms, and showers. The ruins of Honu'apo wharf are located at the rocky, seaward edge of the park. Offshore of the park, pounding waves and strong currents prevail throughout the year, allowing little opportunity for safe recreational swimming, but fishermen report that these rough waters are often productive. Several dirt roads lead through the tall grass and brush in the unimproved portions of the park and converge at Honu'apo Pond. The shoreline here is also rocky, but it is partially protected from the dangerous waters of the open ocean by a small low reef. Many ruins, such as old walls and building foundation slabs, reminders of the once bustling port, can be found near the pond, as well as throughout the entire park. Picnickers and campers also occasionally see white-tailed tropic birds (*koa'e kea*) that nest in the high sea cliffs adjoining the park.

(37)
Ka'alu'alu

A short distance east of Waiohinu a fair road strikes makai, leading to Kaalualu, at one time the landing for west Kau, but now consisting merely of a shallow inlet, where is the Kaalualu Ranch House and a few houses. It is an unprepossessing spot, visited mainly on account of the good plover shooting.

The Island of Hawaii
Henry Kinney, 1913

The shoreline from Honu'apo to the Green Sand Beach at Mahana consists chiefly of sea cliffs that are exposed to the direct assault of the open ocean. In several areas the pounding waves have deposited considerable amounts of white sand on some of the lower lava terraces where, blown by the prevailing winds, the sand has massed to form storm beaches such as those at Waikapuna and Kamilo. Farther down the coast, Ka'alu'alu and Paiaha'a bays are lined with small pockets of green or black sand. All of these shoreline sites once supported small, sparsely populated fishing outposts and have also played important roles in the history of Ka'ū.

WAIKAPUNA, "water of the spring"
On April 20, 1895, a girl was born to a young couple at Haniumalu near the plantation town of Nā'ālehu. Soon after the child's birth her maternal grandmother, Nāli'ipō'aimoku, or Pō'ai as she was known for short, approached her daughter, Pa'ahana, and her Caucasian son-in-law, Nathaniel Wiggin, to ask permission to raise their newborn child in her home. Much to her surprise, her *haole* son-in-law consented, and so it was that Mary Kawena Wiggin became the charge of her grandmother after she was weaned.

Pō'ai was a very remarkable woman. Born in 1830, she was reared in the old culture in Ka'ū where Christianity was introduced at a much later date than in other parts of the island. Among her many talents and accomplishments, she had been trained as a *kahuna lapa'au,* in

a sense a medical practitioner, and had been a practicing midwife all of her adult life. She had attended when Kawena was born. Pō'ai was also accomplished in the hula, and at one time performed as a court dancer for Queen Emma. This was only a part of the rich heritage that she passed on to Kawena—the language, the lifestyle, the values, and the wisdom of the Hawaiian people.

When Pō'ai married in her mid-twenties she became the mother of two step-children and eventually she bore fifteen children of her own. The family kept two homes, one at Haniumalu where they lived during the planting and growing season, and one on the shore at Waikapuna where they lived during the fishing season. No one in the district had lived permanently at Waikapuna since the catastrophic tsunami of 1868, which had not only destroyed all of the seaside dwellings, but had also considerably altered the shoreline. By the time Kawena came to live with her grandmother at Haniumalu, Pō'ai was in her mid-sixties, her own children already adults with families of their own. Nonetheless, she still returned to Waikapuna each summer to gather salt. While they camped at the beach, Kawena, as always, continued to absorb the accounts and the details of everyday living as they had been in former times at Waikapuna and throughout Ka'ū. She was a very thoughtful and attentive child with an exceptionally retentive memory, having been trained by Pō'ai to listen to an elder in silence, never to interrupt, and to ask questions only after an adult was through talking.

Mary Kawena Wiggin, better known to Hawai'i's residents by her married name, Mary Kawena Puku'i, returned to live in her father's home in Nā'ālehu when she was six years old. Pō'ai had died, thus ending Kawena's intensive training and almost total immersion in ancient Hawaiian culture, but she very successfully adjusted to the ways of the Western world without losing her native Hawaiian-ness and understanding of her people. This success has been evident throughout her long association with the Bernice Pauahi Bishop Museum, during which time she has become one of the world's most important twentieth-century interpreters of Hawaiian language and culture.

Mrs. Puku'i has written many articles, and has

KAʻALUʻALU. The extensive tidal flats at the head of Kaʻaluʻalu Bay teem with a great diversity of marine life. Large flocks of shoreline birds congregate in the area to feed on the shallow-water sea life. The deeper waters at the mouth of the bay were once used as a landing to pick up cattle from the *mauka* pastures. Ruins of the loading chute and the holding pens can still be seen on the far point.

authored, co-authored, and collaborated on numerous books and research projects. Her sensitive translations of Hawaiian legends and chants, archival material, and articles from the Hawaiian-language newspapers have appeared in many publications. One of her greatest contributions, which she co-authored with Samuel Elbert, was the *Hawaiian Dictionary,* the definitive work on the Hawaiian language. Other well-known books on which she has collaborated by sharing her knowledge of the culture and the language include *The Polynesian Family System in Kaʻū, Hawaiʻi, Nānā i ke Kumu,* and *The Echo of Our Song.* In June 1976, Mrs. Pukuʻi, along with five other exponents of Hawaiian culture, was

honored by the Honpa Hongwanji Mission as a Living Treasure of Hawaiʻi, recognition befitting this remarkable woman, who was raised by her grandmother from Waikapuna.

The Waikapuna shoreline was never quite the same after the destruction caused by the tsunami of 1868 and also by other tsunami and storms that followed. The fishing community here, actually a fishing outpost supplying food for the *mauka* farming regions, had always had great difficulty obtaining fish and seafood because of the extreme ruggedness of the unprotected shore; but with subsidence of the shoreline and scouring of the beach by the enormous waves, the conditions worsened.

In *Native Planters in Old Hawaii*, Handy and Handy related this account by Mary Kawena Puku'i of some of the changes that occurred at Waikapuna:

On these visits [to Waikapuna by Mrs. Puku'i and her grandmother Pō'ai] they would erect a shelter on the *pahoehoe* lava just above the water holes at the southwest corner of the beach area. In those days there were three water holes. In the highest, the *lua wai inu* (drinking-water-hole), there was good potable water. The next below this, the *lua wai holoi 'umeke* (water-hole-for-utensil-washing), was slightly brackish, but good enough for washing dishes. The one nearest the sea, the *lua wai 'au'au* (bathing-water-hole), was for clothing and body washing. Only this one remains. The water lies at the bottom of a pit in solid lava. It formerly was a larger pool and the water was more plentiful. . . . The tidal wave filled up the other holes, and perhaps the [underground shifting of the] fault reduced the flow of water. Probably this was the reason why all the people moved away.

In those days there was more land behind the sandy beach, and the great rocks had not been thrown up along the edge of the breakers. These came up during storms and tidal waves in the last half century [since 1868]. It was a much more habitable spot. Where there was once a sandy beach is now bare, jagged, sea-worn lava.

The storm beach at Waikapuna rests on a low, wide lava terrace that marks the southern end of the high Māniania Pali sea cliffs. The ordinary surge of the deep offshore waters continually batters the *makai* edge of the terrace, flooding into the numerous tidal pools, while storm surf sweeps across all of the barren, low-lying areas into the sparse shoreline vegetation in the backshore. Fishing is the most popular form of recreation for visitors to Waikapuna because the extremely dangerous shoreline conditions preclude almost all other aquatic activities. No facilities, shade, or shelter exist along this arid, desolate, continually windswept section of coast, and there is no convenient public access.

KAMILO

Along the shoreline between Waikapuna and Kamilo the waves and wind have left a series of small pockets of storm sand on the tops of the low sea cliffs, but about midway between the two places, at Keoneokahuku, an extensive sand drift extends inland across the barren *'a'ā*—a conspicuous landmark. Beyond Keoneokahuku the low sea cliffs drop down to sea level as they approach Kamilo Point.

At Kamilo, a large bay-like indentation in the point has been cut by the waves into an assortment of rocky ponds, points, and channels, most of which are exposed at low tides and awash at high tides. A narrow ribbon of white sand forms a beach along the inland border of the low-lying tidal area that is littered with almost every type of debris that the ocean has to offer: logs, driftwood, ropes, nets, and the usual *'ōpala* from passing ships. Handy and Handy and Puku'i in *Native Planters in Old Hawaii,* described it thus:

East of Ka'alu'alu is Kamilo. Its name means "swirling currents." The currents swept Oregon logs and other flotsam into the small inlet. The bodies of drowned persons came ashore. There was a Kamilopaekanaka side and a Kamilopaeali'i side. Those on the side called paekanaka (peoples'-side) were commoners; but those on the pae-ali'i were the bodies of chiefs, which no commoner dared touch. It was to this beach that messages from loved ones traveling to Puna floated down on the current.

Vegetation in the backshore at Kamilo includes *naupaka, milo,* and ironwood, all of which offer some protection from the elements for the *ulua* fishermen who frequently camp here. Otherwise, the area is barren and windswept with no facilities, water, or convenient public access. Other features of interest nearby include Ho'onoua Pond, a large brackish-water pond with a small rock island, that sits just inland of the beach, and a second, smaller storm sand beach that lines the inlet at Kai'olu.

KA'ALU'ALU, "the wrinkle"

The name is said to refer to the fissures in the lava around the shallow bay which resemble wrinkles when seen from a boat at sea. Ka'alu'alu Bay, one of the few protected embayments in Ka'ū, served for many years as the major port of the district. It was the landing nearest to Wai'ōhinu, once the main village of Ka'ū, which is located about 7 miles inland.

Ka'alu'alu's importance as a port declined considerably with the growth of the sugar industry. Honu'apo Bay to the east was much more accessible and centrally located for the plantations and the mills. It was deepened in the 1870s, and a wharf completed there in 1883, effectively downgrading Ka'alu'alu's status as a district port. However, cattle ranchers continued to use the landing to ship to market the animals they raised in the *mauka* pastures, and fishermen used the bay as an anchorage.

A sizable Hawaiian fishing community once lived on the shores of Ka'alu'alu Bay, but the tsunami of 1868 swept away all of the homes in this low-lying area and few people returned to live permanently. For many years the narrow, inshore portion of the bay had been walled off from the open ocean to form a fishpond, but the tsunami of 1946 destroyed the wall and it was never rebuilt. Still standing on the northern point of the bay, having withstood not only the tsunami of 1946 but those of 1960 and 1975 as well, are the remains of the old cattle-loading chute. Inland from the chute along the edge of the *'a'ā* flow stand the ruins of the long, narrow holding pen. A number of ruins, including an old wooden house surrounded by some low rock walls, are situated across the water on the southern point of the bay.

Ka'alu'alu, under normal weather conditions, is probably the largest and most protected bay in the district of Ka'ū, but it is used primarily as a shoreline fishing area, rather than a boating area because it is not readily accessible over land. Surfers also occasionally ride the break that forms just outside the old cattle-loading chute.

At the head of the bay, the shallow inlet that once formed the old fishpond is now an extensive tidal wetland that attracts both land and water birds and a great diversity of marine life. The masses of debris and driftwood that wash up along Ka'alu'alu's shoreline and rocky points gave rise to the once well-known saying, *Nā mamo piha'ā o Ka'alu'alu*, literally "the driftwood descendants of Ka'alu'alu." The epithet was said derisively of a Ka'ū person with many children because of the abundance of driftwood at Ka'alu'alu. Low tide reveals many places in the bay where spring water bubbles up among the rocks, the source of much of the fresh water that flows into the ocean. *Kiawe* trees line most of the *mauka* sections of the inlet.

Ka'alu'alu Bay is edged almost entirely by lava, but along the northern side of the bay several small coves, one headed by black cinder sand, offer entry and exit points for swimmers, surfers, divers, and net fishermen. At times heavy surf and stormy seas generate rip currents and strong longshore currents, precluding all in-water activities. No facilities exist at Ka'alu'alu, and there is no convenient public access.

PAIAHA'A, "lift and sway [of waves]"

In former times, three places in Ka'ū were famous for surfing: Punalu'u, Kāwā, and Paiaha'a. While surfers still occasionally ride Paiaha'a's waves, the break is no longer surfed regularly. The bay, like its next-door neighbor Ka'alu'alu Bay, is surrounded by private property and located many miles from any paved roads or centers of population, so it is frequented primarily by fishermen who have the four-wheel-drive vehicles needed to reach the area.

A small pocket beach of green sand and pebbles borders a tiny inlet at the head of the bay, but otherwise the shoreline is rocky. The eastern point is an *'a'ā* flow. Nearshore the water is shallow and the bottom rocky, but the deeper waters offshore offer good conditions for swimming, snorkeling, and diving, except when large surf and stormy seas generate rip currents and strong longshore currents, discouraging all in-water activities. No facilities exist at Paiaha'a, and there is no convenient public access.

(38)
Green Sand Beach

Olivine is concentrated as sand on some Hawaiian beaches. The grains are too small to constitute gem stones, but the green sand is valued by collectors. . . . Probably the best locality for olivine sand in the Hawaiian Islands is the beach at Papakolea, on the south coast of Hawaii 3 miles northeast of South Point. There the olivine has been washed out of a littoral cone formed where a lava flow entered the ocean.

Volcanoes in the Sea
Macdonald, Abbott, 1970

Hawaiian beach sand comes in a variety of colors—black, brown, gray, white, green, and red. The composition of the materials from which the sand grains on a particular beach were derived determines the color. The white sand of the vast majority of Hawai'i's beaches is of marine origin, derived from calcareous skeletal material of corals and other invertebrate animals that live in shallow waters. It is commonly called organic sand. Darker colored sands often originate from the land as a result of erosion or weathering. These detrital sands are either fragments of volcanic rock or fragments of specific minerals from the rock.

Ocean waves pounding against lava at or near the shoreline fashion rounded, basaltic rocks of various sizes that settle onshore to form cobblestone and boulder (*pa'ala*) beaches and also pebble (*'ili'ili*) beaches. *'Ili'ili* beaches composed of very small pebbles are often called black sand beaches, but the term "black sand" most commonly refers to volcanic glass. When an *'a'ā* flow enters the sea, steam explosions occur as the water penetrates the hot central part of flow. These littoral explosions, so called because they occur at the shoreline, may form clouds of liquid lava drops that chill on contact with the water or air, becoming volcanic glass sand. Ocean currents then deposit the sand in some sheltered indentation in the shoreline, making a beach. The lit-

GREEN SAND BEACH. The erosive force of the ocean washing into the base of Pu'u o Mahana, a littoral cone, has produced a secluded sand beach. The ocean also "mines" olivines, small green volcanic stones, out of the cinder and deposits them on the sand, giving the beach a distinctive green tint. Green Sand Beach near South Point is the most famous of the olivine beaches of the district of Ka'u.

toral debris may also pile up where the lava flow enters the sea and form a littoral cone. Erosion of the littoral cone often produces a black sand beach at the base of the cone. Red sand beaches result simply from the erosion of littoral cones composed predominantly of red volcanic matter. A few Big Island beaches in the districts of Hilo, Ka'ū, and South Kona show small sprinklings of red sand, but the only major red sand beaches in the Hawaiian Islands are found in the Hāna district on Maui.

Hawaiian lava, like any other type of rock, is made up of minerals and mineral-like substances. One of the most conspicuous of the dark minerals in Hawai'i is olivine, easily recognized by its green color and its glassy luster. Big grains of olivines are often particularly abundant in 'a'ā, from which, along the coast, they are commonly freed as intact grains in the process of erosion. Surf and currents deposit the loose olivines on any nearby beach where they combine with the existing sand. However, when waves wash over the beach a natural placer-mining action causes large concentrations of the olivines to be deposited on top of the sand near the waterline. These accumulations tint the beach a light, but very discernible green.

The famous Green Sand Beach in Ka'ū, at the base of Pu'u o Mahana, a littoral cone formed during an ancient eruption of Mauna Loa, is liberally strewn with olivines eroded from the cone. Most of them are very minute, but occasionally a crystal of gem purity and size shows up to reward a lucky beachcomber.

Pu'u o Mahana, located as it is at the head of an unprotected bay, is exposed to severe assaults on its beach and seaward face during periods of high surf and stormy seas. At these times the ocean not only inundates the entire beach and erodes the cone, but also produces a powerful shorebreak and a very dangerous rip current. During calm periods, swimmers, bodysurfers, divers, and nudists frequent the beach and the sandy inshore waters, and shoreline fishermen try their luck on the rocky points.

Green Sand Beach, or Mahana, as most of the area residents call it, is located 2½ miles from Kaulana Boat Ramp. It is approached over a rutted, secondary access road negotiable by four-wheel-drive vehicles only. To reach the beach itself, one must climb down a low sea cliff. This is not a problem on the south face of the cliff where footing is solid. Other routes, especially those down the high, steep face of Pu'u Mahana, are extremely dangerous because the volcanic material comprising the cone is very loosely compacted, crumbling and sliding easily underfoot. This characteristic has also resulted in severe erosion of the *mauka* side of the hill by drivers using it as an off-the-road vehicle track. In consequence, several ancient Hawaiian sites near the summit are now endangered.

Green Sand Beach has also been labeled Papakōlea Beach, for a nearby inland place name. This isolated spot offers no facilities, no shade, and no water.

(39)
South Point Park

Kalani'opu'u left Kama'oa and went to the shores of Ka'alu'alu and Paiaha'a to fish. Then there came a school of ahi fish to Kalae, and all the chiefs went down to Kalae for the ahi fishing.

Ruling Chiefs of Hawaii
Samuel Kamakau

South Point was known to the Hawaiians as Ka Lae, "the point." It is the southernmost point not only of the Hawaiian Islands, but of all the fifty states. The turbulent converging currents offshore South Point run very deep close to shore, conditions that provide attractive feeding grounds to a wide variety of fish including 'ahi, the yellowfin tuna. 'Ahi are especially sought after by sport and commercial fishermen because, either cooked or raw, this fish is a gourmet's delight. Most local residents consider 'ahi to be the finest fish in the ocean for sashimi, one of the reasons it is always in demand and almost invariably commands very high prices in local markets. Yellowfin tuna, also known in Hawai'i by the Japanese name *shibi*, often grow to 300 pounds; they are regarded as one of the best game fish in Hawaiian waters. They appear seasonally around the islands to feed, usually from July to November, and can often be found in large schools directly off South Point.

Though the ocean surrounding South Point provides excellent fishing grounds, relatively few fishermen are attracted to the area. Strong prevailing winds, commonly turbulent waters, and powerful currents that flow straight out to sea all combine to keep boaters away from this rugged part of the island. The Hawaiians who formerly fished the area were extremely alert to the slightest variations in weather that might indicate hazardous seas, because a canoe swamped undetected at South Point was doomed to drift out to sea with no hope of rescue.

The famous current at South Point is called Hala'ea. In *Majestic Ka'u: Mo'olelo of Nine Ahupua'a,* a historical study, Marion Kelly relates the story of the origin of the name. A greedy chief always watched the fishermen in their canoes off the coast of Ka'ū, and as they returned with their fish, he would rush out in his canoe and demand that they give him their entire catch. One day, however, the fishermen left earlier than usual and returned with a particularly large catch.

> When the greedy chief's canoe approached them, the fishermen separated so their canoes were on both sides of the chief's canoe. The chief called out, "He i'a no? (Do you have fish?)" The fishermen replied, " 'Ae. (Yes)." When the chief demanded, "Ho mai ka i'a! (Throw the fish here!)," from both sides the fishermen threw so many fish into his canoe so quickly that it swamped before the chief realized what was happening. The fishermen quickly paddled away, not stopping to look back. The chief, alone in the swamped canoe, was swept away on the swift current that carries his name, Hala'ea.

This is the inside current that sweeps past South Point and there is no land from there on—to Antarctica. This story gives rise to a saying for someone who has not returned home, *Ua ko'ia paha e ke au o Hala'ea,* "perhaps he is dragged away by the current of Hala'ea."

One of the unique ways by which the Hawaiians apparently fished the grounds, in spite of the Hala'ea current and the powerful offshore winds, was by tying their canoes to land. First they drilled a hole through a rock ledge at the water's edge. Then they passed a strong rope through the hole, securing one end at the hole and the other end to the canoe, and simply let the force of the wind and current pull the canoe out to the desired spot. With the line tied off and the canoe securely moored to the point the fishermen could then bottom-fish the lucrative grounds where it was too deep to anchor and otherwise impossible to remain stationary.

Approximately eighty of these man-made canoe holes still exist at South Point, scattered among the rocks directly below the navigational marker. Although the holes are now only historical curiosities, present-day fishermen practice a variation of the old canoe-drifting technique of fishing at South Point and occasionally at Wai'ahukini by using a toy sailboat to tow a flagline out to the offshore fishing grounds. A 500-foot-long main line supported with floats, usually clorox bottles tied on every 50 feet, is attached to the sailboat and tied to the point. A 6–10-foot steel leader and a baited hook are connected to the main line below each float beginning with the one that is 200 feet from the shore. The relentlessly blowing offshore wind and strong currents stretch the flagline straight out to sea where it usually attracts *ulua* and sometimes *'ahi.* Some fishermen prefer to use only a single hook rigged under the miniature sailboat rather than an entire flagline. One of the most unusual sailhook catches recorded at South Point occurred on June 6, 1966, when Arnold Howard, a long-time Ka'ū fisherman from Punalu'u, landed a 180-pound marlin. Howard hauled the huge fish up the cliff with the assistance of Kahuku Ranch supervisor George Manoa, who happened to be passing by and saw that Arnold needed help. Manoa managed to drop his lasso over the tail of the fish, and together the two men hoisted it up. Two weeks later Arnold repeated his feat, landing a 101-pound marlin, fishing again with a sail-rig at the same location.

The canoe mooring holes are important features of the South Point Complex, a group of archaeological sites that also include numerous carved and natural salt pans, Makalei Cave shelter, Kalalea Heiau, and the Pu'u Ali'i sand dune site. The last Hawaiians to live in the South Point area made their home at Kaulana Bay until just after the turn of the century. The South Point Complex is considered one of the most important records of human occupation in the Hawaiian Islands and has been studied extensively. Many other precontact sites are located in the same vicinity. To the east of the park and inland of the Pu'u Ali'i sand dunes, eight large cairns border a deep water hole, Ka Wai a ka Palahemo or Lua o Palahemo. The water in the hole rises and falls with the tide, but it is said that in former times a layer of fresh water floated at its surface at low tide, providing drinking water for the inhabitants of South Point. Volcanic eruptions or earthquakes may have cut off the water hole from its underground fresh-water sources.

Some modern ruins in the area include the concrete foundations of military barracks used by the army during World War II. They are located along the paved road leading to Kaulana Bay.

Some years later, in 1958, a Navy missile tracking station consisting of four buildings was constructed on 33 acres of land bordering the main South Point road. Located one mile above the cutoff to Kaulana Bay, it was named the Pacific Missile Range Station and was used to track missiles launched from Vandenberg Air Force Base and space launches from Cape Canaveral. Naval operations ended in 1965, but the Air Force took over the facility on a part-time basis and renamed it the South Point Air Force Station. The station was finally closed in 1979.

South Point Park is adjacent to the marine navigational marker, a light atop a 32-foot pole with a red and white checkered diamond daymark, that stands near the tip of the point. The park is undeveloped, offers no facilities, no shelter, and no water. It is fronted, as is all of South Point, by low sea cliffs, precluding all swimming. Strong prevailing winds sweep the area continually, so most of the point consists of large, open pastures with only a handful of low, bent trees at the park. For nonfishermen South Point offers spectacular panoramic views of the coastline and good beachcombing among the piles of debris the ocean has deposited in the numerous coves and inlets to the east. Some pole fishing occurs along the sea cliffs, but fishermen use the point primarily as a mooring site for their boats.

A number of hoists built into the cliffs service the small craft that anchor in the lee of the point. The boats are launched from Kaulana Boat Ramp, a paved, one-lane ramp located at Kaulana Bay, one mile to the east. About half a mile to the west of the point are the ruins of a concrete landing that the county built in April 1955

to service *aku* and *'ahi* boats at South Point. The landing stood only until the coming of the first severe *kona* storms. By January 1956 the storm surf that battered the point had destroyed the landing and left only the top part of the access road intact. Area residents refer to the site simply as Broken Road.

(40)
Wai'ahukini

Where the *'ili'ili* rocks are now, there used to be all white sand. That is where we brought up the canoes. . . . The boat is put up on the beach with rollers.

Archaeological and Historical Survey of . . . Waiahukini . . .
Sinoto and Kelly, 1975

The former fishing village of Wai'ahukini was situated on the shoreline between Pali o Kūlani, a 500-foot-high cliff, and a branch of the 1868 lava flow. In 1954, archaeologists from the Bishop Museum in Honolulu began the first of a series of surveys in the area and discovered that the lava tube shelters at Wai'ahukini contained some of the best examples of stratified cultural layers to be found in the islands, and show evidence of occupation from the earliest period of settlement in Hawai'i to modern times. Most important among the artifacts from these shelters are the types of fishhooks found in the successive layers, which have provided an almost unbroken record of the people who inhabited Wai'ahukini, and demonstrate that the earliest of these inhabitants showed Marquesan cultural traits. Some of the one-piece fishhooks are similar to and indicate a relation with those found in the early cultural layers of sites in the Marquesas Islands—conclusive evidence that at least one segment of the Hawaiian population came from the Marquesas as Hawaiian legends suggest.

Wai'ahukini was first occupied about A.D. 750, but occupation of the area was very likely seasonal or periodic. After about A.D. 1600, people started to build permanent stone structures, such as house walls, house platforms, and large cairns, indicating year-round occupation of the area, but the village still maintained social and economic ties with the productive inland farming regions.

In the 1750s Kalani'ōpu'u, the ruling chief of the Big

74

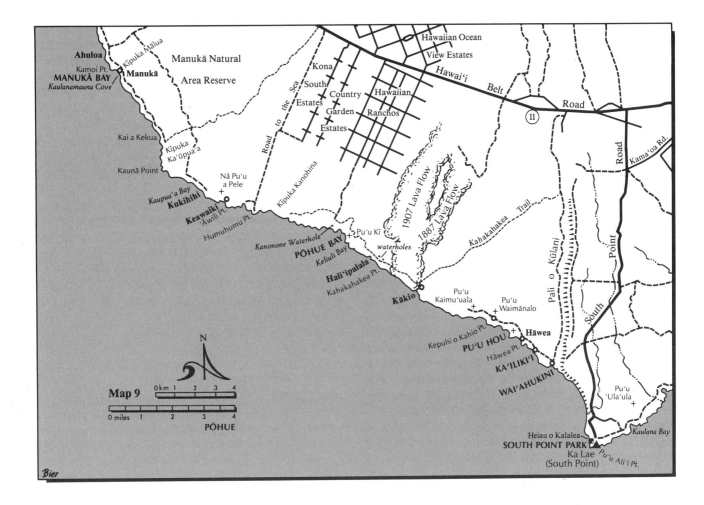

Island, built a residence for himself on the beach at Wai'ahukini, and it was there that he died in 1782, some three years after his confrontation with Captain James Cook at Kealakekua Bay in January 1779. The long-term tenure of Kalani'ōpu'u is clear evidence that the area was highly desirable in the eyes of the Hawaiians. In the Bishop Museum's Department of Anthropology Report 75–1, the most comprehensive work compiled on Wai'ahukini, Sinoto and Kelly offer these reasons for the site's importance.

First, brackish water was available there, an important asset in the dry rugged terrain of south Ka'u. Second, whoever controlled Waiahukini controlled the southern gateway to the eastern half of the island of Hawaii. This was particularly true in the days before there was an inland road over the lava fields between South Kona and Ka'u. The usual route to the eastern half of the island from South Kona was by canoe to Kailikii or to Waiahukini, and then over land on foot. The tradewinds and ocean currents usually rendered the canoe trip around Ka Lae to the windward extremely uncomfortable and at times hazardous. Third, fishing in this general area was excellent at certain seasons, and the coastal villages of (the ahupua'a) Pakini provided shelters for canoes and headquarters for fishermen operating there. Because these villages were located on the most-traveled route around the island, vegetable foods and other supplies were easily obtained from the inland farmers in exchange for fish, salt, and other products of the sea. Thus the coastal villages of Pakini played a prominent role in the district of Ka'u.

By the 1860s, many of Wai'ahukini's residents had moved away. The village's importance as a fish- and salt- supplying center and as a transportation terminal had diminished considerably. Roads were improved, schooners and steamers were replacing canoes, and people were drifting away from the old subsistence lifestyle. The turn of the twentieth century, however, found a tremendously expanded population in Ka'ū because of the development of the commercial sugar industry, and with the population increase came a demand for fresh fish. A handful of former Wai'ahukini families re-inhabited the village along with several non-Hawaiians, and set up commercial fishing operations. These activities apparently continued until the outbreak of World War II, when the village was abandoned for good as a permanent site of habitation. Fishermen and campers continue to visit the area, but there is no convenient access for the general public.

Two sections of beach front the former village, but neither is particularly good for swimming. The eastern section, the white sand beach that is visible from South Point, lies directly at the base of Pali o Kūlani. Almost the entire beach, which is liberally strewn with olivines, is fronted by rocks, but the southern end offers a small opening to the ocean for easy entry and exit. The ocean bottom immediately offshore, however, is a very shallow and rocky shelf on which the surf is often breaking, affording very poor swimming conditions. An extensive field of *naupaka* covers the entire backshore, where considerable amounts of white sand have been blown inland. Two brackish-water ponds are *mauka* of the *naupaka*; the smaller one provided drinking water for the former residents. This pond is called Wai o 'Ahukini, "water of 'Ahukini [a supernatural woman]," and gave the area its name, now shortened to Wai'ahukini.

The western section of Wai'ahukini Beach consists of a mixture of pebbles, cobblestones, and coral with large patches of green sand behind the rocks, especially in the shoreline road that borders the beach. Swimming conditions are poor because of a shallow and rocky bottom offshore, but several small channels through the rocks offer entry and exit points for in-water activities. An extensive *kiawe* grove covers the backshore, providing the only source of shade for miles.

During periods of calm seas, Wai'ahukini offers good inshore snorkeling and diving conditions, and surfers report that occasionally when waves are breaking in the area, there are rideable breaks. However, shoreline fishing constitutes the major recreational pastime. Some of the fishermen make use of the strong offshore, late afternoon winds and fish with sail-hook rigs like those seen at South Point.

Besides providing a variety of recreational opportunities in a remote and isolated setting, Wai'ahukini has the attraction of a unique complex of archaeological and historical sites that have to date remained almost intact. Sinoto and Kelly have strongly recommended that the sites be preserved in their natural state or, if any development at all is to occur, that they be made part of a state or county historical park.

(41)
Ka'iliki'i

The wind was still too strong to allow the canoe to proceed to her voyage; and those who had travelled by land felt too much fatigued to go on without some refreshment and rest. Desirous of spending the Sabbath with the people at Tairitii [Ka'iliki'i], we determined to rest a few hours, and then prosecute our journey by moonlight. We slept tolerably well till midnight, when the wind from the shore being favorable, and the moon having risen, we resumed our journey.

I went with Mr. Harwood in the canoe to Tairitii, which we reached a short time before daybreak; but the surf rolling high, we were obliged to keep off the shore until daylight enabled us to steer between the rocks to the landing place. Some friendly natives came down to the beach, and pointed out the passage to the steersman, by whose kind aid we landed in safety about half past five in the morning.

Journal of William Ellis, 1823

Before the time of good roads and western-style vessels, the usual route from South Kona to the eastern half of the island took one by canoe to Ka'iliki'i or Wai'ahukini, and then overland by foot. The tradewinds and ocean currents usually rendered the canoe trip around

Ka Lae extremely uncomfortable and at times hazardous, and so both Ka'iliki'i and Wai'ahukini served as transfer stations for travelers. Gradually, however, as roads replaced the *mauka* trails and schooners and steamers replaced canoes for hauling cargo and passengers, many coastal stops such as Ka'iliki'i were generally by-passed. As a result, by the 1860s, Ka'iliki'i, no longer attractive as a travel stop, had lost much of its population, but the village was still an important fishing center. Then in 1868, a great eruption from Mauna Loa's southwest rift zone sent lava flowing toward the sea; it destroyed the outer fringes of Ka'iliki'i village as it poured into the ocean between Ka'iliki'i and Wai'ahukini on one side and between Ka'iliki'i and Hāwea on the other. This catastrophic event apparently marked the end of all permanent habitation at Ka'iliki'i. The present jeep road through the area runs between two very large rock-wall structures still standing intact behind the beach. The large enclosed stone-walled complex to the east is thought to have been a community house, and the high-walled, partitioned site to the west, a canoe shed.

Ka'iliki'i Beach borders a small bay set between two rocky points created by the lava flow of 1868. From point to point, pebbles cover the entire foreshore, but a large amount of green sand overgrown with *pōhuehue* makes up the backshore. The olivine content of the *'a'ā* here is very high, and erosion by ocean waves has separated the olivines from the parent rocks and deposited them onshore as green sand. Offshore, the water drops quickly to overhead depths. Although conditions are suitable for swimming, the small bay is unprotected from the open ocean. Surf comes in straight and unchecked, forming rip currents that converge offshore with strong alongshore currents. On occasion the waves are good enough for surfing. Other than its important historical and archaeological attractions, the area is best known for good shoreline fishing. There is no convenient public access to this section of shoreline.

(42)
Pu'u Hou

Along the south shore of Hawai'i, for about 14 miles west of South Point, a row of cinder and ash cones has been built by littoral explosions where lava flows from the southwest rift of Mauna Loa entered the sea. The most recent of the cones is an unusually large one, 240 feet high, known as Puu Hou (new hill), formed by the lava flow of 1868.

Volcanoes in the Sea
Macdonald and Abbott, 1970

On the shoreline of Ka'ū between South Point and Kauna Point, lava flows from the southwest rift zone of Mauna Loa have entered the sea and built a long series of littoral cones. The most recently formed and the largest of these cones is Pu'u Hou ("new hill") which stands 240 feet above sea level. In 1868, a year never to be forgotten in the history of Ka'ū, an eruption broke out on March 27 along the southwest rift zone of Mauna Loa. A massive outpouring of lava from a group of spectacular fountains located about two miles above the present Hawai'i Belt Road streamed down into the *ahupua'a* of Pākini. One branch of the flow, which spared the fishing village of Wai'ahukini, continued on toward the ocean and destroyed part of the village of Ka'iliki'i. A second branch split into two arms on its path to the ocean, surrounding the village of Hāwea, which was thus isolated in a *kīpuka,* an "island" of land encircled by lava. Where the westernmost of the two arms met the sea, a large littoral cone was formed—Pu'u Hou.

In its position on the shoreline Pu'u Hou is continuously assaulted by storm surf and seasonally high waves. The resulting erosion has created three beautiful green sand beaches at its base. The easternmost, the largest and most prominent, contains three distinctively colored materials—black cinder, red cinder, and green olivines. The combination of these three colored sands makes the beach one of the most unusual in the Hawaiian Islands. Seen from a distance, the beach has a distinctly green tint because of the high concentration of olivines, but the black and the red grains in the mixture are evident on closer inspection. Though beautiful, this beach is not safe for swimming. The steep foreshore and the abrupt drop to overhead depths at the water's edge are themselves indications of the hazardous water conditions. High surf causes a powerful shorebreak, undertows, and rip currents. Even during periods of calm seas, persistent longshore currents flow past this completely unprotected stretch of sand.

PUʻU HOU. When ʻaʻā flows enter the sea, steam explosions occur as the water penetrates the hot central part of the flow. These littoral explosions, so called because they occur at the shoreline, eject tremendous amounts of debris. When massive quantities of the debris pile up at the edge of the flow, they form a littoral cone. Puʻu Hou, created by the lava flow of 1868, stands 240 feet above sea level, the highest littoral cone on the Big Island.

The other two long green sand beaches which front the westernmost end of Puʻu Hou, do not contain any red sand. They also appear green from a distance because of the high olivine content. Like the first, they are unsafe for swimming, and for the same reasons. In one protected spot only can swimmers and snorkelers find a place to get wet during calm seas: at the eastern end of the third beach, a rocky point offers enough of a lee to block the prevailing wind and current.

The barren countryside surrounding the littoral cone is just as uncongenial as the shoreline, providing no protection from the elements. Shade, shelter, and fresh water are nonexistent. Hikers walking over Puʻu Hou should exercise extreme caution near the edges because the material comprising the cone is very loosely compacted and slides very easily underfoot.

Low sea cliffs line the shoreline from Puʻu Hou to Kahakahakea, but several storm beaches of white sand cover the rocks below Puʻu Waimānalo and Puʻu Kaimuʻuala. Another pocket of white sand farther west, at Kākio, occupies a small kīpuka, the only low-lying area in the makai edge of the January 16, 1887, lava flow. The contrast of white sand against the dark masses of surrounding ʻaʻā is startling and easily pinpoints Kākio's location from a distance. This rugged reach of shoreline is frequented primarily by ʻopihi pickers and pole fishermen. There is no convenient public access.

The moderately long white sand storm beach at Kahakahakea is liberally strewn with lava fragments, giving it a salt-and-pepper appearance. Boulders and broken lava front the entire length of the beach, which lacks safe entry and exit points. Waves breaking continually over the rocks preclude almost all in-water activities in the deep, current-ridden waters offshore. A number of natural brackish water wells, in addition to a brackish water pond, occupy various cracks and depressions to the rear of the beach. The ruins of a large number of habitation sites are evidence that this was once a thriving Hawaiian fishing outpost. Fishermen are the most numerous visitors to this remote, desolate area.

(43)
Pōhue

Yesterday the lava reached the sea. It appears that in its course that stream of fire has done much damage to the Kahuku Ranch, that vast tract owned by Col. Samuel Norris. The flow is described as having split into three rivers of fire and to have gone over the flows of 1887 and 1868.

Hawaii Tribune Herald
January 15, 1907

Pōhue, "gourd," is a beautiful little pocket of white sand bordering a small sand-bottomed inlet in Pōhue Bay. During periods of calm seas this picturesque beach is one of the safest swimming areas in the district of Ka'ū and offers excellent snorkeling opportunities along the otherwise rocky shoreline. Pōhue Bay's recessed position in the shoreline protects it from dangerous currents under normal weather conditions and for boaters it is known as the best refuge from the wind between South Point and Kaunā Point. However, hazardous conditions occur occasionally when high surf, particularly during *kona* storms, sweeps across the entire bay and funnels unchecked directly into the beach. The moderately steep slope of the sand is a good indication that dangerous water conditions are sometimes encountered. High surf and storm waves create a powerful shorebreak, backwash, undertows, and rip currents.

Along the eastern margin of the bay, a large, rounded littoral cone, Pu'u Kī, dominates the shoreline and slopes gently down to Pōhue Beach. A number of habitation sites of a former Hawaiian fishing community are located on this rocky slope, which offers a magnificent view of the bay and all points along the coast and inland. Here too is the beginning of a vast petroglyph field that stretches beyond Pu'u Kī toward Kahakahakea.

Tucked into the inside corner of the eastern point of Pōhue Bay is a small beach of black sand with a sprinkling of olivines and white sand. Rocks border the sand at the water's edge and boulders cover the bottom offshore, making it a poor swimming beach. Farther east of the bay, fronting the summit of Pu'u Kī, low, flat-topped sea cliffs overlook one of the most productive *ulua* fishing grounds in the district. Local fishermen throughout the Hawaiian Islands know this area as Hosaka Point or simply as Eddie Hosaka. Edward Y. Hosaka was born and raised in Hawai'i and attended the University of Hawai'i at Manoa in the early 1930s. After earning a master's degree in 1934 he became an agronomist with the University's Extension Services, specializing in pasture management. In time he became recognized throughout the Pacific as an authority on pasture grasses for cattle. His work took him often to the Big Island and into the remotest areas of many of the island's large ranches. In these areas, when his work was completed, he often went shoreline fishing, one of his greatest pleasures. Hosaka, regarded as one of the finest *ulua* fishermen of his day, often fished at Pu'u Kī, located on the shoreline of Kahuku Ranch, and it was there at the age of 55 while doing what he loved best, that he suffered a stroke. Taken immediately by his companions to Hilo Hospital, he died on July 23, 1961. Since that date the point has been known as Eddie Hosaka.

In addition to his work for the University, Hosaka was for many years an honorary associate in Botany at the Bishop Museum—and also an author. Probably his best known and most widely circulated work is *Sport Fishing in Hawaii*, first published in 1944 and still considered one of the standard works on fish and fishing in the Hawaiian Islands.

To the west of Pōhue Beach, a storm beach of white sand, lava fragments, coral rubble, and water-rounded pebbles borders a larger inlet of Pōhue Bay. The bottom immediately offshore is a very wide, shallow, and rocky shelf that precludes swimming. Just inland of the beach is a large rectangular brackish-water pond, Kanōnone Waterhole, that is encircled by coconut and *hala* trees. This little oasis in the surrounding desert of barren *'a'ā* stands out very clearly and constitutes Pōhue's most visible landmark.

The Pōhue shoreline is known to some local residents as Glover's Beach, for James W. Glover, a former owner of Kahuku Ranch, who founded the general construction firm James W. Glover, Ltd. The company continues to operate from offices in Honolulu and Hilo and has been acknowledged for many years as one of the major local contracting firms in the Hawaiian Islands. After Glover's death, the ranch was sold under court order by the Hawaiian Trust Company, the executor of his estate, to pay estate debts including inheritance taxes amounting to almost a million dollars. The trustees of the Samuel M. Damon Estate, with an offer of $1,363,630, were the successful bidders in 1958 for the 158,000-acre ranch. Because Kahuku Ranch has controlled access to Pōhue for so many years, some Ka'ū residents also know the area as Kahuku Beach. There is no convenient public access to this shoreline.

(44)
Road to the Sea

After leaving Kapua, we had sailed along close to the shore, till the wind becoming too strong for us to proceed we availed ourselves of the opening [in the rocky shoreline] which Keavaiti afforded, to run the canoe ashore, and wait till the wind should abate, though in so doing we were completely wet with the surf, and spoiled the few provisions we had on board.

A number of conical hills, from 150 to 200 feet high, rose immediately in our rear, much resembling sand-hills in their appearance. On examination, however, we found them composed of volcanic ashes and cinders; but could not discover any mark of their ever having been craters.

Journal of William Ellis, 1823

On the shoreline of Ka'ū, between South Point and Kaunā Point, lava flows from the southwest rift zone of Mauna Loa entering the ocean have formed a series of littoral cones. The largest concentrated group of these cones is situated at the end of Road to the Sea, a cinder road that leads from the Hawai'i Belt Road to the shoreline. The highest of the cones are the two known as Nā Pu'u a Pele ("The Hills of Pele") at Keawaiki. According to Hawaiian legend, these hills were once two young men, chiefs of Kahuku, who excelled in all sports, especially *hōlua* ("sled")-riding. Pele also loved this sport. One day she appeared as a beautiful young chiefess to join in the competition. The chiefs, however, suspected her identity and refused to race with her. Angered, Pele came after them with a lava flow that devastated the once fertile lands of Kahuku as she chased them toward the beach. She overtook the chiefs just inland of Keawaiki and turned them into the hills that bear her name, Nā Pu'u a Pele.

On January 9, 1908, another flow from Mauna Loa reached the sea in the same area, surrounding Nā Pu'u a Pele and creating several smaller littoral cones on either side of the older hills. The ocean has eroded the cone to the south of Humuhumu Point and the one to the south of 'Āwili Point, creating two green sand beaches.

The small pocket of black sand at Humuhumu is liberally sprinkled with olivines, giving it a definite green tint in the sunlight. Swimming is safe under normal weather conditions, but the rocky offshore bottom drops abruptly to overhead depths. Snorkeling and nearshore scuba diving are good around the rocky points. High surf, particularly during *kona* storms, sweeps across the entire beach onto the face of the littoral cone and creates a strong shorebreak, undertows, and rip currents.

The larger and longer pocket of black sand at 'Āwili also is tinted green from the high concentration of olivines. The beach is narrow and steep at its eastern end, but flattens and widens at its western end, where a pocket of shoreline vegetation, mostly *pōhuehue* and *naupaka*, occupies the backshore. Swimming is safe under normal weather conditions, but the rocky offshore bottom drops abruptly to overhead depths. Like the neighboring beach at Humuhumu, high surf and *kona* storm waves make swimming very hazardous.

The beach at Humuhumu Point and the beach at 'Āwili Point are collectively known to most area residents as Road to the Sea. Road to the Sea, a 7-mile-long cinder road, begins at the western edge of Hawaiian

'Āwili. The district of Ka'u is noted for its eroding littoral cones and the volcanic sand beaches that form at their bases. Located inshore of 'Āwili Point, this cone is one of a large concentration of littoral cones at the bottom of Road to the Sea. The two most famous in the area are called Nā Pu'u a Pele, "The Hills of Pele," after the goddess of the volcano.

Ocean View Estates and ends on the shoreline at Humu-humu Point. It is one of the few *mauka-makai* access routes in Ka'ū to the ocean. Ordinary passenger cars traveling slowly can negotiate the road except for the last rugged downhill slope to sea level; so most drivers park above this last section, which requires a vehicle with four-wheel drive, and walk to the shore. Visitors to the area include swimmers and sunbathers during periods of calm seas, and shoreline fishermen who camp and fish throughout the year.

'Āwili Point is said to be one of the better *ulua* grounds when these fish are running in Ka'ū—primarily during the spring and summer months. In 1977, Roy Ogata, a professional photographer from Hilo who is acknowledged as one of Hawai'i's finest *ulua* fishermen, in one night caught twenty-three *ulua* at 'Āwili, most of them ranging in size from 20 to 40 pounds. This is now the Hilo Casting Club record for the most *ulua* caught by one person in one night of fishing. Ogata was born and raised on the Hilo bayfront near the Wailuku Stream bridge and spent much of his youth fishing and diving in and around Hilo Bay. In later years, as he fished in different areas on the Big Island, he heard stories of a warm current that periodically flowed past 'Āwili Point and apparently caused the fish to bite with abandon. On the night that he made his record catch, the ocean was rough, the wind was cold, but the water was warm.

Behind 'Āwili Point, a trail leads from the jeep road across the *a'ā* to Nā Pu'u a Pele and climbs directly over the summits of these massive hills. The view from the top is magnificent in every direction, offering an excellent perspective on the movement of the 1907 lava flow toward Keawaiki below.

The ocean has eroded Keawaiki's rocky shoreline to form a wide, fairly flat tidal shelf that is strewn with large standing rocks and laced with many pools. Behind this *papa* and on the points that border it are several sections of storm beach composed of cobblestones, coral rubble, and scattered pockets of green sand. A series of brackish-water ponds lines the backshore, and a number of habitation sites that comprised portions of the former Keawaiki village also occupies the area. The trail from Nā Pu'u a Pele leads down to Keawaiki, where it crosses the shoreline trail heading back to the beach at 'Āwili. There are no facilities, shade, or fresh water at Road to the Sea, but the area is an excellent place for beachcombing, fishing, and hiking.

Beyond Keawaiki and the remnants of an old bombing target-range marker, a jeep road follows the rocky shoreline toward Kaunā Point, a wide impressive promontory that overlooks deep blue, current-swept waters. Extensive storm beaches, consisting chiefly of white sand, occupy the backshore bordering both sides of the low sea cliffs.

(45)
Manukā

About noon we came [by canoe] to a small village named Manu-Ka where we found our chief Luhea's residence, and where we landed before his house at a small gap between rugged precipices against which the surges dashed and broke with such violence and agitation and with such horrific appearance, that even the idea of attempting chilled us with the utmost dread. We, however, quietly submitted ourselves to their guidance, and were highly pelased to see the extraordinary dexterity with which they managed this landing.

Hawaii Nei 128 Years Ago
Archibald Menzies

In February 1794, Archibald Menzies, botanist with Captain George Vancouver's exploratory expedition to Hawai'i, journeyed by canoe from South Kona to Ka'ū for the purpose of scaling Mauna Loa. In the Bishop Museum's Department of Anthropology Report 75–1, Sinoto and Kelly note the importance of Menzies' visit and observations.

His description of arriving at the first coastal village in Ka'ū in Manuka is worthy of recording here for several reasons. The weather, obviously stormy, was not a deterrent to the Hawaiians who managed the canoe. The equally obviously difficult and hazardous landing, executed with the help of local residents, was accomplished with superb dexterity in the face of what seems today to have been impossible odds against its success. Also Menzies provides us with some indication of the size of population and the activities carried on in an outlying coastal village.

Menzies also provided a vivid description of the village and the surrounding countryside: "As the chief had some arrangements to make, we were obliged in compliance with his request, to remain at this dreary-looking place all night. A situation more barren and rugged can scarcely be imagined."

Today the Manukā shoreline remains just as arid and desolate as described by Menzies, except that the backshore now supports a large grove of *kiawe*, a tree that was not introduced to Hawai'i until 1828. The Manukā archaeological complex includes the former village, a *heiau*, a *hōlua* slide, petroglyphs, and a trail system. Successive lava flows from Mauna Loa almost completely overran the once fertile slopes, prompting most of the residents to move. The village at Manukā continued as a small outpost of fishermen and provided a wayside stop for travelers passing through on foot or by canoe.

The little bay at Manukā is the only low-lying opening in the sea cliffs from Keawaiki to Niu'o'u, a distance of nearly 10 miles, and therefore is one of the few places where the ocean can easily deposit sand on shore. The beach at Manukā consists of coral rubble, lava fragments, and white sand, and is fronted at the water's edge by a low, flat ramp of lava. Brackish water collects in one of the larger splash pools on this rocky shelf and attracts many thirsty insects, especially wasps.

Swimming conditions are poor because directly offshore of the beach the ocean bottom is shallow and rocky. At the surf line, numerous deep fissures in the bottom and an underwater cliff attract an abundance of reef fish and other sea life, affording excellent snorkeling and nearshore scuba diving opportunities. However, at times of high surf water conditions are hazardous, due to rip currents and waves that sweep unexpectedly over the rocky ledges.

The backshore vegetation includes *ēkoa (koa haole), naupaka, pōhuehue,* and a large stand of *kiawe,* which provides some protection for campers, primarily goat hunters and shoreline fishermen. There are no facilities and no fresh water in this dry, wind-swept, isolated area. Access via a jeep road to the shoreline is open to the public, but it is very rugged and negotiable only by four-wheel-drive vehicles. Manukā marks the boundary between the districts of Ka'ū and South Kona.

(46)
Kapu'a

About two p.m. we reached Taureonanahoa, three large pillars of lava, about twenty feet square, and apparently sixty or eighty high, standing in the water, within a few yards of each other, and adjacent to the shore. Two of them were united at the top, but open at their base. We sailed between them and the main land; and about five in the afternoon landed at Kapua, a small and desolate-looking village, on the southwest point of Hawaii, and about twenty miles distant from Kalahiti. Here we had the canoe drawn up on the beach until our companions should arrive.

Journal of William Ellis, 1823

William Ellis and his companions found little to their liking in the small fishing community of Kapu'a. The shoreline wells used by the Hawaiians contained brackish water, a fluid that upset the Caucasian digestive system, and only desolate expanses of lava comprised the surrounding countryside. Ellis observed, "Nothing can exceed the barren and solitary appearance of this part of the island, not only from the want of fresh water, but from the rugged and broken tracts of lava of which it appears to be entirely composed."

Despite the inhospitable appearance of the area to the Western eye, the Hawaiians at Kapu'a, as in many other similar shoreline communities, lived comfortably, fish-

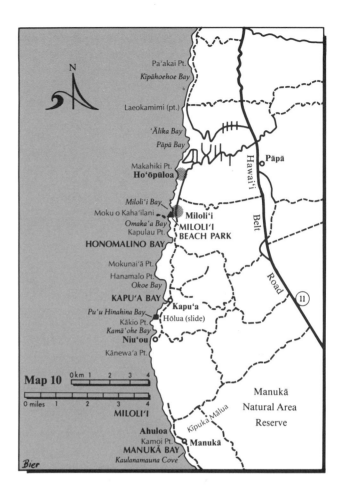

ing in the waters offshore and farming the more fertile lands at the higher elevations. Their homes near the beach centered around three spring-fed brackish wells and a small pocket of sand. The well closest to the ocean was used for storing taro, from which they made poi, and for *palu,* a fishing chum; the water in the middle well was reserved for drinking only; and the third well provided the water for all other domestic needs.

One of the most conspicuous landmarks at Kapu'a, an old dilapidated wooden shack that stands in the large *kiawe* grove, was the homestead of many generations of the Kahele family. Their original Western-style home on the property—a large, two-story house—collapsed in the 1930s during a devastating windstorm, and the smaller building remaining today was constructed in its place. The replacement structure was not large because most of the family by then had moved away from Kapu'a. The last family members to leave the area, the last permanent residents of Kapu'a, moved to Miloli'i during World War II.

Near the Kahele home, a stone wall enclosure with ten coconut trees rooted in it lines the backshore of the beach. This structure served as a holding pen during the early twentieth century, when Kapu'a was a cattle shipping point for the *mauka* ranches. Cowboys on horseback dragged the roped cattle into the ocean and tied them to lighters, which then hauled the swimming animals out to the steamers anchored offshore. There, the cattle were hoisted on board. In later years, the coconut trees were planted inside the corral to protect them from the numerous foraging goats that still roam the miles of open lava.

The pocket of sand fronting the small, protected inlet at Kapu'a is almost tan in color from a generous admixture of olivines, lava fragments, coral rubble, and water-worn pebbles. The relatively flat and rocky ocean bottom just off the beach drops off quickly to overhead depths and provides an excellent swimming area cooled by pockets of intruding fresh water. An abundance of marine life close to shore is an attraction for snorkelers and nearshore scuba divers. Hazardous ocean conditions generally occur only during periods of high surf or *kona* storms.

A small rock island located immediately off the eastern end of the beach was known to the Kapu'a residents as Kalepeamoa ("the cock's comb"). The comb is said to be most visible against the setting sun. Besides protecting one end of the beach, Kalepeamoa also marked the landing at Kapu'a for the steersmen of incoming fishing and voyaging canoes.

On the sand inshore of Kalepeamoa rests another large rock that was known as Pōhaku Ku'ihili ("rock to pound the bark"). The fishermen of Kapu'a fished for *'ōpelu* (mackeral scad) whenever large schools of these fish moved into the nearshore areas. To prolong the life of their *'ōpelu* nets, the fishermen periodically soaked the net fibers in a dye made from the bark of the *kukui* tree, and then allowed the nets to dry. In making the dye, *kukui* bark had to be pounded on a rock before

KAPU'A. At Pu'u Hinahina Bay near Kapu'a is a ski-jump-shaped structure with a 25-foot-long runway and an 85-foot-long ramp. Known as the 'Ahole Hōlua, it is the best preserved hōlua slide in the Hawaiian Islands. Precontact Hawaiians covered the surface of the ramp with *pili* grass and *kukui* oil and then raced down the slide on narrow sleds with hardwood runners. According to tradition, Pele, goddess of the volcano, was an expert rider and often competed with handsome young chiefs in her guise as a beautiful young woman.

being mixed with water. Generations of fishermen used Pōhaku Ku'ihili for this purpose.

A number of other important cultural and recreational sites are located immediately to the south of Kapu'a—Pu'u Hinahina, Kaupō, and Niu'o'u. At Pu'u

Hinahina, a massive *hōlua* with a 25-foot-long runway and 85-foot-long ramp dominates the other shoreline sites nearby. This slide, one of approximately nineteen discovered on the Big Island and forty throughout the state, is in excellent condition and is considered to be the best preserved *hōlua* in the Hawaiian Islands. The structure has suffered only minor deterioration, most of it at the seaward end where it is exposed to the reach of high seas. Visitors to the site need little imagination to visualize the ancient sledding events, with spectators on the terraces cheering for the riders making their runs down the ski-jump-shaped ramp.

Beyond Pu'u Hinahina, another cluster of habitation sites at Kaupō centers around two brackish-water wells and a small bay in the lee of Kākio Point. Several stepping-stone (*pa'ala*) trails converge here, among them one that runs *mauka-makai* and another that crosses the *'a'ā* to Niu'o'u. The backshore shows evidence of use by present-day fishermen who find shelter under a few scattered *kiawe* trees. The seaward vantage point at Kaupō affords a spectacular view inland of Mauna Loa and Hualālai and of the extensive plantations of macadamia nut trees along the Hawai'i Belt Highway.

The pockets of beach fronting Pu'u Hinahina and Kaupō contain considerably more rock and coral rubble than sand, but they still provide easy access to the ocean. Snorkeling and nearshore scuba diving are excellent in the nearshore areas, where marine life is abundant and fresh water seeps out of the ocean floor.

A short stretch of trail across the *'a'ā* at Kaupō leads south to Niu'o'u, once the site of a large coconut grove. Long-time residents of the area generally agree that the last few surviving trees died during the early 1950s, but opinions differ concerning the fate, earlier, of the larger part of the grove. One story tells of a local rancher who cut down almost all of the trees in the 1940s to use the trunks as corral posts for a goat trap. According to another story, goat hunters in the area used the trees for target practice and killed most of them by shooting at the coconut clusters. Others speculate that the grove simply died of old age, the ravages of powerful storms, and damage to the young trees from herds of roaming goats after the few inhabitants at Niu'o'u had deserted the area by the turn of the twentieth century. Whatever the cause or combination of causes, the coconut trees are gone and Niu'o'u is marked today only by a large stand of *kiawe*.

Niu'o'u sits on an old, low-lying *pāhoehoe* flow. It is the only low spot in the sea cliffs between Kākio Point and Manukā where the ocean washes inland freely. High surf coming in over the low *papa* at the water's edge has created an extensive storm beach of white sand speckled with brown and black lava fragments, olivines, and coral rubble. *Pōhuehue* and impatiens line the backshore of the otherwise open stretch of sand, a readily visible landmark. The area is frequented primarily by fishermen.

Immediately to the north of Kapu'a are two more early habitation areas, both fronted by pocket sand beaches nestled into indentations in the rocky shoreline. The beach at Oea, located inshore of a small inlet that opens toward Kākio Point, consists of white sand speckled with olivines, black and brown lava fragments, and coral rubble. This tiny pocket of sand is too small for recreational beach activities, but snorkeling and nearshore scuba diving are excellent offshore where there is an abundance of marine life, especially in areas affected by fresh water intrusion. *Kiawe* dominates at Oea, but *pōhuehue* grows in the backshore and several *puapilo* bushes are located near the *kiawe*. The delicate flowers of the *puapilo* have a very pleasing fragrance that drifts lightly on the evening and early morning air currents.

The beach at Okoe, tucked against the southern face of Hanamalo Point, consists primarily of detrital black sand, but the beach appears gray because of an admixture of white calcareous sand. Boulders front the eastern half of the beach, where it is steepest, while the western end near the *'a'ā* point flattens out considerably. Many barely submerged rocks lie directly offshore, so swimmers and divers must exercise some caution. Otherwise, swimming is excellent. The ocean bottom drops quickly to overhead depths, fine for snorkeling and nearshore scuba diving. Fresh water intrusion occurs in many places. Hazardous water conditions generally arise only during periods of high surf or severe storms. A large *kiawe* grove, with some *kou* and *ēkoa*, occupies the backshore, providing a camping area for fishermen and other visitors to the beach.

Okoe was once the site of an extensive Hawaiian settlement that centered around the beach and the perimeter of the bay. Among the many ruins is a deep well with a with a stone-lined shaft beside the access road to the beach. Several stepping-stone trails are also located nearby. Okoe, like Kapuʻa, was used as a cattle shipping point by the *mauka* ranches, but less frequently.

To reach Okoe, Oea, Kapuʻa, and all of the shoreline sites in this section of South Kona one needs both a vehicle with four-wheel drive and the permission of the owners of the property between the ocean and the highway.

(47)
Honomalino

Ino wa o ka makani o Kauna.
Nānā aku o ka makani malaila.
O Honomalino, malino i ka laʻi o Kona.

There's a storm when wind blows at Kauna.
Just look at the tempest raging there.
Honomalino sleeps sheltered by Kona.

Unwritten Literature of Hawaii
Nathaniel Emerson

Honomalino Bay, one of the most protected bays in South Kona, once supported a large fishing and farming community. Numerous pre-contact cultural sites are located along the perimeter of the bay and in the amphitheater-shaped gulch inland of the sand beach. Many of them are hidden in the dense growth of *kiawe*. Immediately behind the beach, bordering the jeep road, stand the ruins of several holding pens, reminders of more recent times when cattle from the *mauka* ranches were shipped to market by swimming them to interisland

HONOMALINO. Coconut and *kiawe* trees border the beach at the head of Honomalino Bay. During periods of calm seas the bay offers excellent opportunities for swimming and snorkeling. A handful of Big Island families maintain beach homes at this remote South Kona site. Macadamia nut tree orchards comprise much of the upper regions of the Honomalino land division.

steamers anchored offshore. Today, a handful of contemporary beach homes constitutes the extent of the shoreline community.

Low sea cliffs line most of the water's edge of Honomalino, but a beautiful pocket beach is set into the northern corner of the bay. The beach consists primarily of black sand, but it appears gray because of an admixture of olivines and calcareous white sand. A shallow sand bar fronts the beach, but drops off quickly on the seaward side to overhead depths and a flat, rocky ocean bottom. Snorkeling and nearshore scuba diving opportunities are excellent, especially off the rocky points, where the waters harbor a wide variety of fish. Hazardous water conditions generally occur only during periods of high surf or severe southerly (kona) storms. An extensive coconut grove, perpetuated by regular replanting by the area residents, covers both the backshore of the beach and adjoining Kapulau Point. Sand drifts extend a considerable distance from the nearshore vegetation into the inland kiawe grove.

Although the beach at Honomalino is one of the largest in South Kona, long-time residents report that the volume of onshore sand has been eroded dramatically in the twentieth century and that each year more of the beach is washed away. Observers have estimated that during the 1940–1980 period the beachfront has moved inland between 75 and 100 yards. Like many other Big Island beaches whose primary source of sand was a nearby lava flow entering the ocean, Honomalino has inevitably lost sand as a result of the erosive forces of storms and tsunami.

Honomalino Bay cannot be reached from the Hawai'i Belt Highway without a vehicle with four-wheel drive and without crossing private property. There is no convenient public access.

(48)
Miloli'i Beach Park

Miloli'i. Ma ia wahi nui ka niu. Milo i ka 'aha niu no nāli'i. A lākou kanaka 'ike ma kahi a niu. 'Āina nui mai uka a kai. Miloli'i punawai ma kahakai.

Miloli'i. At this place coconuts are huge and sennet fibers are twisted into cordage for the chiefs. Their men know of this as the place of the coconut. A large land area,

from mountain to sea. Miloli'i spring is located at the shore.

Place name notes from Kalokuokamaile
Theodore Kelsey collection

Miloli'i means "fine twist" and is probably a direct reference to the excellent plant fiber cordage once produced at the village. The Miloli'i craftsmen supplied themselves, their neighbors, and their chiefs with 'aha, or sennit, braided from the husk fibers of the coconut, and olonā, cordage prepared from the bark fibers of the olonā shrub. The Hawaiians considered 'aha to be the strongest and most salt-water resistant of their ropes and used it for tying their canoes, whereas olonā was highly prized for making fish nets.

When the residents of Miloli'i put their outrigger canoes and their nets to use, it was often to catch 'ōpelu (mackerel scad), a silver, schooling fish that was an important source of food. The 'ōpelu range in shallow water, usually 20 fathoms or less, from nearshore to a few miles offshore, and tend to gather in specific areas (ko'a) where they find favorable foraging conditions. Before the actual netting began at the various ko'a, the fishermen spent a considerable amount of time feeding the fish, conditioning them to come at the approach of the canoes. Repeated raps with a paddle on the side of the canoe was the sound cue indicating that the canoes and the food had arrived. The parcels of chum, or ka'ai (a few handfuls of bait wrapped in a piece of coconut fiber, with a flat stone for a sinker) were lowered several fathoms into the water and then jerked open to release the contents. As the food showered down, the 'ōpelu darted in to feed.

In order to avoid attracting carnivorous fish such as sharks and eels, the fishermen fed the 'ōpelu a primarily vegetarian diet: the poi scrapings from the calabashes, cooked and pounded taro, sweet potatoes, and breadfruit, and also in post-contact times, papaya, pumpkin, and rice. Often a special flavor was imparted to the chum by adding mashed, cooked 'a'ama crab or raw red shrimp from brackish-water ponds.

In Kona, where 'ōpelu fishing was an important occupation, the fish were fed in this way from May to August, and netting was done from August to December. During the remainder of the year a *kapu* was placed on the fish to allow the schools to regenerate unmolested. When the fish were ready to be taken, the fishermen went out, three to a canoe: the fishermen (*lawai'a*) forward, the feeder (*hanai 'ai*) in the middle, and the steersman of the canoe (*malama wa'a*) in the stern. The big bag *olonā* nets (*'a'ei 'ōpelu*) rested on the gunwales (*mo'o*) and the outrigger booms (*'iako*) of the canoe.

As the fleet of canoes lined up at the *ko'a*, a signal was given to begin the feeding. As soon as the *'ōpelu* were swarming under the boats, the stretching poles (*kuku*) were inserted to hold the nets' mouths round and open, and nets were lowered. When a net was in place, one *ka'ai* was opened directly into the mouth of the net, and as the fish scurried in after the food particles, the net was hauled up to the canoe. As the *lawai'a* pulled, his two companions leaned out on the *'iako* to prevent the canoe from overturning. When all of the nets and fish had been brought on board, the fleet returned to the beach.

Today, the fishing fleet consists of canoes made from imported lumber and powered by small outboard motors instead of paddles and sails, but the traditional *'ōpelu* fishing methods are still practiced, almost unchanged from the methods of generations past, by a few fishermen. The isolated Hawaiian shoreline community at Miloli'i is one of the very last places left in the Hawaiian Islands where the residents still support themselves by fishing and still maintain a firm hold on the traditions that Western civilization has overshadowed almost everywhere else. Many of the older residents still speak Hawaiian among themselves, an infrequent occurrence in contemporary Hawai'i.

It might seem that life at Miloli'i has been forever idyllic and problem-free, but some of the residents have been grappling since the mid-1920s with an issue of major concern: the title of ownership to their land. In April of 1926, a lava flow from Mauna Loa completely overran the neighboring fishing village of Ho'ōpūloa, destroying all of the homes and forcing all residents to relocate. Some of the families settled in Miloli'i, while others moved to more distant parts of the island. Nearly all of the former residents petitioned the county that they be given back their land. In 1931 Governor Lawrence Judd set aside 56 acres in Ho'ōpūloa for a village site, but the County of Hawai'i Board of Supervisors asked him to rescind his order and, instead, let the parcel be subdivided into houselots. The commissioner of public lands, however, pointed out that lots in any such subdivision would have to be sold at public auction, to all bidders. Governor Judd suggested that the Territorial legislature resolve the matter, but it took no action at all.

In 1940 the issue surfaced again in the Territorial legislature. At the legislature's request the Hawai'i County engineer mapped twenty-four house lots in a part of the area that once was Ho'ōpūloa. In 1941 one family moved in; during the next five years, fifteen more lots were occupied, but the families were given no clear indication of terms or title. The situation remained unchanged until 1982 when the State of Hawai'i finally resolved the issue.

Fifty-two acres of land, beginning roughly at the public boat ramp in Miloli'i and following the shoreline toward Ho'ōpūloa, were set aside for the refugees of the 1926 lava flow and their descendants. Subdivision plans for the parcel provide residential lots for these people so that they can once more be part of a traditional fishing community. In order to coordinate the land distribution with the state's Department of Land and Natural Resources, the residents organized a nonprofit group called Pa'a Pono Miloli'i, Inc. The group assists the state in screening applicants for lots, determining eligibility and distribution, and handling any related problems. The Miloli'i/Ho'ōpūloa land issue was finally resolved after fifty-six years.

Miloli'i Beach Park is located on a small, low point of lava next to the public boat ramp in the center of the village. The park consists of a large sandy lot bordered by a seawall, several picnic tables, a small community pavilion, playground equipment, restrooms, and a small grove of ironwood trees at the *makai* edge of the park. Beyond the sea wall, a network of broken lava fingers and pools offers a protected, but rocky area for swimming. Snorkeling and nearshore scuba opportunities are excellent, except during periods of high seas and *kona* storms, when hazardous ocean conditions occur. Just south of the park, a large, natural pond, known locally as Ako Pond, serves as an anchorage for shallow-draft boats.

Approximately one mile north of Miloli'i, another low-lying section of shoreline, at Ho'ōpūloa, contains a small pocket beach comprised of pebbles, lava fragments, and coral rubble. The prevailing water conditions and periodic hazards are almost identical to those at Miloli'i.

The 13-mile reach of shoreline from Ho'ōpūloa to Ho'okena consists primarily of low to moderately high sea cliffs, the seaward edge of a very steep-sloping section of Mauna Loa's southwestern flank. The only sand beaches are a few pockets of storm sand, such as those at Pāpā and 'Ālika. The pre-contact population in this area was comparatively sparse, but habitation ruins can be found in nearly every land division in this area, especially near springs at the shoreline or in the ocean. In the absence of sand beaches, the former residents built canoe ladders, such as those commonly associated with the district of Puna, in order to launch and land their boats over the boulder beaches. A canoe ladder was used at Kīpāhoehoe, where a small fishing outpost once occupied the backshore of the rocky bay. Other rocky beaches such as the pebble-and-cobblestone beach at Ka'ohe were less imposing, but still difficiult to cross carrying a canoe. Today the beach at Ka'ohe, now known as Pebble Beach, is the waterfront of the Kona Paradise Properties subdivision. The large, shifting pebbles are hard to cross with bare feet, and so more fishermen than swimmers frequent the area.

On June 1, 1950, a major eruption began on Mauna Loa along the southwest rift zone. This eruption lasted for three weeks and extruded an enormous amount of lava, a large portion of which poured into the ocean in three separate flows. All three of these flows are located in the reach of shoreline between Ho'ōpūloa and Ho'okena and have become well known landmarks, especially for fishermen at sea who refer to them by number. The Honokua flow, the first flow encountered by a boat traveling south from Ho'okena, is known as First Flow, the Pāhoehoe Flow as Second Flow, and the Ka'apuna Flow as Third Flow. These flows were the source of a number of small black sand and olivine beaches in a section of shoreline that was otherwise primarily rocky sea cliffs. All of these tiny pockets of black volcanic cinder, however, are exposed to the direct assault of the open ocean and are battered by high surf and *kona* storms. They are not safe for swimming except when the ocean is very calm. There is no convenient public access to any of them.

(49)
Ho'okena Beach Park

Ho'okena i ka la'i,
Honomū a 'o nā manu,
'Ike 'ia 'o ka lihi,
Alia 'oe a pulale mai.

'O Kupa Landing,
Hanohano i ka la'i,
Ho'ulu 'ia no, Ho'okena,
Ho'oheno ka mana'o,
Nā kupa o ka 'āina,
Ho'olu i ka maka o ka malihini
Ho'olu i ka maka o ka malihini.

Ho'okena is peaceful
And the birds flock to Honomū
And glance about shyly.
But don't you rush.

Cooper Landing,
Its glorious solace and
Ho'okena's charm are
Cherished in the thoughts
Of the natives of the land.
Charm, too, in the eyes of visitors.
Charm, too, in the eyes of visitors.

"Kupa Landing"
Traditional song

The first steamship in the Hawaiian Islands, promptly labeled *mokuahi* or "fire ship" by the Hawaiians, arrived in 1836. However, canoes and sailing ships continued to dominate the interisland and circle-island trade and mail runs until the middle of the century. Then, with the establishment of the Inter-Island Steam Navigation Company and the Wilder Steamship Company, steamers became the vessels most frequently seen at the numerous local landings. The regular calling of a steamer at a particular landing often resulted in the

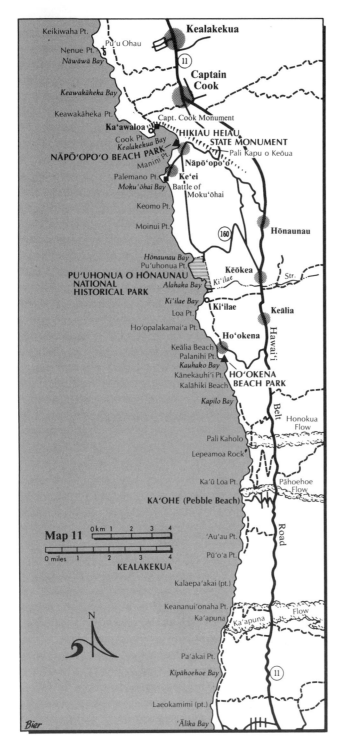

Map 11
KEALAKEKUA

rapid development of a trading community, and this is what happened at Hoʻokena, a tiny fishing village on the shore of Kauhako Bay.

The major village in the area was Kalāhiki, but Kalāhiki's exposed, rocky shoreline south of the bay did not offer a protected landing site, especially during periods of high seas. Hoʻokena's more sheltered location, with its sandy beach on the shore of Kauhako Bay, was much more attractive and, by the early 1880s, a landing, a wharf, and a macadamized road connecting the site with the *mauka* government road had been constructed. Hoʻokena grew into a busy trading village, with its own jail, courthouse, and school. The landing was named Kupa Landing for Henry Cooper, road supervisor of the District of South Kona from 1871 to 1880. (Kupa is the Hawaiianized version of the English name Cooper.)

One of Hoʻokena's most famous nineteenth-century visitors was British author Robert Louis Stevenson. Stevenson, a frail, sickly man, spent the last six years of his life in the South Pacific in his almost life-long search for good health. He arrived in Hawaiʻi in 1889. In April of that year, Stevenson spent a week relaxing in the home of Judge Nahinu in Hoʻokena. In his journal *Travels in Hawaii*, Stevenson described his landing from a lighter at the isolated Hawaiian village:

On the immediate foreshore, under a low cliff, there stood some score of houses, trellised and verandaed, set in narrow gardens, and painted gaudily in green and white; the whole surrounded and shaded by a grove of coco palms and fruit trees, springing (as by miracle) from the bare lava. In front, the population of the neighborhood were gathered for the weekly incident, the passage of the steamer, sixty to eighty strong, and attended by a disproportionate allowance of horses, mules, and donkeys; for this land of rock is, singular to say, a land of breeding. The green trees, the painted houses, the gay dresses of the women, were everywhere relieved on the uncompromising blackness of the lava; and the rain which fell, unheeded by the sightseers, blended and beautified the contrast.

The boat was run in upon a breaker and the passengers ejected on a flat rock, where the next wave submerged us to our hoses. There we continued to stand, the rain drenching us from above, the sea from below, like people mesmerized; and as we were all (being travelers) tricked

90

HO‘OKENA BEACH PARK. Ho‘okena was once an important interisland steamer landing. Today little remains of the once-thriving village. Automobiles and trucks eventually replaced steamers as the island's means of transporting people and freight, and, in a move that was repeated in many other areas of the Big Island, the residents left the shoreline and relocated *mauka* along the main highway.

out with the green garlands of departure, we must have offered somewhat the same appearance as a shipwrecked picnic.

Ho‘okena continued to be an important interisland steamer landing well into the twentieth century, until automobiles and trucks traveling over improved circle-island roads began to link the Big Island's once remote coastal areas directly with the major port in Hilo. Trucks replaced the steamers to transport the cattle, the coffee, and the other produce of the Kona coast. By the mid-1930s, high surf and storms had demolished the

landing at Ho‘okena, and most of the Hawaiian families had abandoned the village and moved up closer to the *mauka* highway, the new center of activity. Today, only a handful of people maintain shoreline residences at Ho‘okena, although a small fleet of canoes at Ho‘okena Beach is still used to fish for *‘ōpelu* and *‘ahi* in the offshore waters. Near the beach pavilion an old gas lamp standard is one of the few vestiges of the former village.

Ho‘okena Beach Park occupies the northern corner of Kauhako Bay, a wide, open bay bounded by moderately high sea cliffs. A large pocket beach at the park consists of very fine, black detrital sand blended with white calcareous sand, giving the beach a gray color. Low sections of rock front most of the shoreline, but sandy entry and exit points for swimmers, snorkelers, and nearshore scuba divers are located at the southern end of the beach and at the northern end near the ruins of the old landing. The *ʻōpelu* fishing canoes beached on the backshore also launch and land through the small sand channel near the former landing. The waters of Kauhako Bay are generally calm enough for most in-water activities, but hazardous conditions occur during periods of high surf and *kona* storms. Hoʻokena Beach Park contains parking, restrooms, showers, picnic tables, a small coconut grove, and a number of shade trees.

Beyond the sea cliffs, on the southern side of Kauhako Bay, a large, level fan of lava at Kalāhiki extends into the ocean, terminating at Limukoko Point. In his travel guide *The Island of Hawaii*, Henry Kinney briefly described the Kalāhiki area as it appeared in 1913: "A very poor trail leads makai of this cliff to the Kalahiki village, a small settlement on the south side of the bay, which may also be reached by a better trail on top of the bluff. Here are traces of a four terrace heiau. Beyond this there is no practical trail leading south."

A long, wide storm beach composed of white sand liberally strewn with coral rubble and lava fragments wraps completely around Limukoko Point, and is a highly visible landmark on this otherwise rocky coast-line. An extensive section of shallow reef fronts the entire length of Kalāhiki Beach, offering excellent fishing opportunities, but little inducement for swimming. Surf breaks frequently on the outer edge of the reef and sweeps in over the shoreline rocks, generating small rip currents. Shoreline plants on the backshore include *pōhuehue, kamani, kou,* and coconuts, while the extensive ruins of Kalāhiki village inland of the beach are overrun by *ēkoa, kiawe,* and *ʻopiuma*. *ʻOpiuma* trees, common to the shoreline areas in this region of South Kona, are sometimes called Manila tamarinds although they are from tropical America. The Hawaiians observed that the tree's black seeds resembled commercial pellets of opium and named the tree *ʻopiuma*. There is no convenient public access from Hoʻokena to Kalāhiki.

To the north of Hoʻokena Beach Park, a low, wide lava bench borders the entire length of Keālia Beach. A long, narrow storm beach composed of coral rubble and pockets of white sand is located behind the bench. The rocky shoreline is poor for swimming, but excellent for snorkeling and nearshore scuba diving. Approximately a dozen beach homes occupy the backshore. Keālia Beach is accessible by public road or simply by walking the shoreline from Hoʻokena Beach Park.

(50)
Puʻuhonua o Hōnaunau

Ua nani Hōnaunau Paka e kū nei,
O ka heke no ia o nā Kona.

Ulu wehiwehi i ka lau o ka niu,
A me ke kole maka onaona kaulana nei.

O ka laʻi auau a ʻo Kapuwai,
O upolu i ka ili a ka malihini

O Aleʻaleʻa i ke ehu o ke kai,
O ke kūkilakila Hale o Keawe.

Haina ia mai ana ka puana,
Kaulana mai nei Hōnaunau Paka.

Beautiful is Hōnaunau Park standing
At the fore of the Kona districts.

Festive are the coconut tree leaves
And the famous, beautiful-eyed surgeonfish.

Swimming in the calm of Kapuwai
Wets the skin of the visitors

The ocean spray drifts over Aleʻaleʻa Heiau,
Hale o Keawe Heiau stands majestically

Tell the refrain again,
Famous is Hōnaunau Park.

"Hōnaunau Paka"
Traditional song

The Hawaiian *kapu* system in pre-contact times strictly regulated the lives of both commoners and chiefs and imposed harsh penalties, often death, for infractions of the rules. The Hawaiians believed that their gods took offense at any broken *kapu* and that catastrophies such as lava flows, earthquakes, and tsunami were penalties for wrongs left unforgiven. For this reason, *kapu* breakers were relentlessly pursued and were usually unable to hide undetected for any length of time. If they managed to avoid capture, the law breakers did have one alternative for salvation: the *pu'uhonua*, place of refuge.

One or more *pu'uhonua* existed on each of the eight major Hawaiian islands, but the Big Island offered at least six, one for each of the island's major districts: Hilo, Puna, Ka'ū, Kona, Kohala, and Hāmākua. The most famous of all of these sites, the Pu'uhonua o Hōnaunau, the place of refuge in the Kona district, is located on a large point of land in Hōnaunau Bay. The

6-acre sanctuary contains many tidepools, coconut trees, and a *heiau*, Hale o Keawe, which was restored in 1968 at its original site.

Pu'uhonua o Hōnaunau is separated from the remainder of Hōnaunau by a massive stone wall that measures 1,000 feet long, 10 feet high, and 17 feet wide, a truly remarkable example of dry-stone masonry. Construction of the wall, the Great Wall as it is commonly called, occurred in the mid 1500s. Hōnaunau was also the home of the ruling chief of the area, and the grounds of the royal residence adjoin the Great Wall of the *pu'uhonua*. Keone'ele, the small beach located in a cove

HŌNAUNAU. Powered by an outboard motor, a modern outrigger canoe makes its way through a channel in the reef to the boat ramp in Hōnaunau Bay. The deeper waters seaward of the rocks to the right harbor a wide variety of fish and other marine life and offer some of the best nearshore snorkeling on the Big Island. The reconstructed *heiau* associated with Pu'uhonua o Hōnaunau National Historical Park is visible on the far point at the *makai* edge of the coconut grove.

93

near the northern end of the Great Wall, served as a royal canoe landing.

Many early visitors to the Hawaiian Islands mention the Pu'uhonua o Hōnaunau in their writings. Missionary William Ellis wrote in 1823 in his journal:

> These puhonuas were the Hawaiian cities of refuge, and afforded an inviolable sanctuary to the guilty fugitive, who, when flying from the avenging spear, was so favoured as to enter their precincts.
>
> This had several wide entrances, some on the side next the sea, the others facing the mountains. Hither the manslayer, the man who had broken a tabu, or failed in the observance of its rigid requirements, the thief, and even the murderer, fled from his incensed pursuers, and was secure.
>
> To whomsoever he belonged, and from whatever part he came, he was equally certain of admittance, though liable to be pursued to the gates of the enclosure.
>
> Happily for him, those gates were perpetually open; and as soon as the fugitive had entered, he repaired to the presence of the idol, and made a short ejaculatory address, expressive of his obligations to him in reaching the place with security.
>
> In one part of the enclosure, houses were formerly erected for the priests, and others for the refugees, who, after a certain period, or at the cessation of war, were dismissed by the priests, and returned unmolested to their dwellings and families; no one venturing to injure those, who, when they fled to the gods, had been by them protected.

Missionaries like Ellis and other early observers likened the *pu'uhonua* to the ancient biblical cities of refuge. The latter were actual cities where people lived and worked, while the Hawaiian *pu'uhonua* was not a city. In the Hebrew cities the accused stood before judges and priests, and if he was found guilty, he was sent back home for punishment. If he was found innocent, he remained in the city of refuge until the high priest in his home district died. In an Hawaiian *pu'uhonua*, on the other hand, the accused, guilty or not, was absolved and set free within a matter of hours or days to return home in complete safety. During times of war the *pu'uhonua* also served as a haven for children, women, the aged, and the defeated, offering a temporary sanctuary until the conflict ended. Although the *pu'uhonua*

occasionally afforded shelter to groups of people, it was never a city or even a village, but rather a designated area administered by priests and their attendants. The misnomer "city of refuge," however, quickly became the accepted definition of *pu'uhonua*, and the *pu'uhonua* at Hōnaunau, the best preserved of any in the Hawaiian Islands, was soon widely known as the City of Refuge.

The City of Refuge became an official park in 1920 when the County of Hawai'i leased the land from the Bishop Estate, the landowner. In 1955, thirty-five years later, Congress authorized acquisition of the site as a national historical park, and on July 1, 1961, the City of Refuge National Historical Park was established. The 180-acre tract includes the *pu'uhonua*, the grounds of the royal residence, and the village sites of Hōnaunau and Ki'ilae, the two fishing villages that supported the chief-in-residence. The new park was well received by both residents and visitors alike, but many Hawaiians objected to the continued use of the name City of Refuge and a campaign was mounted to change the name. Finally in 1978 Congress authorized the name that had been requested by the Hawaiian community, and the City of Refuge became officially Pu'uhonua o Hōnaunau National Historical Park.

Pu'uhonua o Hōnaunau is one of the Big Island's most popular visitor attractions. It offers an excellent opportunity to visualize and experience pre-contact Hawaiian culture in a natural setting. Facilities include a visitor center, restrooms, drinking water, an interpretive trail system, a picnic area, and parking. The park is on the shoreline of Hōnaunau Bay, one of the best snorkeling and nearshore scuba diving areas on the Big Island. The waters offshore of the park harbor a wide variety of fish and other marine life. Cold pockets of intruding fresh water are common. Fishermen and other persons wishing to catch fish or other sea life for food should check for restrictions at the visitor center; they will also need to notify the park personnel if they are planning to fish after dark.

Snorkelers, nearshore scuba divers, and swimmers are encouraged to enter the waters of Hōnaunau Bay near the one-lane public boat ramp at Kapuwai, adjoining Pu'uhonua o Hōnaunau, rather than from the park itself. The park includes a small pocket beach of white sand, Keone'ele, located on the shoreline of the royal residence. As a former royal canoe landing, Keone'ele was a sacred area, and to maintain the historical integrity of the beach, the park regulations discourage sunbathing and other recreational activities at the site. If necessary, however, Keone'ele may be used as a shoreline entry/exit point.

During the winter months, high surf and *kona* storms make ocean conditions hazardous at both Kapuwai and Keone'ele, precluding almost all in-water activities. Occasionally, experienced surfers find the waves offshore the *heiau* good enough to ride. In the southern portion of the park, around the picnic area, storm sand beaches form much of the backshore. The heavy winter surf that creates the storm beaches often poses a hazard to people strolling near the water's edge, and so during periods of high surf, park personnel post signs warning of high-washing waves. The winter surf not only deposits sand onshore at the southern end of the park, but also washes away some of the existing sand at Keone'ele. The winter months, however, are an excellent time for whale-watching. Every year, the official marine mammal of the state of Hawai'i, the humpback whale, winters in the islands and can often be seen near the shore at the southern end of the park.

(51)
Ke'ei

At noon we hired a Kanaka to take us down to the ancient ruins at Honaunau in his canoe—price two dollars—reasonable enough, for a sea voyage of eight miles, counting both ways. In one place we came upon a large company of naked natives of both sexes and all ages, amusing themselves with the national pastime of surf-bathing. Each heathen would paddle three or four hundred yards out to sea, (taking a short board with him), then face the shore and wait for a particularly prodigious billow to come along; at the right moment he would fling his board upon its foamy crest and himself upon the board, and here he would come whizzing by like a bombshell! It did not seem that a lightning express train could shoot along at a more hair-lifting speed.

Mark Twain in Hawaii
Walter Frear, 1947

In 1866, the *Sacramento Union*, a California newspaper, dispatched a young reporter to Hawai'i to survey and file stories on the history and the life style of the islands. Mark Twain was that reporter. He stayed in Hawai'i for months and visited many of the famous historical sites such as Pu'uhonua o Hōnaunau that still attract visitors today. During a one-hour canoe ride from Nāpō'opo'o to Hōnaunau, Mark Twain and his companion were paddled past the extensive shallow reef at Ke'ei, where they paused to watch a large group of the local residents out surfing. Today, the reef at Ke'ei remains a popular surfing site and provides some of the biggest waves and the longest rides along the entire reach of coastline from Nāpō'opo'o to Hōnaunau.

Ke'ei is also a place of historical significance, for it was the scene of the Battle of Moku'ōhai, Kamehameha I's first battle in his drive to gain control of the Big Island. In 1782, at the death of his uncle, Kalani'ōpu'u, the ruling chief of Hawai'i, Kamehameha was awarded custody of the war god Kūkā'ilimoku and the god's temples, whereas the late chief's son, Kiwala'ō, inherited the kingdom. Shortly thereafter, without consulting Kamehameha, Kiwala'ō redivided the lands of the island of Hawai'i, depriving Kamehameha and other high chiefs of extensive holdings that had previously been theirs. This action, coupled with other insults, led to a struggle for power between Kamehameha and Kiwala'ō and culminated in a major battle at Moku'ōhai on a rocky plain near Ke'ei. Kiwala'ō himself was killed during the fighting, and his forces were routed.

The battle of Moku'ōhai gave Kamehameha rule over half the island of Hawai'i, securing for him the districts of Kona, Kohala, and part of Hāmākua. He interpreted this victory as a sign that the gods supported him and favored him to rule not only the Big Island, but all of the Hawaiian islands. That dream finally became a reality in 1810 when Kamehameha gained supremacy over the entire group of islands and established the Kingdom of Hawai'i.

The village of Ke'ei today consists of a cluster of shoreline homes located principally in the lee of Palemanō Point. Ke'ei Beach, a white sand beach speckled with black lava fragments, sits between the village and the point. Although the beach itself is attractive, the ocean bottom immediately offshore is very shallow and rocky. A small sandy channel at the extreme northern end of the beach that was cleared by area residents is the

KEʻEI. This peaceful setting is a part of the panorama that greeted Captain Cook on his return to the Hawaiian Islands in 1779. Cook sailed into Kealakekua Bay, passed Keʻei Beach, and anchored in the lee of Pali Kapu o Keōua, the high sea cliff in the distance.

only site suitable for swimming. The extensive expanse of shallow reef fronting the beach stretches offshore for nearly 300 yards and provides good opportunities for a wide range of activities including snorkeling, surfing, and all types of fishing, including torch fishing. The backshore is undeveloped and overgrown with *kiawe* and *ʻopiuma*.

On the southern side of Palemanō Point, a long narrow storm beach of white sand lines the otherwise rocky shoreline. This area attracts primarily fishermen and beachcombers. The view from the tip of the point of Kealakekua Bay and points inland is spectacular.

Just north of Keʻei village is an undeveloped section of shoreline. The low sea cliffs here are a popular area for picnicking, fishing, and swimming. The waters offshore are excellent for snorkeling and nearshore scuba diving.

(52)
Nāpōʻopoʻo Beach Park

Ea mai ka makakai heʻenalu,
Kai heʻe kakala o ka moku,
Kai ka o ka nalu nui,
Ka huʻa o ka nalu o Hikiau,
Kai heʻenalu i ka awakea

The spray of surfing, rises
While wave upon wave strikes the island.
From the high waves
Foam washes against Hikiau Heiau.
This is a surf to ride at noon.

"Hele Mele He'e Nalu"
Traditional chant

Nāpō'opo'o Beach Park adjoins the village of Nāpō'opo'o. The most prominent feature in the park is Hikiau Heiau, the temple where Captain James Cook was received by the Hawaiians and honored as the god Lono. The ships of Cook's expedition, his third into the Pacific, came to anchor in Kealakekua Bay on January 17, 1779. The captain and a landing party went ashore near the *heiau*. Less than a month later, Cook was killed in an incident at Ka'awaloa, a village site on the northern side of Kealakekua Bay. Although the Ka'awaloa area is not accessible to the public except from the ocean, a 27-foot white obelisk erected near the spot where Cook was slain, can easily be seen from Nāpō-'opo'o Beach Park. Twelve rounded metal posts linked by chains surround the monument, which is fronted by a concrete jetty. The plaque on the obelisk reads:

In memory of the great circumnavigator Captain James Cook, R.N., who discovered these islands on the 18th day of January AD 1778 and fell near this spot on the 14th day of February AD 1779. This monument was erected in November AD 1874 by some of his fellow countrymen.

Two other signs at the site read:

This jetty was erected by the Commonwealth of Australia in memory of Captain James Cook, R.N., the discoverer of both Australia and these islands.

and

In commemoration of the 200th anniversary of the arrival in the Pacific Ocean of Captain James Cook, R.N., on his voyage of discovery 1768–1771 in the bark Endeavor. Presented by Swedish American Line on the occasion of a visit by M.S. Kungsholm to Kealakekua Bay, April 1st, 1969.

One-mile-wide Kealakekua Bay with its rich diversity of marine life and bottom features provides snorkelers, scuba divers, and glass-bottom boat passengers with excellent opportunities for first-hand observation of and contact with Hawai'i's nearshore undersea habitat. In 1969 the State of Hawai'i set apart the entire bay as the Kealakekua Bay Marine Life Conservation District to preserve and protect the underwater features and the life forms that inhabit them from depredation by a constant swarm of visitors. The conservation district is divided into two sub-zones, A and B. In Subzone A, the area inshore of a straight line drawn from Ka'awaloa Point to the northern end of Nāpō'opo'o Beach Park, all consumptive activities including the removal of coral, rocks, and shells, are prohibited. In Subzone B, the area between the Subzone A line and a straight line drawn from Ka'awaloa Point to Manini Point, fishing is permitted for any finfish by hook-and-line or throw-net, and for *akule, 'ōpelu,* and crustaceans by any legal fishing method except traps. The 315-acre conservation district is also known as the Kealakekua Bay State Underwater Park.

The beach at Nāpō'opo'o Beach Park consists primarily of pebbles, cobblestones, and boulders, with only a narrow strip of sand at the water's edge fronting the rocks. The sand, a blend of olivines, white calcareous sand, and black lava fragments, appears gray when dry. Residents of the area report that the present narrow strip was formerly a much larger beach. In August 1959, Hurricane Dot swept across the bay, partially eroding the beach and depositing onshore many of the rocks that now cover the sand. Despite its limited area and generally rocky appearance, the beach at Nāpō'opo'o attracts many sunbathers and swimmers. Occasionally, bodyboarders and bodysurfers ride the small shorebreak.

The small 6-acre park is the only public beach park with facilities that are conveniently accessible to the local residents from the nearby *makai* and *mauka* communities. In addition, non-local visitors come to the park in droves—both sightseers and water enthusiasts. Although many snorkelers are brought to the Kealakekua Bay State Underwater Park on commercial tour boats from Keauhou and Kailua, Nāpō'opo'o Beach

Park also serves as the chief entry/exit point for many other snorkelers and scuba divers who prefer to organize their own diving excursions. In addition to the activity in the park itself, the wharf and warehouse area of the old Nāpōʻopoʻo Landing nearby is used for single- and multi-hull boats of sailors and fishermen. Thus traffic in the whole neighborhood is often heavy. Facilities in the beach park include a picnic pavilion, restrooms, picnic tables, showers, a basketball court, and parking. Inland of the beach, the park is undeveloped; a large, stagnant pond is surrounded by tall grass, false *kamani*, coconut palms, date palms, and many large *ʻopiuma*.

To the south of the old Nāpōʻopoʻo Landing, Manini Beach, a storm beach, wraps around the northern point of Kahauloa Bay. An easily visible landmark on the otherwise rocky shoreline, Manini Beach consists of coral rubble that high surf and *kona* storms have washed inland over the rocks at the water's edge. Surfers occasionally ride the waves on the *mauka* side of the point, but only when the surf is big and breaks far enough out to allow them to clear the rocks safely. A large portion of the point behind the beach belongs to the state and is labeled on most maps as Nāpōʻopoʻo Park, but the area is undeveloped and overgrown.

A small shoreline community also backs a part of Manini Beach, and it was here that Iolani Luahine, one of the foremost exponents of the ancient hula in the twentieth century, was born on January 31, 1915. Her father decided that one of his children, Harriet Lanihau, would learn and carry on the traditions of their Hawaiian forebears; so, as an infant, she was sent to live in Honolulu with her grandmother Juliet Luahine. At the age of six months, with the approval of her parents, she was given the name Iolani Luahine, which she carried until she died.

Juliet Luahine, an accomplished dancer from the court of King Kalākaua, started Iolani's formal education in the hula when the child was four years old. Her training in the sacred dances, chants, and ceremonies of her ancestors continued until 1937, when Juliet Luahine died. The years following the death of her teacher and foster mother were spent in public performance and in perfecting what she had learned, until she became known and honored as a living legend in the performance of the ancient hula. Finally, in the early 1960s, she moved back to Nāpōʻopoʻo and took up residence in the house where she was born. In these later years she performed publicly only on infrequent occasions, but she remained an invaluable link with the past by conducting workshops on the hula and its associated arts and traditions. Iolani Luahine died on December 10, 1978, at the age of 63 and was buried at Hawaiian Memorial Park on Oʻahu.

At the northern end of Kealakekua Bay, the lowlands of Kaʻawaloa, once the site of a major Hawaiian settlement, are now overrun with *kou, ēkoa, kiawe,* and *ʻopiuma*. The Captain Cook Monument stands on the edge of a large, open cove on the Kaʻawaloa shoreline at the northernmost corner of Kealakekua Bay. This cove offers one of the most sheltered natural anchorages on the Kona coast, providing a fairly deep bottom and safety in almost all weather. Kealakekua Bay is subject to hazardous ocean conditions, particularly during periods of high surf and *kona* storms, but the cove at Kaʻawaloa almost invariably remains calm. Under ordinary weather conditions, the area attracts commercial dive tours.

The 8 miles of rugged shoreline from Kaʻawaloa to Keauhou consist primarily of low sea cliffs covered with *kiawe* and other dense shoreline vegetation. A number of small white-sand storm beaches cover the rocks near the Kaʻawaloa lighthouse, Nenue Point, Keikiwaha Point, and Kainaliu. The most conspicuous coastal feature along this reach is Puʻu Ohau, a 230-foot-high cinder cone located just north of Nāwāwā Bay. Puʻu Ohau, a landmark for Kona fishermen who know it as Red Hill because of the dominant color of its lava, marks the shoreline boundary between the districts of South Kona and North Kona.

(53)
Keauhou

Aia i Heʻeia la,
E ka nalu e heʻe ana.

Heʻe ana i ka nuku la,
Hoʻi ana i ka lala.

Naʻu i kikaha la,
Oia ae kai.

Ahe kuhi hewa koʻu la,
Aia i ka poli

Haina ka puana la,
O halala i ka nuku manu.

It is at Heʻeia,
That there are waves to surf.

Surfing in on the broken wave,
Returning on the diagonal one.

It is for me to glide upon,
Toward the edge of the shore.

It has been a misjudgment on my part,
It is there in the heart.

This is the story told
Of Halala, the beak of the bird.
"Heʻeia"
J. Kalahiki
© by Charles E. King

In 1813 or 1814 (historians are uncertain of the precise year) the high chiefess Keōpūolani, the highest-ranking wife of King Kamehameha I, gave birth to her third child, a son, in a house on the shore of Keauhou Bay. According to traditional accounts, the child, Kauike-aouli, was stillborn, but was brought back to life by Kapihe, a *kahuna* from Kalapana in the district of Puna who happened to be at Keauhou. Kapihe took the apparently lifeless infant outside the house to a boulder nearby and placed him in a depression in the top of the stone. There Kapihe revived the baby by fanning him, sprinkling him with water, and reciting a chant for the living. Kauikeaouli grew into a healthy man who eventually ruled the Kingdom of Hawaiʻi as Kamehameha III from 1825 until his death in 1854. On March 17, 1914, the Daughters of Hawaiʻi conducted a ceremony at Keauhou to mark the one-hundredth anniversary of the birth of Kamehameha III; they considered this to be the correct birth date. In attendance for the occasion were Queen Liliʻuokalani, Prince Kūhiō, and many other dignitaries of the day. A bronze plaque, still in place at the site, was affixed to the boulder on which the apparently lifeless infant was revived. In 1925 the Daughters of Hawaiʻi acquired the title from the Bishop Estate to the small parcel of land containing the

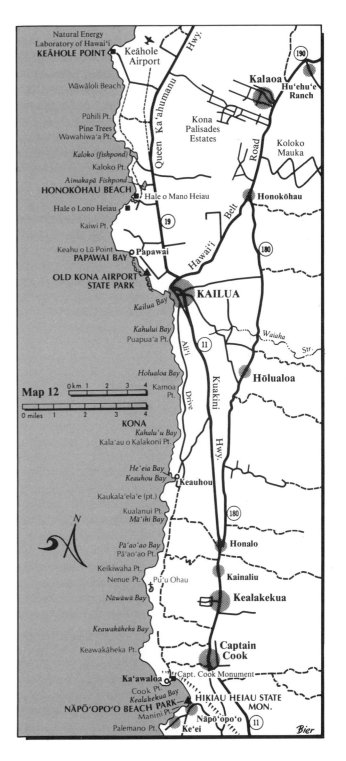

99

Kauikeauoli Stone and the birthplace for the sum of $50. The site is now maintained as a memorial.

The greatest memorial to the birth of Kauikeaouli, however, is the Keauhou Hōlua, which begins on the hillside directly above Keauhou Bay and, in former times, ended at the shore of Heʻeia Bay, just north of Keauhou. This *hōlua*, or sledding run, was originally almost a mile in length—the longest such structure known. Its construction on Kaneaka Hill was ordered by Kauikeaouli's father, Kamehameha I, then the reigning monarch of the Hawaiian Islands. Over the years the lower portion of the slide was destroyed, and a golf course now occupies the site; but the *mauka* portion remains intact, although in disrepair. The large inclined stone ramp can be most easily seen where it meets Aliʻi Drive opposite the entrance to the golf course.

In his book *Hawaiian Games for Today*, Donald Kilolani Mitchell offers the following description of the sport known as *heʻe hōlua*:

A narrow sled (papa hōlua), some 12 to 18 feet long, fitted with a pair of hardwood runners, was used by the chiefs to race downhill. The hōlua slide for this exciting sport was a steep hillside. It was usually necessary to add stones and earth to the depressions in the natural slope to construct a smooth, even course. The finished slide was then covered with pili grass to provide a slick surface for the sled runners.

Stories from days gone by tell of chiefs and chiefesses racing downhill in competition singly or side by side. Most of the riders lay prone on the mat-covered surface of the sled. Others crouched with the hands holding the supporting rods. They planted one foot against a brace constructed for that purpose and thrust the other foot beyond the rear of the sled in order to touch the surface of the slide as needed to guide the sled.

Many of the slides are located near famous traditional surfing areas, such as Heʻeia Bay. This has led some observers to speculate that there may have been a direct competitive connection between surfers and downhill racers. Perhaps, at the moment a surfer caught a wave a referee on shore signaled the sled rider at the top of the slide to begin his run, and when the contestants reached the ends of their respective rides, they would run for a common finish line between the beach and the end of the slide.

Keauhou Bay affords one of the most protected anchorages on the Kona coast and is the site of a small boat harbor and a public boat ramp. Support facilities in the area include a marine railway, a hoist on the dock, restrooms, fresh water, and parking for vehicles with trailers. At the northern corner of the bay is a small beach park, complete with picnic tables, restrooms, showers, and a sand volleyball court. A tiny pocket of pebbles fronts the park, the only beach in Keauhou Bay. Although the remaining shoreline in the bay consists primarily of sea walls and lava, the waters of the inner bay are excellent for swimming and snorkeling, the only real danger being the private and commercial boat traffic moving in and out of the harbor and boat ramp areas.

Heʻeia Bay, located just around the northern point of Keauhou Bay, offers another excellent site for swimming, snorkeling, and nearshore scuba diving, although again, the beach is rocky, with only a small pocket of pebbles and black sand. Entry and exit are more difficult than over a sandier beach, but the water is usually very clear and the bay harbors a wide variety of marine life. During the winter months, high surf often closes the entrances to both Heʻeia and Keauhou bays, and conditions are then extremely hazardous for swimmers and boaters alike.

Experienced surfers occasionally find some of these waves good enough to ride, especially if the swell is from the west. Although the backshore of Heʻeia Bay is undeveloped and overrun with *kiawe* and *ʻopiuma*, the entire bay area is surrounded by residential and resort development. A public right-of-way, as well as public parking, can be found on Manukai Street. A public pedestrian walkway follows the low sea cliffs from Heʻeia Bay to Mākoleʻā Beach fronting the Kona Lagoon Hotel. This section of shoreline provides an excellent view *mauka* of the Keauhou Hōlua.

Many long-time Kona residents know Heʻeia Bay as Walker Bay, a name dating from the 1930s. During the early part of that decade, Reverend Shannon Walker, the pastor of Central Kona Union Church in Kealakekua, acquired several parcels of land at the head of Heʻeia Bay. A youth camp he built on the point had four cabins, a combination meeting hall/cafeteria, and several auxiliary buildings. Walker tapped the brackish-water spring *mauka* of Heʻeia's pebble beach for the camp's bathing and toilet needs and obtained drinking water by catchment. Such dual water systems were common in the area until the 1960s, when county water lines were installed. Although Walker's camp has long since given way to other development, the name Walker Bay is still often used for Heʻeia.

(54)
Mākoleʻā Beach

He wahine a Makoleā no Kahaluʻu no. O kana kane o Kepakaʻiliula. Oia ke kaikamahine uʻi hoʻokahi a puni o Hawaiʻi nei.

Mākoleʻā was a woman from Kahaluʻu. Her husband was Kepakaʻiliula. She was the most beautiful young maiden in all of Hawaiʻi.

Place name information by Kalokuokamaile
Theodore Kelsey collection

Mākoleʻā Beach takes its name from Mākoleʻā Heiau located on the grounds of the Kona Lagoon Hotel. The *heiau* in turn took its name from a legendary beauty, the chiefess Mākoleʻā, who is said to have dwelt on the site. This particular *heiau*, one of ten in a comparatively small area, was for women, according to one authority, and offered them, among other things, a place to pray for fertility. Little remains of the structure today beyond its perimeter walls and small portion of an interior platform.

Mākoleʻā Beach is a mixture of black sand, pebbles, some white sand, and coral rubble. The beach, though at the head of a small cove, offers very limited opportunities for swimming. A very shallow, rocky shelf comprises the entire cove bottom from the water's edge to the surf line offshore. The few nearshore depressions among the rocks allow for little more activity for adults than wading. A rip current runs almost continually along the south point of the cove. Generated by the water from the incoming surf that flows through the shallows, the current drains back into the deeper waters offshore. During periods of high surf or *kona* storms, the rip current is especially swift and powerful, often creating an undertow as it passes through the breaking

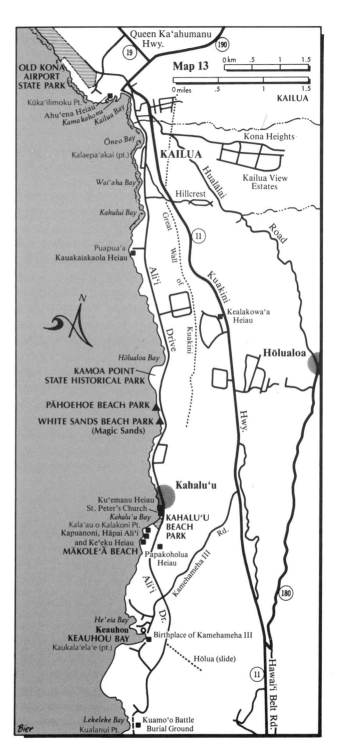

101

waves. Beyond the surf line, strong alongshore currents prevail. Mākoleʻā Beach is frequented chiefly by sunbathers, children playing in the wash of the waves, and occasionally by fishermen.

The shoreline between the Kona Lagoon Hotel and the Keauhou Beach Hotel, a low wide tidal flat of *pāhoehoe* covered with protruding rocks, depressions, and rises, harbors a large population of marine life. Many sections of the flat are dry at low tide and flooded at high tide. Two small adjoining pockets of white sand provide limited space for sunbathing.

Kahaluʻu Beach Park

Further south still is Kahaluu, a particularly interesting and possibly the most beautiful village in Kona.

The Island of Hawaii
Henry Kinney, 1913

Kahaluʻu, blessed with an excellent water supply and fertile soil, supported a large pre-contact population of both commoners and chiefs. Many house sites, *heiau*, other habitation ruins, and petroglyphs are located at or

KAHALUʻU BEACH PARK. Tourists and local residents alike enjoy the beach at Kahaluʻu, the largest white sand swimming beach between Kailua and Keauhou. The shallow nearshore waters offer excellent opportunities for snorkeling and occasionally for surfing. Many Hawaiian ruins are located in the area, particularly on the shoreline between the park and Keauhou Bay.

near Kahaluʻu Bay, which was a focal point for the community. Probably the most striking feature on the shoreline is the ruin of the great breakwater that once entirely enclosed Kahaluʻu Bay and Kealialia, the tidal lagoon *makai* of the Keauhou Beach Hotel. Known as Pāokamenehune, the "menehune breakwater," the structure originally formed a semicircle, 3,900 feet long. Most of the huge boulders of which it was constructed have been scattered by the endless batterings of high surf, storm waves, and tsunami.

Tiny and much-photographed, St. Peter's Catholic Church still stands on the shoreline of Kahaluʻu Bay. Beside it is another important site, Kuʻemanu Heiau, where the chiefs prayed for good surfing conditions. After surfing, they rinsed off in an adjoining spring, Waikuʻi, which is now a stagnant pond. Another larger pond nearby located to the rear of the beach was known as Waikuaʻala.

Kahaluʻu Beach Park became an official county park in 1953, when the Bishop Estate, the former landowner, leased the property to the County of Hawaiʻi. Thirteen years later, in a dedication ceremony held on September 24, 1966, Richard Lyman, a trustee of the Bishop Estate, presented Mayor Shunichi Kimura with the deed to the property, thereby assuring Kona residents of a permanent public beach park in the area. Since then, all of the remaining shoreline property south from Kahaluʻu Bay to Keauhou Bay has been developed for residential and resort purposes and is now known inclusively as Keauhou-Kona.

Kahaluʻu Beach Park is one of the most popular swimming and snorkeling sites in the district of Kona. It attracts large crowds of beachgoers, many coming in family groups, particularly on weekends and holidays. The white sand beach speckled with black lava fragments provides a good area for sunbathing and is also an easily negotiated entry/exit point to the bay offshore. The bay offers excellent opportunities for snorkeling and nearshore scuba diving in waters that are protected by a fringing reef and are generally current-free under ordinary ocean conditions. In addition to swimmers, snorkelers, and scuba divers the bay attracts local fishermen, who use surround-nets, hukilau nets, and throw-nets to catch their favorite fish. The bay has

never been designated a conservation district because it has always been a source of seafood for Hawaiian fishermen.

During periods of high surf, experienced surfers and bodyboarders may find some excellent waves at the seaward edge of the reef in the outer area of Kahaluʻu Bay. These same waves, however, generate an extremely powerful rip current that runs north from Kuʻemanu Heiau, along the rugged shoreline rocks, and out into the deeper waters beyond, where it dissipates. A person who has been caught in this rip and finds himself being towed out to sea can regain the safety of the beach only by swimming south around the surf line and then riding back in with the incoming waves. Many unwary and uninformed visitors, however, when trapped in the rip, attempt to swim against the current, often to the point of exhaustion when they cannot swim another stroke or even tread water—critical difficulties that may lead to drowning. Others caught in the rip, finding that they are being swept away from the beach, attempt to go ashore through the heavy surf pounding against the shoreline rocks; these attempts invariably prove equally disastrous. County lifeguards and fire department rescue personnel make more rescues at Kahaluʻu Beach Park than at any other beach in Kona. They suggest that rip current victims who go with the current and then float offshore beyond the surf until help arrives stand the best chance of survival.

Kahaluʻu Beach Park lies along Aliʻi Drive. Facilities include picnic pavilions, restrooms, showers, drinking water, a lifeguard tower, and a parking area.

(56)
White Sands Beach Park

Laʻaloa. A *heiau* here called Leleiwi (bone altar); the famous priest Hāwaʻe, who served under chief Ehukaipo, lived here. *Lit.*, very sacred.

Place Names of Hawaii
Pukui, Elbert, and Mookini, 1974

Situated on the shoreline of the land division of Laʻaloa is a large pocket of white sand, one of the largest onshore sand deposits along the 7-mile reach from

WHITE SANDS BEACH PARK. This small pocket of sand bordering Ali'i Drive is the most popular bodysurfing and bodyboarding site in North Kona. During periods of high surf the pounding shorebreak erodes the beach very quickly, leaving only exposed lava bedrock in its wake. This dramatic change often occurs overnight and has given rise to a variety of alternate names for the beach, including Vanishing Sands, Disappearing Sands, and Magic Sands.

Keauhou to Kailua. During periods of high surf, usually during the winter months, violent wave action will wash away the sand down to bare rock within twenty-four hours, causing the beach literally to disappear overnight. When the heavy surf subsides, normal wave action and ocean currents will slowly move the sand from the offshore reservoirs and redeposit it onshore. The accretion process often extends over a period of several months before the beach once again contains its usual volume of sand, and may be slowed or reversed by later assaults by high surf. The periodic flushing of this body of sand as it is moved offshore and onshore keeps it free of debris and very white. Over the years, the unique characteristics of this beach have been reflected in a number of different names, the most popular of which are Disappearing Sands Beach, Vanishing Sands Beach, Magic Sands Beach, and White Sands Beach. The County of Hawai'i prefers the last of these names, so the site is called White Sands Beach Park.

This very small park borders Ali'i Drive. Facilities

include restrooms, showers, a lifeguard tower, and a parking lot. A coconut grove in the backshore provides some shade for sunbathers and picnickers. A shallow sand bar that fronts the entire beach slopes gently to the deeper waters offshore, providing a safe swimming area. Throughout the year, a small shorebreak on the sand bar produces waves suitable for novice bodysurfers and bodyboarders. The attractive white sand of the beach, the park facilities, and the gentle shorebreak combine to make this one of the most popular parks in Kona, a favorite with visitors and residents alike. During the summer months and on weekends and holidays throughout the year, the park is usually crowded from end to end with sunbathers and bodysurfers.

When high surf rolls into Kona, however, the shorebreak at White Sands Beach Park is very strong and generates a powerful rip current that usually runs north into the open ocean. This becomes a serious hazard and occasionally results in near-drownings. The county lifeguards and Fire Department resuce personnel who are called to help report that they treat more injuries at this beach than at any other in Kona. When the shorebreak closes out, experienced bodysurfers move to the break directly outside the point fronting the comfort station where some of the best bodysurfing waves in the Hawaiian Islands can be found. The point break can hold rideable surf up to 10 feet and spectators line the shore to watch the big-wave bodysurfers in action. During the winter months the annual Magic Sands Bodysurfing Championship, the only bodysurfing contest held on the Big Island, attracts large crowds.

Just south of White Sands Beach Park is a small rocky cove. Snorkeling and nearshore scuba diving offshore the cove are excellent.

(57)
Pāhoehoe Beach Park

A wide trail leads south from Kailua, passing through a pretty stretch of country, near the beach, and through many villages. In the past there were many heiaus here. The villages are in order, north to south, Kahului, Kaumalumalu, Pahoehoe, and Laaloa.

The Island of Hawaii
Henry Kinney, 1913

Pāhoehoe Beach Park, located in the land division of Pāhoehoe and situated near the deserted Pāhoehoe village complex, occupies a small, narrow parcel of shoreline property shaded with *kiawe* trees. A low sea wall lines the entire seaward edge of the park, a barrier against the erosive forces of the occasionally powerful surf that pounds this area. Below the wall, the one tiny pocket of white sand and coral rubble in the rocky shoreline is not a good beach for swimmers. The park is frequented primarily by picnickers and fishermen. Facilities include picnic tables and parking.

(58)
Kamoa Point State Historical Park

After the death of Captain Cook and the departure of his ship, Kalaniopu'u moved to Kainaliu near Honua-'ino, and after some months to Keauhou where he could surf in the waves of Kahalu'u and Holualoa.

Ruling Chiefs of Hawaii
Samuel Kamakau

The 4-mile stretch of shoreline from White Sands Beach Park to Kailua Pier is notched by many little inlets, bays, and coves. A few are lined with white sand, but most of them are fronted by pebbles, boulders, or simply solid rock. This rocky reach attracts many fishermen and surfers, but only a few swimmers, snorkelers, and nearshore scuba divers. The best surfing breaks have been named for well-known landmarks on shore, such as Banyan's for the huge banyan tree on the grounds of the Kona Bali Kai, Lyman's for the nearby Lyman family home, Kona Tiki for the Kona Tiki condominium, and Honl's for the nearby Honl family home. Of all these various breaks, Lyman's provides probably the most consistent surf throughout the year and some of the biggest and longest rides. The waves here break off the northern side of Kamoa Point and roll into the waters of Hōlualoa Bay, making an excellent left slide that is just as popular with surfers today as it was long ago with the Hawaiians. During periods of high surf the break attracts not only large numbers of surfers and bodyboarders, but an enthusiastic crowd of spectators who line Ali'i Drive—a good vantage point from which to witness the big-wave surfing. Spectators also watch the action from Kamoa Point, where remains of a surfing *heiau*, bathing pools, and other important archaeological sites are hidden in the dense thicket of *'opiuma, kamani, naupaka,* and other shoreline vegetation. In December 1980 the State of Hawai'i acquired 12 acres on the northern half of Kamoa Point to preserve this historically important area. The property remains undeveloped.

The Lyman home, from which the popular surfing break at Kamoa Point gets its name, is prominently located on another point of Hōlualoa Bay inshore of the break. Barbara and Howard Lyman purchased the property on Poinciana Point and built their home in 1956, and ever since, the surfing break has been "Lyman's."

A long-time friend and frequent visitor to the Lyman home is Lei Collins, the curator of Hulihe'e Palace in Kailua. One day while relaxing on the *lanai* of the newly completed home and gazing out across the water, a song suddenly began to form in her mind. She retired to the Lyman's study and soon emerged with a beautiful new song that has become a standard for many Hawaiian groups. It is entitled "Laimana," the Hawaiian version of the English name Lyman.

'Ike aku i ka nani
Ka home a'o Laimana
Home kau i ka nuku
Home piha hau'oli
Home piha hau'oli

He koho kula kaimana
Aloha nei i ka la
Ua ohu oi au pa'a
Nā kealoha o ka 'aina
Nā kealoha o ka 'aina

Nanea me na hoaloha
Ma ka ili kai o Kona
No Kona ke kai malino
O Hualālai ko makua.
O Hualālai ko makua.

Eo mai kou inoa
Ka home a'o Laimana
Home kau i ka nuku
Home piha hau'oli
Home piha hau'oli

I have seen and admired the beauty
Of the Lyman home,
Home gracing the entrance of the bay,
Home so full of happiness,
Home so full of happiness.

I gaze at the splendor of the horizon
Like diamonds, sparkling in the sun.
Enchantment, so binding, leads you here.
You have found a home at last.
You have found a home at last.

We relax with friends
On the shore of Kona
Favored by the gentle sea
Beneath Hualalai, beloved mother.
Beneath Hualalai, beloved mother.

We sing praises to your name
Home of the Lymans
Home gracing the entrance of the bay
Home so full of happiness.
Home so full of happiness.

"Laimana"
© by Lei Collins, 1956

(59)
Kailua

Kailua, now capital of Owhyhee, was the seat of government of the group after the conquests of the renowned Kamehameha I, who, it will be remembered, died here. It is situated within a wide bay, with a safe roadstead and good anchorage.

Travels in the Sandwich and Society Islands
S. S. Hill, 1856

The town of Kailua is the Big Island's most popular tourist destination. Its location on Kailua Bay at the foot of the island's third-highest mountain, Hualālai, has long attracted visitors, who enjoy not only its beauty, but its seemingly endless days of sunshine. In addition to its excellent weather for sightseeing, sunbathing, and swimming, Kailua also offers a wide variety of other recreational opportunities, such as snorkeling, deep-sea fishing, tennis, golf, and just about every other amenity desirable in a major resort destination.

Kailua is located in the Big Island's vast district of

Kona. The district begins on the shoreline at Manukā and extends some 86 miles to 'Anaeho'omalu. Pu'u Ohau, a cinder cone between Kealakekua and Keauhou, marks the boundary between North and South Kona. The word *kona* in Hawaiian means leeward and each of the other major islands also has a *kona* or leeward district. The word is also commonly used throughout the islands to indicate weather conditions originating from the southern or leeward direction, such as "a *kona* wind," or "a *kona* storm."

During the twentieth century, traveling to the town of Kailua has become synonymous with traveling to the district of Kona, so much so that one rarely speaks of "going to Kailua" on the Big Island; instead one invariably "goes to Kona." This situation was further reinforced after World War II when the newly constructed airport at the edge of town was named the Kona Airport rather than the Kailua airport, so people flying to Kailua always said they were flying to Kona. Then in 1957, the U.S. Postal Service changed the town's postal designation from Kailua to Kona. The change was made because literally thousands of letters a week intended for residents of Kailua in the Ko'olaupoko District of O'ahu were ending up in Kailua in the Kona District of the Big Island. The change, however, was protested by the Kona Civic Club whose members felt that the name Kailua should be preserved. They suggested the compromise name Kailua-Kona and sent petitions to that effect to Washington. The petitions were acknowledged and on July 13, 1957, the postal designation for the town of Kailua became officially Kailua-Kona.

This solved the mail dilemma, but it misled many people into believing erroneously that the name of the town had also been changed to Kailua-Kona, so today the town, still officially bearing the original, but unusued, name of Kailua, is called either Kona or Kailua-Kona. Fortunately for the residents of the village of Kailua on Maui, their small rural community has a Star Route designation at the Ha'iku Post Office, and so the third Kailua in the Hawaiian Islands was never involved in the controversial name-change episode.

Prior to the development of tourism, farming provided one of the economic mainstays of the Kona district, and probably the area's most famous agricultural product was and still is its internationally renowned coffee. Coffee plants were originally brought from Brazil and the Philippines in the early 1800s and successfully planted in the Kona district on the island of O'ahu, but the industry soon shifted to the Big Island's Kona district. Coffee berries do not flourish in direct sunlight, and in other parts of the world, shade trees are planted to protect them. But planters discovered that the *mauka* slopes of Hualālai not only offered good climate and soil, but enough cloudiness to allow the coffee trees to grow unshaded on the mountainside. The first commercial crop was harvested in 1845 and weighed in at 248 pounds.

Coffee subsequently developed into an important industry on the island, and today the Big Island supports the only commercial coffee industry in the United States. Although the trees bear annually, there are three or four pickings per year because the berries ripen unevenly. The growers prune the trees to heights of 12 feet for convenience of picking, which is done completely by hand. The harvesting season opens in September, peaks in October, then dwindles through the holidays. The freshly picked berries are odorless and tasteless; the heat applied during roasting and brewing releases the famous aroma and flavor.

Prior to the development of tourism, ranching also provided one of the economic mainstays of the district, and for years the town of Kailua served as a major shipping point for many of the large *mauka* ranches. Originally, cattle-loading operations were conducted by cowboys on horseback driving the animals to the water's edge and then swimming them to an interisland steamer anchored at a safe depth. Then, one by one, the cattle were hoisted on board the ship into an open deck corral for the voyage to the slaughterhouse in Honolulu. In later years, when the pier was improved and modified, cattle were penned on the structure and then loaded through a chute onto a barge. However, wave action in the bay often made this operation difficult. Finally, the Kona ranchers who had been using Kailua Pier abandoned the site in favor of the deep-draft harbor that had been developed in the late 1950s at Kawaihae. In 1966 the Hawai'i Cattlemen's Association advised the state that they had no further use for the cattle pens on the pier, and in November of that year, a private contractor removed the fences and concrete flooring.

Today, Kailua Pier, under the administration of the State Division of Harbors, is still in constant use as a landing by many commercial and privately owned boats. The perpetual activity centered around the pier has made it one of the most popular visitor attractions on the shores of Kailua Bay. The pier also hosts annually a number of competitive events that have gained world-wide recognition, including the Hawaiian International Billfish Tournament, originated in 1959, and the Ironman Triathlon World Championship, held first in 1978 on Oʻahu and moved to Kona in February 1981. Many sportsmen consider the waters off the Kona coast to be the world's best sport fishing area for big-game fish, such as Pacific blue marlin, striped marlin, yellowfin tuna, dolphin, wahoo, and bonito. The Hawaiian International Billfish Tournament attracts four-man teams from all over the world to participate in this annual summer event. The Ironman Triathlon World Championship, the most famous and highly publicized of modern triathlons, has developed into the premier event of its kind, attracting some of the world's greatest multi-sport athletes. During the grueling one-day competition, Kailua Pier serves as the base of operations for each segment of the swim-bike-run event.

Immediately north of Kailua Pier is a small cove of white sand that is known as Kamakahonu, "the eye [of

KAMAKAHONU. In Hawaiian Kamakahonu means "the turtle eye." The name is said to have originated from a rock, now located under nearby Kailua Pier, that was shaped like a turtle. This area was the final home of King Kamehameha the Great, who lived here from 1812 until his death on May 8, 1819. The calm, shallow waters of Kamakahonu Beach, one of the safest swimming sites in Kona, is a favorite place for Kona residents to bring their little children.

the] turtle." Long-time residents of the area recall that a rock formation resembling a turtle once topped a small, low-lying projection of *pāhoehoe*. In 1915 the first pier was built over the formation. For many years, the turtle-like formation remained visible, but eventually it was covered when concrete was used to fortify and expand the pier's foundations. Some observers believe that it was this turtle formation in the lava, now buried, that gave rise to the name Kamakahonu.

Kamakahonu is probably best known as the site of the last home of King Kamehameha I, the great Hawaiian leader who successfully unified all of the islands and established the Kingdom of Hawai'i. In 1812 Kamehameha moved his royal residence from Honolulu to Kailua and took up residence on the bay, first at Kalake'e, where Hulihe'e Palace now stands, and soon afterward at Kamakahonu. A massive, crescent-shaped stone wall that stretched from the present pier to the shoreline beyond Ahu'ena Heiau enclosed the grounds of Kamehameha's royal residence, which included a number of thatch and stone dwellings for the king, his wives, and their attendants. In this complex the king lived and conducted matters of personal and government concern until his death on May 8, 1819.

After the death of Kamehameha, a number of sayings referring to the king emerged among the Hawaiians. Several contained specific references to Kamakahonu or Kamakaokahonu, the complete noun phrase of the place name. Two of these were posed in the form of riddles, and the answer to both is Kamehameha:

Ku'u ali'i, ho'i nō a ka maka o ka honu, make.
My chief who returned to the eye of the turtle and died.

and

Ua hānau ia o ka lani i nuna o Kamakaokahonu.
Ua hānai ia o ka lani i nuna o Kamakaokahonu.
Ua make o kalani nui i nuna o Kamakaokahonu.

The chief was born at Kamakaokahonu.
The chief was raised at Kamakaokahonu.
The great chief died at Kamakaokahonu.

The multiple references to the place name Kamakahonu in the second riddle at first seem inaccurate because historians have determined that Kamehameha was born and raised in the district of Kohala. Tradition says the chief was born at Kapakai in the land division of Kokoiki, where his parents were camped with the army of Kalani'ōpu'u, and that immediately after his birth, he was taken to 'Āwini, a remote valley high in the mountains, where he was raised in seclusion during his early childhood. Long-time Kohala residents, however, still recall that a canoe landing at Kapakai was called Kamakahonu and that the place in 'Āwini where Kamehameha lived was also called Kamakahonu. This appears to give credence to all three statements in the second riddle.

Less than one year after the death of Kamehameha, on April 4, 1820, the first company of Congregational missionaries from New England stepped ashore at Kamakahonu, landing on the rock outcropping now beneath the pier. For many years after the missionaries' arrival, this particular arm of *pāhoehoe* was known as Hawai'i's Plymouth Rock. In 1964, the entire Kamakahonu area was designated by the U.S. Department of the Interior as a National Historic Landmark.

Although the Kailua waterfront has been altered by the construction of the pier and the adjoining sea wall protecting Ali'i Drive, the cove of white sand at Kamakahonu fronting the King Kamehameha Hotel has remained intact and still provides the most protected swimming area on the shoreline of Kailua Bay. The small pocket beach slopes very gradually into the deeper waters offshore, and is an excellent place for little children to swim. Before 1960, when development of the area into a resort complex was completed, Kamakahonu Beach served as a canoe landing and boat yard for many of Kailua's fishermen and was also one of the favorite places among local families to spend a day at the beach. Although the boats are now launched and landed from the ramp on the pier, the beach still attracts many residents with little children from Kailua and the surrounding *mauka* communities. No public facilities exist on the beach itself, but public restrooms are located on the pier.

At the southern end of the sea wall near Hulihe'e Palace, another small pocket of white sand, tucked into the shoreline of Kailua Bay, is known to most long-time Kona residents as Kanuha Beach. The Kanuha family, descended from a long line of Kailua chiefs, formerly owned a parcel of property *mauka* of this shoreline site. A very shallow, rocky shelf fronts Kanuha Beach, so the area is used chiefly as a landing for racing canoes and sailing craft rather than as a swimming site.

(60)
Old Kona Airport State Recreation Area

From the point where the Honokohau Trail leaves Kailua a poor trail leads makai over the lava to the lighthouse. Hence it continues along the beach for a couple of miles. After passing several old stone mausoleums, the trail passes an abandoned grass house where is a stone wall, the remnants of the heiau Keohuulu. Still further north is a cocoanut grove, where there were several heiau, notably that of Palihiole. There were several kuulas here, one particularly powerful one, the idol of which is still remembered as having been in a fair state of preservation, only one arm missing, when a Christian priest took it from the cave where it was kept. Since then, say the inhabitants, the fishing has been comparatively poor. In the grove are two cocoanut stumps which served as gallows for the first execution conducted by hanging in Hawaii. A chief, Kekuakahaku, was the victim.

The Island of Hawaii
Henry Kinney, 1913

Not long after the end of World War II, the Territory of Hawai'i constructed the Kona Airport on the open shoreline immediately north of the town of Kailua. The land had belonged to the Lili'uokalani Trust, but was condemned for public use. At the northernmost end of the site, a small Hawaiian community of 'ōpelu fishermen lived in a cluster of homes in a large coconut grove. Behind the homes were several large brackish-water ponds from which the fishermen gathered tiny red shrimp to mix in the *palu*, or chum, used for catching 'ōpelu. Several springs and one well provided water for drinking and for other domestic needs. The fishermen kept their canoes and boats at Kamakahonu in Kailua, where a protected, sandy cove offered a safe site for landing, unloading catches, and beaching their crafts. The 'ōpelu fishing community, known to its residents as Makaeo, fell victim to the airport along with the beautiful coconut grove and its attendant ponds. Today, only one small brackish-water pond remains.

By 1960 the Kona Airport had become obsolete for the types of aircraft and the volume of traffic that it was handling. The runway, even when extended as far as possible with a 1,500-foot addition to its original length, was still too short to safely accommodate DC9s with a full load of passengers, fuel, and cargo. Take-off and landing weight restrictions were imposed on the large aircraft, forcing them to carry less than a full load and adding costs and inconvenience for the airlines. In addition, navigational problems were aggravated because of insufficient space to accommodate the necessary components for an Instrument Landing System (ILS). Without an ILS, much higher visibility was needed by incoming and departing aircraft. By the 1960s the nearby town of Kailua had greatly expanded with residential and resort development, leading to many complaints about take-off and landing noise. In 1970 the Kona Airport was finally closed, and the new Keāhole Airport began operations on the vast expanses of barren lava at Keāhole Point.

The State of Hawai'i converted the 120-acre-site of the old Kona Airport into a park that is formally known as Old Kona Airport State Recreation Area. Most Kona residents refer to the area simply as Old Airport. Facilities in the park include picnic pavilions, restrooms, showers, drinking water, and unlimited parking on the old runway. The county has leased the southern portion of the recreation area surrounding the old terminal building, and there provides restrooms, tennis courts, and athletic fields for organized sports and other community events.

The shoreline of Old Kona Airport State Recreation Area consists of a long, wide storm beach of white sand situated between the rocks at the water's edge and the length of the old runway. A few scattered inlets and sand channels offer swimmers entry and exit points when the ocean is calm. This rocky reach of coast is fully exposed to high surf and southerly storms, both of which create hazardous water conditions. Offshore, a shallow reef shelf provides Kona surfers with a popular surfing break that they call Old Airport. Snorkelers and nearshore scuba divers enter and leave the water at a small, partially protected cove that is commonly called Pawai Bay located at the northern end of the beach. A narrow channel leads to the deeper waters offshore. A few scattered coconut and beach heliotrope trees offer some protection from the sun, but most of the shoreline is open and unshaded.

Beyond the park boundary at the southern end of this rocky shoreline, a small, sheltered sandy inlet provides the most protected place for little children to swim. The inlet lies just north of the lighthouse. A small storm beach of white sand at its head can be easily reached by walking along the water's edge from the park. This area was once a popular camping site for local fishermen and their families, but a developer purchased the prime beachfront real estate and put a stop to all camping and trespassing. This turn of events was disturbing for a number of local residents because they were then left with only one public beach camping site in the entire Kona district, the tiny beach park many miles away in remote Miloli'i. A group of the irate campers, under the leadership of Herman Paakonia, decided to confront the developer and publicize their concerns by erecting a tent city on the site. They named their community Kūkā'ilimoku Village after the nearby point on which the lighthouse is located. Kūkā'ilimoku, the most famous of the Kū war images owned by Kamehameha I, means "Kū, snatcher [of] islands," a name the group thought appropriate for their village.

After several months and a number of confrontations at the site between police and the villagers, Paakonia and two other men were arrested for trespassing. At the trial in January 1981, they were found guilty of the charge and given suspended sentences. This action led to the dissolution of Kūkā'ilimoku Village, but did not dampen the spirit of resolution that had been kindled among the community members and their supporters. A group known as Friends of Kuka'SPOKA, an acronym for Kūkā'ilimoku and State Park at the Old Airport, has continued the protest under the leadership of Jerry Rothstein. This concerned group monitors the movements of the developer on his property and presses for the public's right of access through certain disputed portions of the shoreline. A state shoreline survey following the Kūkā'ilimoku trespass trial determined that approximately 8 acres of beachfront property claimed by the developer actually belong to the state. Friends of Kuka'SPOKA believe the actual figure may be even higher.

(61)
Papawai
Beyond the main [coconut] grove are a few isolated trees near the edge of the flow. Here was the heiau of Pauai, and here the trail ends.

The Island of Hawaii
Henry Kinney, 1913

The rocky 3 miles of shoreline between the Old Airport State Recreation Area and Honokōhau Harbor consists of a succession of *pāhoehoe* hills and depressions interspersed with a number of coral rubble and white sand storm beaches. In one low-lying area there is a small, shallow, sandy pool that is backed by a pocket of white sand shaded by *milo* and *kiawe*. This site is known as Papawai and has been designated by the Lili'uokalani Trust, the landowner, for use as a camp site for the beneficiaries of the trust. Queen Lili'uokalani (1838–1917), the last reigning monarch of the Kingdom of Hawai'i, created the trust to assist needy orphaned children of Hawai'i and decreed that "all of the property of the Trust estate, both principal and income, shall be used by the Trustees for the benefit of orphan and other destitute children in the Hawaiian islands, the preference to be given to Hawaiian children of pure or part aboriginal blood." In accordance with the Deed of Trust, the Queen Lili'uokalani Children's Center helps each youngster under its care to become a part of a family and to grow into an independent adult. One of the center's special project areas is located in the land division of Keahuolū and includes a meeting hall and the shoreline campsite at Papawai. Use of the site is regulated by the trustees and the executive director.

The trust decided to develop the Kona property at Keahuolū in 1974 and began making improvements in the area in 1975 with the construction of an access road from Queen Ka'ahumanu Highway. Prior to this time, the trust had been leasing Papawai to Captain Beans Beans, a tour boat operator from Kailua. During the mid-1960s, Beans had been taking snorkeling and picnic tours to 'Alula Beach at Honokōhau, but selection of Honokōhau as the site for a major state harbor forced him to find another suitable location. Beans decided on Papawai, arranged to lease the area, and ran his snorkeling and picnic tours there until the early 1970s.

At that time he sold his snorkeling business and concentrated exclusively on his glass-bottom boat and dinner cruise operations, for which he was famous until his death in April 1983. During the period when Beans used Papawai, it was commonly called Beans Beach, a name still familiar to many local residents. Papawai, is probably best known to long-time Kona residents as Pawai. When the Lili'uokalani Trust decided to develop the area, it was found in the course of their research that Pawai was actually a shortened version of Papawai; so they restored the older name to the site.

(62)
Honokōhau

From the trail running north toward Makalawena a side trail runs makai to the Honokohau village, which consists of about a dozen houses by the beach. Here is a large cement pan, formerly used for the manufacture of salt from sea water, north of which are some rock drawings. Makai thereof, by a couple of cocoanut stumps, are the scant remains of a heiau, "Hale o Kane." Directly in front of the houses are some excellent specimens of the papa konane, or checker boards used by the ancient Hawaiians.

The Island of Hawaii
Henry Kinney, 1913

The shoreline of Honokōhau once supported a sizeable Hawaiian settlement, as evidenced by the remains of numerous archaeological features. Archaeologists from the Bishop Museum in Honolulu have identified over 200 sites that include almost every known type of pre-contact structure, indicating a population of several hundred people. The most significant sites include temples, images used to attract fish, house platforms, trails, stone planters, canoe landings and shelters, assembly grounds, salt pans, petroglyphs, burial sites, and three fishponds—'Ai'ōpio, 'Aimakapā, and Kaloko. The Honokōhau settlement demonstrates the close relationship between the early Hawaiians and their environment and is regarded as an important historical and archaeological complex. The National Parks and Recreation Act of 1978 provided for the establishment of the Kaloko-Honokōhau National Cultural Park to preserve the integrity of the entire area, but to date, no further progress has been made.

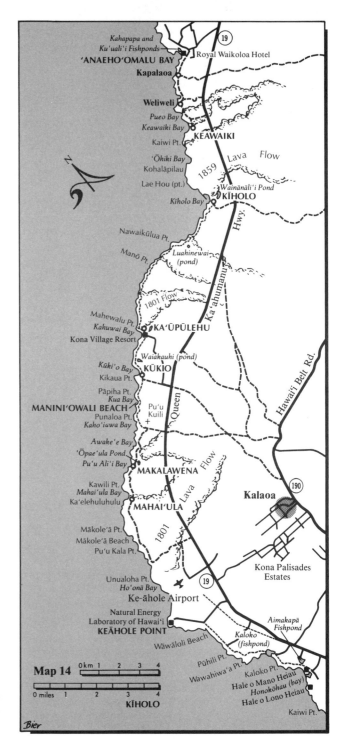

112

'ALULA BEACH. This secluded little pocket of white sand is located at the entrance to Honokōhau Harbor. In spite of an abundance of fresh water intrusion, the nearshore waters are excellent for snorkeling during periods of calm seas. The beach also provides a good vantage point for watching the boat traffic moving in and out of the harbor.

The three fishponds were at the heart of the Honokō-hau settlement's activity. One of them, 'Aimakapā, is the largest on the entire Kona coast. In addition to its historical significance, 'Aimakapā, with 20 acres of open water and 15 acres of marsh, today provides an important habitat for native and migratory waterbirds, two of which, the *āe'o* (stilt) and the *koloa* (Hawaiian duck), are on the endangered species list. Although the Big Island's land area is larger than the rest of the Hawaiian islands combined, the island has very few wetland areas suitable for native waterbirds; the two most important are 'Aimakapā and 'Opae'ula, located a scant 10 miles north at Makalawena.

Kaloko fishpond, though less important as a water-bird habitat, is an excellent example of the Hawaiians' ingenuity in adapting the existing environment to meet their needs. They built a 750-foot-long seawall across the mouth of a natural embayment, thus enclosing the 11-acre fishpond, which was not only an excellent source of fish but also apparently was a site favored by Hawaiian chiefs, if we can judge from the clustering of especially large, well-made structures and complexes surrounding the pond.

The Kaloko area is also well known as a possible burial site of Kamehameha I. When the great king died on May 8, 1819, at Kamakahonu, his royal residence in

Kailua, his body was prepared according to ancient custom, which required the separation of the flesh from the bones. The sacred bones were then placed in a container and taken in secret to a hidden burial site, which, according to some accounts, was a cave at Kaloko. To this day, however, the exact site has never been discovered or revealed.

The third fishpond in the Honokōhau area is 'Ai'ōpio, on the shoreline immediately north of the entrance channel to Honokōhau Harbor. This small circular pond was created by the construction of a low sea wall between Maliu Point and Honokōhau Beach. It is bordered by a cluster of fishermen's homes and a number of archaeological sites.

Honokōhau Beach, a long, curving stretch of white sand peppered with fragments of black lava, extends the full length of Honokōhau Bay. A low lava shelf at the water's edge lines most of the shore, but the comparatively rock free central portion of the beach offers an adequate swimming site for most beachgoers. The shallow, rocky ocean bottom immediately offshore lies within a semicircle of fringing reef that dissipates surf and prevailing currents and is a good place for snorkeling. 'Aimakapā fishpond is directly inland of Honokōhau Beach, which serves as a narrow barrier between the pond and the ocean.

The northern end of the beach consists of a rocky point backed by a dense thicket of shoreline vegetation. A trail leads from this area *mauka* across the barren lava field to a brackish-water pool that is known as the Queen's Bath. A number of large rock cairns surround the cool, spring-fed pool, a refreshing place to rinse off after a swim.

Although Honokōhau Beach is commonly frequented by pole fishermen, net fishermen, snorkelers, surfers, and swimmers, nudists come here in such numbers that Honokōhau is often described as a complete-tanning or a clothes-optional beach. Nudists are attracted to the area because it is close to the population centers in Kona, yet far enough removed to allow them a moderate amount of seclusion. In addition, all of the groups that come to the area usually co-exist peacefully; so the nudists are not subjected to the amount of harassment they have encountered in other places. For these reasons, Honokōhau Beach has become an important

shoreline site for the nudist community, a low-profile but widespread minority in Hawai'i.

To reach Honokōhau Beach, most beachgoers park near Maliu Point at the entrance to Honokōhau Harbor and follow the shoreline past 'Ai'ōpio fishpond. The nearest public facilities are located at the boat harbor.

Honokōhau Small Boat Harbor was authorized by the River and Harbor Act of 1965, but the actual construction of the complex was not completed until March 1970. During the summer of 1978 an expansion project was initiated to enlarge the harbor basins and to provide additional boat ramps, loading docks, and moorings. Improvements were made to the washdown area, the vehicle and trailer parking areas, the repair yard, and the access road. The excess excavated material was deposited in a large depression in a state-owned lava field 1,000 yards south of the harbor. Contractors completed the expansion project in 1980.

On the southern side of the entrance to Honokōhau Harbor, behind a small, protected cove, are several brackish-water ponds and a number of archaeological sites that are known as the 'Alula Bay Complex. The cove shelters a crescent of white sand speckled with fragments of black lava—a secluded spot for sunbathing and for viewing the boat traffic moving in and out of the harbor. With its shallow ocean bottom of sand and rock, the cove is also a good place for swimming. Snorkeling and nearshore scuba diving are excellent along the rocks bordering the beach. A small stand of *kiawe* and *ēkoa* in the backshore provide a little shade. Places of fresh water intrusion are frequently encountered in the deeper waters offshore in Honokōhau Bay. Most local residents know this little cove as 'Alula Beach. Public facilities are available in the boat harbor.

(63)
Keāhole

The fishpond of Paaiea. This was a very large fishpond extending from Kaelehuluhulu, adjoining the little fishing hamlet of Mahaiula, and as far as Wawaloli on the boundary of Ooma.

This pond was not far from Ka-Lae-O-Keahole, (fisherman's point) which is the extreme western point, or cape on the island of Hawaii, and on which there was a lighthouse.

To mariners of the days of sailing crafts, this point was a test of skillful navigation; the wind and tide and current, all combining to thwart the mariner's effort to round the cape, and make the entrance into Kailua Bay.

This fish-pond of Paaiea was three miles long, and a mile and a half wide. The fishermen going to Kailua and further south, often took a short cut by taking their canoes into the pond and going across, thus saving time and the hard labor of paddling against the Eka, a strong sea breeze from the south, and also against the strong current from Keahole.

Kona Legends
Eliza D. Maguire, 1966

The 4 miles of rocky shoreline from Kaloko to Keāhole Point are backed by a long, sandy stretch of storm beach that is frequented by beachcombers, campers, fishermen, sunbathers, and surfers. The two most popular sites on the beach are Pine Trees and Wāwāloli Beach.

Just north of Wawahiwa'a Point, a number of brackish-water ponds border the jeep road that follows the shoreline. A tall, dense thicket of mangrove has completely overrun the largest of the ponds and is a distinctive landmark in an area that otherwise contains only low-lying vegetation. From a distance, the mangrove can be imagined to resemble a stand of pine trees, and it was this resemblance that gave the area its popular name, Pine Trees.

Pine Trees is one of the best and most popular surfing sites in Kona. The main break is located directly offshore of the mangrove thicket in a shallow, rock-bottomed bay. During periods of calm seas, the deeper offshore areas offer some excellent cave-diving opportunities and are frequented by commercial dive classes, who come in by boat. Surfers and other visitors generally reach Pine Trees in four-wheel-drive vehicles, following the shoreline jeep road from its intersection with the Natural Energy Laboratory of Hawai'i road. The entire area is undeveloped and has no facilities.

Wāwāloli Beach is located where the Natural Energy Lab of Hawai'i road meets the ocean and curves north toward Keāhole Point. This coastal site is said to have been named for the *kupua* Wāwāloli, a demigod who often changed from a *loli*, or sea cucumber, into a man to make love to the girls who visited the seashore near his home. An excellent version of this legend can be found in Eliza Maguire's book *Kona Legends*. Archaeologists also know Wāwāloli as the site of an ancient habitation complex that contains a small pool, several ruins, and an ancient paved trail.

Wāwāloli Beach, a storm beach that is an excellent place for sunbathing, affords little opportunity for in-water activities. In the rocky shoreline fronting the beach is a shallow, protected tidal pond especially attractive to young children. Many families find their way to this area, preferring the seclusion of the undeveloped surroundings to the crowds in the developed public beach parks.

Wāwāloli Beach is easily accessible in an ordinary passenger car from the Natural Energy Lab of Hawai'i road, which intersects Queen Ka'ahumanu Highway. Visitors to the area should check with the security guard in the kiosk near the highway to determine the hours that the gate is open to the general public.

The Natural Energy Laboratory of Hawai'i, a complex that includes a laboratory building, a power center, a warehouse, and an administration building, was established by the State Legislature in 1974 at Keāhole Point. Scientists at the facility are studying methods of using the ocean as a source of electrical power in an effort to at least reduce Hawai'i's dependence on petroleum. The major alternate-energy project occupying the researchers is called OTEC, an acronym for "ocean thermal energy conversion." OTEC uses the temperature difference between warm water on the surface of a tropical ocean and cold water from the depths to generate electricity. Keāhole Point is regarded as one of the best OTEC research sites in the world because it is near cold, deep ocean water as well as year-round warm surface water. While the principle is simple, the expense of the hardware and a number of unresolved technical problems must still be overcome before the method will be practicable. Work continues on these problems and others at the Natural Energy Lab of Hawai'i, the only operational OTEC center in the United States. The research complex is not open to the general public on a walk-in basis, but may be visited by interested parties who make arrangements through the administrative offices.

The 4½ miles of rocky shoreline from Keāhole Point

to Mahai'ula consist of low sea cliffs, some of them veneered by storm beaches of black sand. Mākole'ā Beach, situated in a cove to the south of Mākole'ā Point, is the only beach along this stretch of coastline that actually slopes into the ocean. Rocks line the water's edge at the southern end of the beach, but the northern end is rock free, providing a good entry/exit point. Several small brackish-water ponds fill depressions in the backshore between the sand and the lava. Beneath the sand, a large layer of consolidated mud suffers some erosion from incoming waves and often clouds the inshore waters, but otherwise, nearshore conditions are usually good for swimming and snorkeling. During periods of high surf, particularly during the winter months, large waves roll unchecked onto the unprotected beach, generating hazardous currents and washing violently over the rocks. Three small rock islets protrude above the surface of the ocean between the beach and Mākole'ā Point.

Mākole'ā Beach can be reached in a four-wheel-drive vehicle by following the access road which begins immediately north of Keāhole Airport and crosses one branch of the 1801 lava flow, the most recent flow from Hualālai. The beach is undeveloped and has no facilities. There is no shade.

(64)
Mahai'ula

Mahai'ula, he wahi e noho ai ka po'e lawai'a. He inoa mai'a. Malia paha he mai'a i kapa'ia he mai'a 'ulu'ulu. Aia ma Kekaha. He one kahi o ka niu e ulu nui ana. A'ohe nui o kanaka.

Mahai'ula, a place where fishermen dwell. A name of a type of banana. The naming of the banana results perhaps from the fact that the banana is reddish. There at Kekaha is the sandy spot where the coconuts grow to enormous size. There are not many people at this place.

Place names by Kalokuokamaile
Theodore Kelsey Collection

Mahai'ula, once the site of a small but thriving fishing community, is probably best known as the location of the shoreline retreat of Alfred Kapala Magoon, a prominent part-Hawaiian businessman. By the time Magoon

acquired the property during the 1930s, the Hawaiian fishermen at Mahai'ula had moved away, although one family returned periodically to tend to their family burial cave. Pre-contact Hawaiians commonly placed their dead in lava tubes. These sites, known as burial caves, are found in many areas of the Big Island. Magoon respected the old ways, and during his long tenure on the property he never disturbed the caves or their contents.

Although the Magoon family members and their friends visited Mahai'ula frequently throughout the year, the traditional month for everyone to gather was August, to celebrate A. K. Magoon's birthday. He and his wife, Ruth Puanani, were renowned for their hospitality, and the festivities at Mahai'ula often lasted for days on end. In later years, Helen Desha Beamer, a close family friend and one of Hawai'i's finest Hawaiian composers, wrote a beautiful song entitled, "Mahai'ula." The first and last verses are as follows:

Haele a'e kaua la
*   i ke kono a ka makemake*
E kipa e luana e ho'onanea
*   me Puanani a me Kapala.*

He nani a he nani maoli no
Mahai'ula i ka la'i
Hali'i mai la i ka loa
Me ke kai kahakai ki'i
*   lihilihi i ke one*
E ō e Puanani me Kapala ko inoa.

We two go up there
    by invitation and wish
To visit, to enjoy, to relax
    with Puanani and Kapala.

Beautiful, really beautiful
Mahai'ula in the calm
Spread out into the distance
And the shorebreak draws
    lacy pictures in the sand.
Oh answer, o Puanani and Kapala,
    to your names.

After the death of A. K. Magoon, his son, George Alan Magoon, inherited the property. During the three-year period from 1968 to 1971, the Mahai'ula home became the base of operations for a scuba diving center and was called the Kona Diving Lodge. The lodge catered primarily to tourists, who were offered diving lessons and excursions, as well as the usual accommodations. When the lodge closed, management of the estate was left to Roy Damron, the diving instructor, who has since run the business as a low-key beach hideaway for small, private groups of no more than a dozen or so people. Although a handful of divers still make use of the facilities each year, nudists comprise the majority of visitors.

Mahai'ula Beach is a beautiful, moderately steep crescent of white sand at the head of a deep, well-protected bay. The shallow inshore ocean bottom slopes gently offshore. Alternating pockets of sand and rock offer excellent swimming and snorkeling opportunities. Beyond the confines of the bay, scuba divers explore the "Arches," a series of spectacular underwater tunnels and caves, and a sunken ship. During the winter months, heavy surf often breaks completely across the mouth of the bay and produces some excellent waves for surfing. Many surfers consider the break that forms off Kawili Point, at the north end of the bay, to be one of the best right slides on the Kona coast.

Many pre-contact archaeological sites are located on or near the shoreline at Mahai'ula, but probably the most famous is Pōhaku o Lama, a stone fish goddess standing in the ocean almost at the water's edge. At certain times of the year fishermen brought her offerings to ensure their luck at sea. During the months of May, June, and July, the water around the rock occasionally turns red. In former times the Hawaiians believed this meant that the deity was menstruating. Such "red tides," usually caused in Hawai'i by great masses of tiny organisms called dinoflagellates, still occur at Mahai'ula, generally during the spring months. The phenomenon manifests itself as a brownish-red streak that reaches from the ocean bottom to the surface of the sea and drifts with the light currents in the bay.

The small cluster of dwellings at Mahai'ula, as well as the coconut groves at both ends of the beach, are visible from Queen Ka'ahumanu Highway, but there is no convenient public access to the beach.

Around the southern point of Mahai'ula Bay is Ka'elehuluhulu, another beach that was known to the Magoon family as Second Beach. Ka'elehuluhulu consists of white sand speckled with black lava fragments. A wide sandy opening in the shoreline rock provides a good entry and exit point to an excellent swimming and snorkeling area offshore, where an arm of broken lava curving into Mahai'ula Bay protects Ka'elehuluhulu from most adverse ocean conditions.

In 1977 Ivar "Little Joe" Kaipo, president of a tour company called Hawai'i Untouched, Inc., leased a parcel of land at Ka'elehuluhulu and began bringing visitors to the area, where they could enjoy a relaxing day at an isolated beach. His facilities included a snack bar and restrooms. Kaipo then obtained an easement for a road to his shoreline site and in 1979 constructed a private paved road across the barren expanses of lava.

(65)
Makalawena

Makalawena. A beautiful set of bays with many legends. Makalawena was the most prominent town of this area back in the first decade of this century. Essentially a fishing village, it boasted a church, school, store, and 7 or 8 houses at one time. All houses were wiped out in the 1946 tsunami. Only one house was rebuilt, that of Annie Una. Her last husband, Porto, still lives at Makalawena. Raising goats and chickens, and going fishing are his principal occupations.

"Na Ala Hele"
State Dept. of Land and Natural Resources, 1973

The Makalawena shoreline consists of several coves and inlets that are separated by a series of broken lava points but united by a long, continuous, curving sand beach. From the mid-point of the beach, south to the barren lava flow separating Makalawena from Mahai'ula, extensive sand dunes line the backshore. The fine clean white sand of the dunes is covered by *pōhuehue* and *kiawe*. In some descriptions of the area, this portion of the beach is called Pu'u Ali'i Beach, but in common usage the place name Makalawena generally means the entire length of this magnificent beach.

The largest inlet, where the sand dunes are highest, offers the best place for swimming at Makalawena. Although the other coves and inlets are equally shallow and protected, their shorelines and ocean bottoms tend to be rockier and less inviting. Snorkeling and scuba diving are popular offshore activities in this area, which is noted for octopus and shells. During the winter months, big surf causes mild erosion of the beach and occasionally generates some excellent surfing waves. The preferred break for board surfing is located directly offshore a stand of ironwoods in the backshore. The next break to the south is frequented primarily by body-surfers.

In addition to its excellent shoreline recreational resources, Makalawena is also noted as the site of 'Opae'ula Pond, an ancient Hawaiian fishpond that is now one of the Big Island's most important waterbird sanctuaries. The 12-acre pond is immediately inland of the small cluster of fishing shacks on the beach and contains large numbers of *'opae'ula*, or red shrimp, which the Hawaiians caught and mixed in their *palu*, or chum, that was used for netting *'ōpelu*. The waterbirds also feed on the *'opae'ula* that inhabit the pond. The Big Island has very few wetlands suitable for native waterbirds, and so 'Opae'ula Pond plays a vital role in the preservation of many of these birds. It is the most important site for the endangered Hawaiian stilt (*ā'eo*) and also provides a habitat for coots, ducks, and black-crowned night herons, and a feeding ground for golden plovers, wandering tattlers, doves, mynahs, sparrows, and cardinals.

MAKALAWENA. Some of the most extensive sand dunes in the Kona district line the backshore of beautiful Makalawena Beach. Once the site of a Hawaiian fishing village, the area is now visited by swimmers, sunbathers, and surfers. Inland of the beach is 'Opae'ula Pond, one of the Big Island's most important refuges for shoreline birds.

Along the rocky shoreline between Makalawena and Manini'ōwali are some small scattered pockets of white sand and coral rubble, notably at Awake'e and Kaho'iawa bays. These areas are frequented primarily by shoreline fishermen and skin divers.

(66)
Manini'ōwali

There is a little bay by this name of Maniniowali situated between Kukio and Awakee. This bay is like a turquoise gem along this barren lava coast. The water is always a turquoise blue. There is a stone in the form of a woman imbedded in the sand at the edge of the beach, which also bears the name of Maniniowali.

Kona Legends
Eliza D. Maguire

Manini'ōwali Beach is located immediately to the north of Pu'u Kuili, a 342-foot-high cinder cone that constitutes the most prominent shoreline landmark for miles in either direction. The beautiful white sand beach slopes gently into the deeper waters offshore and provides the district of North Kona with one of its finest swimming beaches. On the shallow sand bar that fronts most of the beach, a small shorebreak forms occasion-

MANINI'ŌWALI. Many Kona residents consider Manini'ōwali to be one of the best swimming beaches on the Big Island. Located immediately north of Pu'u Kuili, a shoreline cinder cone, this wilderness beach is only accessible to vehicles with four-wheel drive. Manini'ōwali, a legendary princess, was turned to stone at the water's edge. The beach was named in her honor.

ally, with waves that appeal to bodysurfers and body-boarders. The rocks bordering both ends of the beach attract snorkelers, nearshore scuba divers, and shoreline fishermen.

During the winter months, heavy surf and southerly storms often intrude on the serenity of Manini'ōwali and generate hazardous ocean conditions such as rip currents and surf that sweep across the rocks. High winter surf also completely washes away the sand, often within a 24-hour period, leaving behind only the exposed lava bedrock. The surf carries the sand offshore where it settles into the huge sand reservoirs on the ocean bottom. Once the heavy wave action has subsided, the beach begins to rebuild and finally stabilizes until the next erosive onslaught. During such winter storms at Manini'ōwali, experienced bodysurfers occasionally find some excellent waves to ride.

Manini'ōwali Beach is surrounded chiefly by state lands, but the area is undeveloped and can be reached only by a vehicle with high clearance or with four-wheel drive. A jeep road from Queen Ka'ahumanu Highway leads *makai* to the base of Pu'u Kuili. No shade or facilities exist at this remote site, where *pōhuehue* and scattered *kiawe* comprise the primary shoreline vegetation. In some descriptions of the area, Manini'ōwali is called Kua Bay, a map name that has been assigned to the beach.

(67)
Kūki'o

Kahawaliwali, the Princess, was turned into a long stone about thirty feet high, which stands in the sea. The lower part has two sections, and it is said they represent her legs through which the sea flows continually.

Kona Legends
Eliza D. Maguire

The place name Kūki'o means to "stand [and] defecate," and while *kama'āina* of the area are in agreement on the definition, there is little accord on the *mo'olelo*, or story, explaining the origin of the name. Many interesting explanations have been offered, most of them amusing, but few seem to have any shred of historical accuracy. Kūki'o is mentioned in the traditional legend of Manini'ōwali, a romantic account of three people

involved in a love triangle who were turned to stone by a powerful *kahuna*, Kikaua. The three unfortunate persons were Manini'ōwali, a beautiful girl from Manini'ōwali; Uluweuweu, Maini'ōwali's betrothed from Kūki'o; and Kahawaliwali, the chiefess with whom Uluweuweu fell in love. The stone formation with its two-legged base that once was Kahawaliwali constitutes one of the most prominent shoreline landmarks at Kūki'o. It stands in a shallow, sandy cove at Kikaua Point. Numerous other small lava formations on the point also project above the ocean's surface and enclose the cove with a natural rock barrier. The picturesque cove provides the best swimming at Kūki'o and has long been used by Hu'ehu'e Ranch, the owner of the surrounding lands, as a picnic and camping site for its employees and guests. A *kiawe* grove shades the small recreational park in the backshore.

Kūki'o Beach, a long ribbon of white sand, stretches from Kikaua Point almost the entire length of Kūki'o Bay and ends at a narrow finger of the 1801 lava flow from Hualālai. A continuous, low-lying bench of shoreline rock lines the beach from one end to the other, offering few suitable entry and exit points to the waters offshore. Kūki'o Beach is not highly regarded as a swimming area, but provides good opportunities for fishing. During the winter months, waves are occasionally good for surfing and bodysurfing. A number of small brackish-water ponds line the backshore where coconut, *kiawe, pōhuehue,* and *kauna'oa* grow. There is no convenient public access to any of the Kūki'o area.

(68)
Ka'ūpūlehu

Ka'ūpūlehu. Literally, the roasted breadfruit ('ū is short for 'ulu). Pele met two girls, Pāhinahina and Kolomu'o, roasting breadfruit here. Only Pāhinahina shared her breadfruit. That night Hualālai erupted near Hu'ehu'e and destroyed the village, but spared the home of Pāhinahina.

Place Names of Hawaii
Pukui, Elbert, and Mookini

Ka'ūpūlehu once supported a large fishing community, but apparently the 1801 lava flow from Hualālai destroyed much of the village, which had been centered around Kahuwai Bay. Many ruins of ancient dwellings are found near the shoreline, as well as a large field of petroglyphs with many unique and still-unexplained figures.

During the twentieth century, a few Hawaiian fishermen and their families lived at Ka'ūpūlehu until the devastating tsunami of 1946 swept in and wiped them out. From then on, the area was visited mainly by the wild goats and pigs that formerly roamed in great numbers, and occasionally by fishermen and boaters. Then, in 1956, a wealthy yachtsman named Johnno Jackson and his wife Helen happened to sail past Ka'ūpūlehu during a visit to the Hawaiian Islands. They put into Kahuwai Bay at Ka'ūpūlehu and soon decided that they had found an ideal location for a small, secluded luxury resort village.

During the early 1960s, construction began on a complex that eventually became the Kona Village Resort. Ka'ūpūlehu at the time was accessible only by aircraft or boat, so Jackson's first priority was the construction of a 2,600-foot landing strip to expedite transportation of the laborers to and from the work site and that could later be used to bring in guests. He purchased an LCVP, a military landing craft capable of carrying vehicles and personnel, and used it to transport much of the lumber, materials, and equipment that his project demanded. He built a power generating plant, and he sank a 550-foot well shaft for water. While construction was in progress, Jackson lived aboard his schooner, anchored in Kahuwai Bay. During a particularly bad storm, high winds and heavy surf forced the boat into the shallow reef and rocks bordering the bay, destroying the craft beyond repair, but Jackson salvaged as much of the wreck as he could and converted it into the Shipwreck Bar, still a popular attraction in the resort village. The original complex, completed in June 1964, was named Jackson Village.

Because of the huge financial obligations involved in transforming his tropical dream-resort into a reality, Jackson brought in Signal Oil Company as a partner. The resort's name was changed to Kona Village Resort, and Signal Oil eventually bought Jackson out. Since Signal Oil's purchase the resort has changed ownership several times, but it continues to offer first-class, luxury accommodations in a secluded shoreline setting providing a wide variety of amenities and recreational opportunities. The resort has also preserved and incorporated the rich historical background of Ka'ūpūlehu in its contemporary activities.

Kaūpūlehu Beach consists of two beaches: a storm beach south of the resort and a good swimming beach fronting it. The storm beach is a long narrow strip of white sand bordered by a low bench of shoreline rock. Although swimming conditions are poor in this area, skin diving and occasionally surfing are excellent on the broad shallow reef offshore. Almost all aquatic activities are centered at the northern end of Ka'ūpūlehu Beach in Kahuwai Bay, where a white sand beach speckled with fragments of black lava offers good swimming and snorkeling. A deep, natural channel provides access to the bay and the beach for motor boats and sailing craft. Fresh water intrusion occurs in several places, but most noticeably at Waiokane Spring located beside a large, submerged rock fronting the Shipwreck Bar. A number of brackish-water ponds are located in the backshore at Ka'ūpūlehu. One of the largest is Waiākuhi, which borders the southern end of the beach; it is overgrown by mangrove. There is no convenient public access to any of the Ka'ūpūlehu shoreline.

To the north of Ka'ūpūlehu and the Kona Village Resort is a long, rounded point that is variously known as Kalaemanō, Laemanō, and Manō Point. A large branch of the 1801 lava flow from Hualālai divided inland of the point, one part flowing across its southern margin at Ka'ūpūlehu and the other, across its northern edge at Kīholo Bay, leaving the central portion of the point untouched. In this lower central area, heavy surf has deposited a large amount of white sand and coral rubble on the low sea cliffs. These storm beaches sitting on top of the older flow are bordered by *kiawe* and are easily visible from Queen Ka'ahumanu Highway 1½ miles inland. On this central part of Kalaemanō are a number of natural *kaheka*, or shallow rock basins, that fill up with salt water during high surf. When the water evaporates, the salt is left behind. Kalaemanō, then, was a good source of salt for the people of the Hawaiian fishing communities to the north and south of the point, who would gather salt there especially after several days of high westerly surf which always filled the *kaheka*.

(69)
Kīholo

Ke pā mai nei e ka Mumuku,
Ka makani o launiu o Kekaha
Ka hea mai a Kīholo i ka laʻi
Auau i ke kai konahenahe.

The Mumuku wind is blowing.
The coconut leaf-rustling wind of Kekaha
The serenity of Kīholo calls us
To swim in the gentle sea.

"Puʻu Waʻawaʻa"
Traditional song

Kīholo Bay is a long, wide bay that stretches for 2 miles from Luahinewai Pond at the south to Waināmāliʻi Pond at the north. Along the backshore are several private homes, many archaeological sites, and a long expanse of undeveloped shoreline that offers a wide variety of recreational opportunities. Many fishermen and campers visit the area, particularly on weekends and holidays. They come for swimming, snorkeling, spear fishing, lay-netting, throw-netting, pole fishing, salt gathering, hiking, and occasionally surfing.

Probably the most popular spot at Kīholo is Luahinewai, the huge spring-fed pond located at the southern

KĪHOLO. Luahinewai, a deep, cold freshwater pool on the shore of Kīholo Bay, is a traditional swimming site for travelers passing through the area. A black sand beach separates the pool from the ocean. Lae Hou, "New Point," the long promontory in the distance across the bay, was formed during an eruption of Mauna Loa. When the lava reached the shoreline in 1810, it filled an enormous fishpond that had belonged to Kamehameha I.

end of the bay. Coconut and *naupaka* surround this beautiful, pristine pond set between a black sand beach and the edge of a rugged lava flow. Luahinewai attracts not only the campers at Kīholo, but also many boaters who anchor off the beach and swim ashore. Apparently, this oasis was just as popular in times past with the Hawaiians. In his book *Ruling Chiefs of Hawaii*, Samuel Kamakau, reporting on a journey to Kawaihae by the high chief Keoua and his party, noted that "they left Kailua and went as far as Luahinewai at Kekaha, where they landed the canoes." In another account in *Fragments of Hawaiian History*, John Papa Ii observed, "Early Thursday morning, the ship sailed, pausing at Luahinewai (Kiholo) to bathe and visit that strange water in the lava. After an enjoyable stop at the water with the pretty pebbles, they again sailed."

Three black sand and pebble beaches are located along the southern margin of Kīholo Bay near Luahinewai. All drop quickly to overhead depths, but during normal, calm water periods, swimming is good at all of them. Hazardous conditions occur when high surf and winter storms generate heavy shorebreaks and rip currents. The remaining shoreline to the small embayment where the private homes and fishponds are located is mostly rocky, with many tidepools and scattered pockets of black sand and coral rubble. Along this reach, a large coconut grove, the landmark for the favored surfing break in Kīholo Bay, grows near the water's edge. Surfing conditions on the shallow reef shelf in this part of the bay are generally best early in the morning during the winter months. As the rising sun begins to warm the land, the difference in temperature between the land and the ocean results in an onshore sea breeze that causes choppy, poorly shaped waves.

At the northern end of Kīholo Bay, a shallow sheltered embayment adjoins a large brackish-water lagoon, Wainānāli'i Pond. Both the bay and the pond are important feeding and sleeping sites for sea turtles, especially the green sea turtle. The migrant green sea turtle travels regularly from its breeding grounds in French Frigate Shoals in the Northwestern Hawaiian Islands to the eight major islands in the Hawaiian Archipelago. This turtle, as well as all sea turtles and their nests, are protected by state and federal wildlife laws and may not be harassed or harmed in any way.

Other important nearshore feeding and sleeping areas on the Big Island where turtles seek sanctuary are Pelekane in South Kohala and Kamehame, Punalu'u, and Ka'alu'alu in Ka'ū. People who are concerned with protecting these animals from human predators have proposed that turtle habitats such as these be designated as marine sanctuaries for all sea turtles.

Wainānāli'i Pond, the 5-acre lagoon at Kīholo, lies between the edge of the 1859 lava flow from Mauna Loa and a sand and boulder spit approximately a quarter of a mile in length. The flat-bottomed pond, lined with several small coconut palms, averages 10–12 feet deep and opens into Kīholo Bay at its southern end. The pond is an easily recognizable landmark from the Kīholo Bay Lookout on Queen Ka'ahumanu Highway, the aqua-colored pond waters a bright spot of color against the dark lava.

One of the most interesting descriptions of the 1859 lava flow that formed the northern margin of Kīholo Bay is found in the November 9, 1859, edition of the Hawaiian newspaper *Ka Hae Hawai'i*. The original Hawaiian account, by J. H. Kaakua, was translated by Mary Kawena Pukui:

Concerning the Lava Flow

It will be well for me to tell what I have seen concerning the lava flow at Wailea and at Kiholo in North Kona, and you will tell those who have not seen it. The flow began to go seaward in the month of February of this year, from the northwest side of Mauna Loa. It reached Wailea first, and from there it turned south to Wailoa, and continued on to the deep sea, smooth lava extending into it to about forty chains or more in length. This new point has been named Lae Hou. There is a long point there called Koena Limu. It is an old point and shorter than Lae Hou. The flow turned on the south side of Wailoa and went to Kiholo where it covered the pond. Then it turned again to the west, where a new point is burning now. Lae Hou is a long point, but this one is shorter. The lava has not finished building it, but it is now in the depths of the sea. I think it is about forty or more fathoms deep where it is burning, and from that burning spot it is about fifty fathoms to shore. The sea there is very hot and any fish that comes there dies. This is the news concerning these doings of the volcano.

In the year 1810, the Kiholo pond was built, during the

reign of Kamehameha I. It was a fishpond in which many of the deep sea fish were kept and in this year, in the reign of Kamehameha IV, Kiholo is closed by the lava. It is now only a heap of lava rocks.

This is another thing. The Protestant church that stood at Kiholo was removed when the lava flow drew near. The people thought that it would be burned down, so they razed it and took the lumber away lest it be destroyed. There is a circle of lava rocks surrounding it and the spot where the church stood remains like a grave. I believe that if the church had not been razed, it would not have been destroyed anyway.

Lae Hou is marked on most maps today as Hou Point. Kamehameha I's fishpond at Kīholo, destroyed by the 1859 lava, was one of the wonders of its day. Missionary William Ellis described the pond during his circle-island journey in 1823:

About four in the afternoon I landed at Kiholo, a straggling village, inhabited principally by fishermen. This village exhibits another monument of the genius of Tamehameha. A small bay, perhaps half a mile wide, runs inland a considerable distance. From one side to the other of this bay, Tamehameha built a strong stone wall, six feet high in some places, and twenty feet wide, by which he had an excellent fish-pond, not less than two miles in circumference. It was well stocked with fish and water fowl were seen swimming on its surface.

Though the lava destroyed the immense fishpond and dramatically altered the entire shoreline, Kīholo continued to provide a haven for a small community of fishermen who relocated their homes to an untouched point of the bay south of the flow. During the 1890s, this area developed into a commercial landing after Robert Hind and Eben Low acquired the lease for Puʻu Waʻawaʻa Ranch from the Republic of Hawaiʻi. Located directly *mauka* of the bay, the ranch used Kīholo as its cattle-shipping point. Living accommodations were built in the area where the private homes are located today, and this site served also as a base of operations on the shoreline. The cattle were herded to Shipping Pen Beach, the black sand beach before Luahinewai, where they were tied alongside lighters and rowed to the steamers waiting offshore. Puʻu Waʻawaʻa Ranch discontinued use of

this landing about 1935 when improved roads made it possible to truck the cattle to the pier in Kailua.

Commercial activity continued on a smaller scale at Kīholo with the annual harvesting of *awa* and *moi* from the comparatively small fishponds left in the wake of the 1859 lava flow. Pigs were raised, and small herds of cattle were fattened on *kiawe* beans. The tsunami of 1960, however, ended all commercial operations at Kīholo, wiping out everything there in its path. Since then, a few of the private shoreline homes have been rebuilt. The part of the bay fronting the homes is a poor swimming beach, being very shallow and rocky. Copious fresh water intrusion is encountered in the nearby ponds and lagoon, as well as in many parts of the bay. As a result, a surface layer of fresh water, often several degrees colder than the bottom water, commonly floats over much of Kiholo Bay, especially near Hou Point.

(70)
Keawaiki

Eia la he kono mai Keawaiki
E kipa e nanea e hoʻolau kanaka
E paʻina ai hoʻi me ia kini
Keiki aloha a Hawaiʻi
Ke punahele hoʻi ʻoe nā makou.

He nani a he ʻoluʻolu ʻiʻo no
Ia home i ka ʻae kai
I laila ʻoe e ola ai
Keiki aloha a Hawaiʻi
He punahele hoʻi ʻoe nā makou.

Here is an invitation from Keawaʻiki
To visit, to relax, to gather together,
To feast with this company.
Beloved child of Hawaiʻi
You're a real favorite of ours.

Beautiful and truly pleasant
This home by the sea's edge
There may you prosper
Beloved child of Hawaiʻi
You're a real favorite of ours.

"Keawaiki"
Helen D. Beamer

The "beloved child of Hawaiʻi" and the "real favorite" that Helen Desha Beamer described in her song

"Keawaiki" was Francis Hyde I'i Brown, the long-time owner of a 15-acre parcel of shoreline property at Keawaiki. Brown was the grandson of John Papa I'i, a distinguished high-born Hawaiian who, from childhood until his death, served Hawaiian royalty—the families of Kamehameha I and Kamehameha II and in the court of Kamehameha III. I'i, an early convert to Christianity and one of the first Hawaiians to learn to read and write, is probably best known for his invaluable work, *Fragments of Hawaiian History*.

Francis I'i Brown, businessman, politician, and sportsman, acquired his estate at Keawaiki during the late 1920s and used the site as a retreat for himself and his friends, many of whom were celebrities of the day. After World War II, Brown made his home at Kalāhuipua'a, a piece of shoreline property he had purchased in 1932, located approximately 8 miles to the north. In 1956, he sold his Keawaiki estate to his nephew Zadoc Brown who in 1975 gave it to his surviving children. The Brown estate centers around a large fishpond immediately inland from the beach. Residences and an extensive coconut grove surround the pond, at least half of which has been filled in with sand and other material pushed *mauka* over the years by tsunami and heavy surf. The pond once was a source of mullet and milkfish, but now supports only tilapia.

Keawaiki Bay is a wide, open embayment that is partially protected at its southern end by a shallow reef. The reef extends into the bay and acts as a barrier against the prevailing waves and winds, but when *kona* storms and winter surf roll in, water conditions become hazardous. The beach at Keawaiki consists primarily of black sand and pebbles which form low dunes at the northern end, where the beach abuts the 1859 lava flow from Mauna Loa. White sand is mixed with the black at the southern end of the beach. The ocean bottom in the inner bay is shallow and mostly rocky. Conditions are good for swimming, snorkeling, net-fishing, and diving.

Just north of Keawaiki is Pueo Bay, a small crescent-shaped embayment that was formed by the 1859 lava flow. The lava backing the beach is devoid of vegetation at the shoreline, so this area is entirely unshaded. The beach consists of a mixture of black lava pebbles and white coral fragments. Fresh water intrudes into the bay, but swimming, snorkeling, and skin diving opportunities are excellent. During the winter months, the offshore waves are occasionally good enough for experienced surfers to ride. Similar surfing conditions exist at nearby Weliweli. A trail *mauka* of the beach leads to several small brackish-water ponds in a gulch that is covered with vegetation.

(71)
'Anaeho'omalu

Anaehoomalu Bay is the most striking feature of this section of coastline. With a broad white sand beach, large grove of coconut trees and numerous tidepools and brackish water ponds, it is an area of exceptional natural and aesthetic value.

West Hawaii Coral Reef Inventory
ORCA, 1981

A long, curving white sand beach speckled with black lava fragments lines the edge of 'Anaeho'omalu Bay, the site of the Sheraton Royal Waikoloa Hotel. Between the beach and the hotel, an extensive coconut grove fringes two fishponds, Ku'uali'i and Kahapapa, that were once reserved for the exclusive use of Hawaiian royalty. The fishermen who lived in the area maintained the ponds and the fish stocks, primarily mullet, to provide delicacies strictly for the pleasure of royal travelers sailing along the coast—hence, most likely, the place name 'Anaeho'omalu, which means "restricted mullet." Signs explaining the historical significance of the area are placed along the paved walkway around the ponds. Fishing and swimming are not allowed in the ponds. Many other interesting archaeological sites, including a large petroglyph field, a portion of the Ala Loa, or King's Highway, and numerous habitation ruins are located at 'Anaeho'omalu. The boundary between the districts of North Kona and South Kohala is just south of 'Anaeho'omalu.

'Anaeho'omalu Bay is located within the land division of Waikoloa, a vast 31,000-acre tract that was purchased from Richard Smart, the owner of Parker Ranch. Waikoloa Village, located 6 miles inland from 'Anaeho'omalu, was the initial increment of the Waikoloa development during the early 1970s. It now includes single-family homes, condominium units, a golf course, and other amenities. The Sheraton Royal Waikoloa

'ANAEHO'OMALU. Several windsurfers relax on the sand after riding their sailboards. 'Anaeho'omalu Bay is a popular West Hawai'i site for windsurfing and a wide variety of other ocean sports. The beach is reached easily from the drive leading to the Sheraton Royal Waikoloa Hotel, visible through the coconut grove. Two large Hawaiian fishponds are located between the beach and the hotel.

Hotel, on the beach, is the largest hotel on the Big Island with more than 500 rooms in a pair of six-story wings. It opened in July 1981. The hotel complex includes a championship 18-hole golf course designed by Robert Trent Jones, Jr.

The long crescent of white sand that lines 'Anaeho'omalu Bay slopes gently into the deeper waters offshore, where swimming, snorkeling, nearshore scuba diving, net-fishing, windsurfing, and occasionally surfing are excellent. Hazardous water conditions occur only during storms or during periods of high surf. A beach service center at the northern end of the beach offers equipment rentals and instruction for hotel guests and any other interested visitors. At the southern end of the beach, a small park complex provides the general public with restrooms, showers, and picnic tables. Public parking is located immediately inland of the facilities.

Adjacent to the public park is the Parker Ranch Recreational Beach, a private beach park for the use of Parker Ranch employees and their guests. The property on which the Sheraton Royal Waikoloa Hotel stands was formerly owned by Parker Ranch. Facilities include a private home, four picnic pavilions, and restrooms.

The southern half of 'Anaeho'omalu Bay is a series of lava outcroppings and sand pockets, the largest of which is the sloping white sand beach at Kapalaoa. The offshore bottom is shallow and rocky, but offers good opportunities for swimming and fishing. The sand dune formations on the backshore extend into the *kiawe* that fringes the shoreline.

To the north of 'Anaeho'omalu Bay a storm beach of white sand and coral rubble lines a wave-washed bench that contains many tidal pools. This beach leads to Waiulua Bay, a narrow, shallow bay along the edge of the Kanikū lava flow. The northern margin of the bay consists of low *'a'ā* sea cliffs, whereas the low-lying southern margin consists of a rocky bar covered with a layer of white sand and coral rubble. The bar separates the bay from a series of brackish-water ponds. The inner portions of the bay are rocky, affording only fair swimming conditions, but the entire bay supports a wide variety of marine life and is an excellent place for snorkeling and nearshore scuba diving. Fresh water flows into the sea from a number of springs along the shoreline. During the winter months waves outside the bay are occasionally good enough for surfing.

(72)
Kalāhuipua'a

From Puako to Kalāhuipua'a is about four miles. The traveler cannot mistake the road in this district, as the paths are always plainly marked. The road to Kalahuipua'a is along the sea beach, and is in good order. A few shrubs are growing along the route, but on my left I had nothing but a sea of lava. At this place there are several waterholes and two small groves of coconut trees.

George Bowser, 1880

The land division of Kalāhuipua'a may have appeared to nineteenth-century travelers as little more than a "sea of lava," with several waterholes and a few coconut trees, but to the Hawaiians this coastal region was an important source of food and contains a wealth of archaeological sites that attest to its use. The most outstanding features at Kalāhuipua'a are the beautiful fishponds that are still in use and productive, providing active examples of ancient Hawaiian aquaculture. Francis I'i Brown, the last individual owner of Kalāhui-

pua'a, upgraded and modified the ponds, keeping them functional and operational after his purchase of the property in 1932. The ponds and the fish in them were described by Helen Desha Beamer in her song "Ke Keawaiki Hula."

'Au'au i ka wai
O kahi punawai i ka pu'u pele
Ia wai aniani hu'ihu'i
Lamalama ke kino ke ea mai.

Ua inu a kena
I na wai o ka'aina
Ua'ai i na i'a ono loa
Mai Kalahuipua'a a ke kai.

Bathe in the fresh water
of that spring in the lava hollow
This water glassy and chill
Glowing the body on emerging.

Drink till satisfied
of the waters of the land.
Eat the most delicious fishes
From Kalahuipua'a by the sea.

In 1972 Brown sold his estate to Mauna Lani Resort, Inc., a development company that improved the ponds and successfully integrated them into the resort development. The Mauna Lani Bay Hotel, a 350-room hotel that opened on February 1, 1983, offers its guests entrées of fresh fish that are farmed and harvested in the Kalāhuipua'a ponds. The spring-fed ponds are also an integral part of a 27-acre historic preserve that provides public access to the ponds, to other important archaeological sites, and to the shoreline.

Kalāhuipua'a is also well known for another important feature, the Ala Loa, a well-preserved straight trail constructed for use by cattle and pack animals in the 1890s. It is also known as the King's Highway and the Ala Mamalahoa Trail. Near the shoreline, the Ala Loa at one time extended uninterrupted from Kīholo to Kawaihae. A few sections of the trail have been incorporated into some of the major thoroughfares used today, but much of it remains in its original state even though population centers have shifted and land-use patterns have changed. One section that is still in excellent condition extends for nearly 7 miles from the clubhouse on

Map 15

0 km 1 2 3 4
0 miles 1 2 3 4

Waiaka'ilio Bay
Kohala Estates
Honokoa Gulch
270
Kai'ōpae Pt.
Honokoa
Akoni Pule Hwy.
KAWAIHAE
Kawaihae
PU'UKOHOLĀ
HEIAU NAT'L
HIST. SITE
Kawaihae Harbor
Pelekane Beach
'Ohai'ula Beach
SPENCER BEACH PARK
Kawaihae Rd.
Mau'umae Beach
Wai'ula'ula Pt.
19
Ka'aha Pt.
Wai'ula'ula Gul.
KAUNA'OA BEACH
Mauna Kea Beach Hotel
Kauna'oa Pt.
Hāpuna Bay
Kānekanaka Pt.
Waialea Bay
HĀPUNA BEACH
STATE RECREATION
AREA
Hōkūloa Church
Puakō Bay
Waimā Pt.
Puakō Rd.
Kapuniau Pt.
Puakō
Lae o Panipou (pt.)
PUAKŌ
Pauoa Bay
petroglyphs
Makaīwa Bay
Wa'awa'a Pt.
Waikoloa Village
Mauna Lani Resort
Honoka'ape Bay
Lūlāhala Pt.
Ka'ahumanu
KALĀHUIPUA'A
Wailulua Bay
Ka'au'au Pt.
Kahapapa and Ku'uali'i Fishponds
Royal Waikoloa
Hotel
Waikoloa Road
'ANAEHO'OMALU
BAY Kapalaoa
Queen
Weliweli
Pueo Bay
19
Keawaiki Bay
'Ōhiki Bay
KEAWAIKI
Bier

natural and historic sites found along trail routes is also a concern of the organization. Nā Ala Hele is particularly involved with the *makai* trails between Kailua and Kawaihae; so the group worked closely with Mauna Lani Resort, Inc., in obtaining the nomination of the Kīholo-Puakō Trail to the state register of historic places. Hikers may locate the Ala Loa on the south side of the golf clubhouse and maintenance facilities.

The Francis I'i Brown Golf Course, an 18-hole championship golf course, includes two distinct 9-hole complexes—the front nine on rugged *'a'ā* lava and the back nine on smoother *pāhoehoe* lava. International golfing enthusiasts have described it as one of the world's finest courses, a fitting tribute to Francis I'i Brown, the last individual owner of Kalāhuipua'a and one of Hawai'i's most respected sportsman. He is particularly remembered for his efforts to bring championship golf to the islands. On August 1978, Brown was named posthumously to the Hawai'i Sports Hall of Fame, the highest athletic honor the state can bestow on any native son.

The view from the course is spectacular in every direction. Immediately at hand are numerous intricate and unique lava formations that one local golfer with religious leanings described as Pele's Cathedral, an appropriate name for the volcanic artistry demonstrated by the goddess of the volcano. At the southern end of the course, this poetic description is further reinforced where the *'a'ā* flow meets the ocean in a beautiful section of low sea cliffs eroded into an irregular series of inlets, arches, caves, and rock islets. Visible in the distance are Hualālai, Mauna Loa, Mauna Kea, and Kohala, four of the five great volcanoes that have created the Big Island. Only Kīlauea, hidden to the east of Mauna Loa, cannot be seen. To the west, across 'Alenuihāhā Channel, the immense volcano Haleakalā that comprises the entire eastern half of Maui, is often clearly visible. The strong, positive sense of volcanic presence at Kalāhuipua'a, in its central position among these five volcanoes and the spectacular lava formations, inspired Emma de Fries, a Hawaiian scholar, to suggest the name Mauna Lani, "heavenly mountain," for the resort development. In 1980 this name was officially adopted.

When the Mauna Lani Bay Hotel opened in 1983, the major public access to the Kalāhuipua'a shoreline was

the Francis I'i Brown Golf Course at Mauna Lani to Kīholo in North Kona. Through the efforts of Nā Ala Hele, this stretch of Ala Loa, commonly known as the Kīholo-Puakō Trail, was placed on the Hawai'i Register of Historic Places in May 1983. Nā Ala Hele, a nonprofit group interested in the preservation of Hawaiian trails, was incorporated in 1979 under the leadership of Deborah Chang Abreu. It also functions as intermediary between the general public and developers and governmental agencies to resolve problems of access over certain intricate trail systems that once served as communication routes over the entire island. Protection of

KALĀHUIPUAʻA. Visitors at Mauna Lani, the resort complex at Kalāhuipuaʻa, swim and snorkel in the placid waters of Nānuku Inlet. Public access to the beach is over a paved trail that leads from the resort's historical park to the shoreline. Before its development, Kalāhuipuaʻa was the home of noted island businessman Francis Iʻi Brown. The magnificent 18-hole Mauna Lani Golf Course was named in his honor.

opened at the same time. This access passes through a historic preserve and a public park, with a parking area at the northeast corner of the preserve. A paved walkway leads to the beach. The widest section of beach and the most protected swimming area are at Nānuku Inlet, a wide, shallow, sandy-bottomed cove enclosed by a natural semicircle of low, broken lava. A number of large *milo* trees line the white sand beach, which is speckled with tiny lava fragments and olivines from the nearby *ʻaʻā* lava flow. Outside Nānuku Inlet, a well-developed reef offers many excellent opportunities for snorkeling and diving during periods of calm seas. Dur-

ing the winter months, when high surf often forms on the offshore reef, surfers find suitable waves at a number of breaks between Pauoa Bay and Makaiwa Bay.

At the southern boundary of the Mauna Lani property, Honokaʻape (also spelled Honokaʻope) Bay contains a large pocket of gray sand, a mixture of white sand and black lava fragments. The shoreline of Honokaʻape Bay consists primarily of low lava sea cliffs, but one low-lying section in its southern corner has a beach. The southern end of the beach is shallow and protected by the outer point of the bay, but the remainder of the beach is open to the ocean and drops quickly to overhead depths. Swimming, snorkeling, nearshore scuba diving, and fishing are excellent except during periods of high surf, a regular occurrence during the winter months, when ocean conditions are hazardous. The undeveloped backshore supports a groundcover of *pōhuehue* and a grove of *kiawe* in which a portable toilet and a picnic table have been placed for beachgoers. The lava flow directly behind the beach slopes very gently inland away from the sea cliffs nearby. For this reason, the winds blowing into Honoka'ape have pushed huge amounts of sand a considerable distance inland. This long, rectangular corridor of low sand dunes is an easily recognizable landmark at Honoka'ape. Honoka'ape Beach can be reached by following the shoreline trail from the fishponds past Makaiwa Bay and around the edge of the golf course.

Pauoa Bay, at the northern boundary of the Mauna Lani property, has good waves for surfing. Snorkeling and nearshore scuba diving are also good during calm seas. The inner bay is shallow and rocky and is bordered by a crescent beach comprised mainly of pebbles and cobblestones with several sandy pockets. Pauoa Bay can be reached by following the shoreline from Nānaku Inlet, an interesting walk past small pockets of sand interspersed among lava outcroppings, tidal pools, and a series of brackish-water ponds on the backshore. Direct public access to both Pauoa and Honoka'ape bays will be opened concurrently with the developments planned for these areas.

(73)
Puakō

Puakou is a village on the shore, very like Kawaihae, but larger. It has a small harbor in which native vessels anchor. Coconut groves give it a verdant aspect. No food grows in the place. The people make salt and catch fish. These they exchange for vegetables grown elsewhere.

Makua Laiana: The Story of Lorenzo Lyons
Emma L. Doyle, 1945

The residential community of Puakō, which dates from the early 1950s, begins at Puakō Bay and extends for 3½ miles of shoreline along the paved extent of Puakō Road. A large wave-washed bench of rock fronts almost the entire length of this long stretch of low-lying coast,

but the irregular beach contains many small points, inlets, coves, and tidal pools, all of which are suitable for pole fishing, net-fishing, spearfishing, snorkeling, and in some areas, swimming. For sunbathers and beachcombers, there is a narrow white sand beach almost the full length of the bench. Public access to Puakō Beach is available from the boat ramp in Puakō Bay, from six rights-of-way along Puakō Road and at the end of the paved road, where surfers also occasionally find waves suitable for riding. The surfing break fronts the Ruddle estate, so surfers generally refer to the site as Ruddle's. Fresh water intrusion from shoreline springs in this area often forms a layer of cool, brackish water on the surface of the ocean. The only true fringing reef of consolidate limestone on the Big Island fronts this section of the shoreline, an excellent site for nearshore scuba diving.

Two sites of historical interest along Puakō Road are a field of petroglyphs and Hokuloa Church. The extensive petroglyph field, thought to contain some of the oldest carvings on the Big Island, is marked by a Hawai'i Visitors Bureau warrior sign. Hokuloa Church, also easily found, was originally dedicated on March 21, 1859, and is one of fourteen churches built by the Reverend Lorenzo Lyons. Lyons, known to his Hawaiian congregations as Makua Laiana, "Father Lyons," had an excellent command of the Hawaiian language and composed many songs before his death in 1886. His most famous composition is the poignant and haunting song, "Hawaii Aloha," which was rediscovered during the 1970s and has become a powerful musical statement of the uniqueness of the Hawaiian culture, the beauty of the Hawaiian spirit, and the need to preserve both. "Hawaii Aloha" crosses every barrier, bridges every prejudice, and reaffirms the privilege of every person who calls these islands home to be counted as a Hawaiian. The song has become the unofficial state anthem of the Hawaiian Islands, and today any local gathering of import invariably concludes with everyone joining hands and singing the first verse and the chorus:

E Hawai'i, e ku'u one hanau e,
Ku'u home kulaiwi nei,
'Oli no au i na pono lani e,
E Hawai'i, aloha e.

E hauʻoli na ʻopio o Hawaiʻi nei.
ʻOli e! ʻOli e!
Mai na aheahe makani e pa mai nei,
Mau ke aloha, no Hawaiʻi.

O Hawaiʻi, o sands of my birth,
My native home,
I rejoice in the blessings of heaven.
O Hawaiʻi, aloha.

Chorus Happy youth of Hawaiʻi,
Rejoice! Rejoice!
Gentle breezes blow,
Love always for Hawaiʻi.

Nā Mele o Hawaiʻi Nei
Elbert and Mahoe, 1970

(74)
Waialea

From Kawaihae to north Kona prevail also the "mumukus"—that is, a down rush of trade wind from Waimea, sweeping away all land and sea breezes in the wild rush of dust and fury.

Thrum's Hawaiian Annual, 1894

Waialea, commonly misspelled and mispronounced as Wailea, is one of the Big Island's most beautiful white sand beaches. The beach slopes gently into deeper waters offshore and offers excellent opportunities for swimming, snorkeling, and nearshore scuba diving. Many families, especially those with little children, pre-

WAIALEA. During the winter months, storm surf erodes the beach at Waialea, further exposing the shoreline rocks. During the summer months, the sand returns. This popular site is known to most Big Island residents as Beach 69.

fer the more sheltered conditions at Waialea to those at neighboring Hāpuna, where the longer, straighter beach is more exposed to the open ocean. During periods of high surf, particularly during the winter months, surfers and bodysurfers often ride an excellent break that forms off the northern point of Waialea Bay. However, the most popular recreational activity at Waialea is sailing, and throughout the year the beach attracts many wind-surfers and sailors of single- and multi-hull craft. The beach offers almost ideal conditions for launching, landing, and sailing the wide variety of portable and trailerable sailing crafts that are used in Hawaiian waters. The beach is flat, sandy, and not extremely wide. The shoreline access road terminates at the back-shore, a short distance from the water. Favorable winds and ocean conditions are the norm. Hazardous ocean conditions generally occur only in the winter months during periods of high surf. Extremely gusty winds blow occasionally from January through March and only infrequently during the summer.

Waialea Beach is undeveloped, having no facilities other than a portable toilet. The backshore consists of a small, unpaved parking lot fronting a cluster of beach homes and a large forest of *kiawe* that extends all the way to Hāpuna Beach. Inland of the beach, a narrow paved road joining Hāpuna Beach State Recreation Area with Puakō Road runs parallel to the shoreline. Prior to the opening of the Queen Ka‘ahumanu High-way in 1975, this road was the major route to Puakō. Public utility poles along the paved road are numbered consecutively in ascending order starting at Hāpuna. The pole closest to the dirt road leading to Waialea is number 69, so Waialea Beach is commonly known to many Big Islanders as Beach 69. This name frequently surprises and amuses visitors hearing it for the first time because of the contemporary sexual innuendo implied by the number 69.

(75)
Hāpuna Beach State Recreation Area

In addition to the fisheries related uses, the Kaunaoa Beach and Hapuna Bay Beach are heavily used by board and bodysurfers. Both beaches and especially Hapuna Bay Beach, are subject to occasional very heavy storm wave activity and swimming and surfing under these conditions is extremely hazardous.

West Hawaii Coral Reef Inventory
ORCA, 1981

The beautiful white sand beach at Hāpuna stretches for over half a mile between the points of lava that form its boundaries. During the summer months, the beach is more than 200 feet wide—the widest white sand beach on the Big Island. High winter surf often erodes the beach considerably, but still leaves beachgoers more than enough sand for various activities. About midway along the beach, a lava promontory that was known to Hawaiian fishermen as Ihumoku (the "bow [of the] ship") crosses the sand and effectively divides the beach in half. To the north of this rocky point, the backshore is undeveloped and privately owned, but the developed backshore to the south is Hāpuna Beach State Recreation Area. Facilities in the beach park complex include half a dozen A-frame shelters that provide lodging for four persons in each shelter, paved parking lots, picnic pavilions, restrooms, showers, and paved walkways to the beach.

The long, wide, flat white sand beach at Hāpuna provides more than ample space for its many visitors. The beach slopes gently into the deeper offshore waters, where there are excellent opportunities for swimming, snorkeling, and nearshore scuba diving. A shallow, pro-tected, sand-bottomed cove at the northern end of the beach is an ideal place for little children to play in the water. Professional diving instructors also use this area to introduce novice snorkelers and scuba divers to the ocean.

At the southern end of the beach, enthusiastic swim-mers have great fun jumping and diving into the ocean from several places in the sea cliffs. Plunging feet first into the water with the least possible splash was a popu-lar ancient Hawaiian sport known as *lelekawa*. During the winter months, high surf often generates some excel-lent waves, particularly at the southern end of the beach, but state law permits only bodysurfing at Hāpuna, thereby eliminating the serious conflicts that arise when board surfers compete with bodysurfers and swimmers for the same site. Fishing is good for both net and pole fishermen off the rocky points bordering the

HĀPUNA BEACH. This idyllic shoreline scene highlights all of Hāpuna's most attractive features: a beautifully landscaped park with extensive public facilities; a long, wide white sand beach; and a cool, inviting ocean. The beach, however, does not have a lifeguard. During periods of high surf, the number of drownings at this beautiful beach is one of the highest in the Hawaiian Islands.

beach. Hāpuna is in the driest area of the entire Big Island (on the average less than 10 inches of rainfall a year). Sunbathers, therefore, can expect more sunny days here than at any other shoreline site on the island.

The combination of ample, well-maintained public facilities, excellent beach conditions, and the wide range of possible shoreline activities have made Hāpuna Beach State Recreation Area the most popular and widely visited beach park on the Big Island. Visitors and residents often travel many miles, from as far away as the Hilo and Puna districts, particularly on weekends and holidays, to spend the day at Hāpuna. The large numbers of beachgoers pose no problems during the summer months when the ocean is calm, but during the winter months, usually from October through April, there are very serious water safety problems. High surf strikes the beach, generating a pounding shorebreak and extremely powerful, shifting rip currents. Many individuals, particularly out-of-state visitors unfamiliar with Hawaiian waters, attempt to swim or bodysurf during such hazardous conditions and find themselves unable to cope. Some even lose their lives.

Hāpuna Beach has no professional lifeguard coverage. Over the years, the regular beachgoers have made numerous rescues, but these volunteer rescuers are not always there. An emergency telephone in the park can be used to summon rescue assistance from the Hawai'i Fire Department, but by the time rescue men reach the scene from Kawaihae or Waimea, it is often too late. Because there is no full-time, professional lifeguard stationed on this beach, particularly during the critical winter months, more drownings occur at Hāpuna Beach State Recreation Area than at any other developed beach park in the entire State of Hawai'i. Swimmers unfamiliar with the beach and the hazards of Hawaiian surf would be well advised to stay out of the water completely during periods of rough or high seas. *Do not take a chance and become one of the annual drowning statistics.* Other hazards in area include Portuguese man-of-war and other jellyfish that blow inshore during storms. Powerful winds, particularly common in the months of January, February, and March, can also pose a danger, carrying inflatables and people on them out to sea.

During the calm summer months, Hāpuna Beach State Recreation Area is the site of the Big Island's Rough Water Swim, an annual event since 1979. The roughly circular course of 1.1 miles utilizes the entire width of the bay from point to point, and attracts many participants.

When the Territory of Hawai'i first opened Hāpuna Beach as a public park, it did not have title to a large triangular portion of the park property immediately south of Ihumoku, the rock promontory that divides the beach. This section of land, part of the land division of 'Ōuli owned by the Parker Ranch, was subsequently acquired through the cooperation of Alfred Wellington Carter, the manager of the Parker Ranch from 1899 to 1937. In recognition of his assistance the park was named A. W. Carter Beach Park, but this name was eventually changed in favor of Hāpuna Beach State Recreation Area when the property was developed and improved with public facilities.

(76)
Kauna'oa

Bill, Solomon, Michael, and I sat on a bench at the old YMCA cottage and discussed Kaunaoa Beach. Michael said that he did not use the beach too much when he was young but some people used to catch akule there. Bill said his family went there almost every weekend. The whole family would come down and throw net or use gill net. They would come down many times on mule or horseback. He could remember as a child racing horses up and down the beach.

Re: Second Trail Walk, Mauna Kea Beach Hotel
Akau vs. Mauna Kea Properties, 1977

Within Kauna'oa Bay is one of the Big Island's most beautiful beaches. Kauna'oa Beach is a long crescent of white sand between two lava points at the head of the bay. Before the area was "developed," Hawaiian fishermen used the beach for surround-net, lay-net, and huki-lau-net fishing. The rocky points bounding the beach were ideal for crabbing, throw-netting, and shellfish gathering. Although Kauna'oa apparently never supported a permanent village, there is considerable archaeological evidence, particularly at Ka'aha Point to the north, that the area was extensively used in pre-contact times. House sites, fishermen's shelters, campsites, stone wall enclosures, garden plots, graves, and a shoreline trail complex that joined the bay with the once populous neighboring villages of Puakō and Kawaihae have been identified. Kauna'oa Bay was also a nesting site for hawksbill turtles, the only sea turtle in Hawaiian waters that still nests, although infrequently, at a few scattered island beaches. Many older fishermen recall that the turtles were most commonly seen on shore at the southern end of Kauna'oa Beach and at Keonehonu, "the turtle sand," a former black sand beach in a small bay to the north of Ka'aha Point. Green sea turtles, although they reproduce and nest primarily on French Frigate Shoals in the Northwestern Hawaiian Islands, are still common visitors to Kauna'oa Bay.

Kauna'oa Bay is today best known as the site of the Mauna Kea Beach Hotel, one of the most elegant resorts in the Hawaiian Islands. Internationally famous for its superb accommodations and fine dining, the hotel offers a wide variety of amenities, including golf on an 18-hole championship course, tennis, and sailing. The idea for the resort came originally from former Governor William F. Quinn during a campaign to encourage tourism on the neighbor islands. Laurance S. Rockefeller, recognizing the possibilities, arranged to lease the beachfront property from Parker Ranch. His Mauna

Kea Beach Hotel, overlooking the bay was dedicated on July 24, 1965.

Kauna'oa Beach, a long, flat, wide, curving white sand beach, slopes gently into the deeper offshore waters, excellent conditions for swimming and snorkeling. During periods of high surf, particularly during the winter months, bodysurfers ride the shorebreak, while board surfers frequent the point break at the northern headland of the bay. However, high surf also brings with it hazardous water conditions, including a pounding shorebreak that can cause severe neck and back injuries. A powerful rip current usually runs out of the center of the bay toward the southern point, but it often shifts position depending on the size and direction of the swell. Although no professional lifeguards are stationed at Kauna'oa Beach, the beach attendants employed by the hotel often serve in that capacity and, over the years, have rescued many swimmers in distress.

Public facilities at the resort include ten paved parking spaces for the public at the southernmost end of the hotel's parking lot, a pedestrian right-of-way adjacent to a service road to the beach, and restrooms with showers at the protected southern end of the beach, the best area for families with little children. The public access and facilities were installed and opened in October 1981, the result of a suit filed in 1973 against the Mauna Kea Land Corporation by four plaintiffs. William Akau, Sr., Solomon Akau, Thomas Kealanahele, and Alika Cooper contended that their traditional rights of access to the shoreline had been violated when the coastal trails at Kauna'oa Beach were closed to the public by the development of the hotel complex. After seven years of litigation, an agreement was finally reached in May 1980. A year later the parking spaces, the pathway to the beach, and the comfort station were completed. The agreement also allows public access over the shoreline trail through the *kiawe* growth separating Kauna'oa Beach from Hāpuna Beach.

The 1½-mile reach of shoreline north of Kauna'oa, between the Mauna Kea Beach Hotel's golf course and Spencer Beach Park, contains two pockets of white sand, one at Wai'ula'ula and another at Mau'umae. Wai'ula'ula Beach, at the base of the gulch of the same name, borders the northern boundary of the Lurline Matson Roth estate. Wedged between two lava points, the sand slopes gently into the deeper waters offshore and offers good opportunities for swimming, snorkeling, diving, and shoreline fishing. Occasionally, heavy storm waves wash the beach almost entirely away, leaving a salt water pond in the gulch.

Mau'umae Beach, inland of Keawehala Point, is excellent for swimming, snorkeling, and shoreline fishing. The large flat pocket of white sand slopes gently offshore and is backed by low dunes covered with coconut and *kiawe*. Mau'umae Beach is accessible from a public foot trail that originates at Spencer Beach Park. There is no convenient public access to Wai'ula'ula, but a public right-of-way to the beach will be opened concurrently with the planned residential development immediately inland.

(77)
Spencer Beach Park

After breakfast, I visited the large heiau or temple called Bukohola. It stands on an eminence in the southern part of the district, and was built by Tamehameha about thirty years ago, when he was engaged in conquering Hawaii, and the rest of the Sandwich Islands.

He had subdued Maui, Lanai, and Molokai, and was preparing from the latter, to invade Oahu, but in consequence of a rebellion in the south and east parts of Hawaii, was obligated to return thither.

When he had overcome those who had rebelled, he finished the heiau, dedicated it to Tairi, his god of war, and then proceeded to the conquest of Oahu. Its shape is an irregular paralelogram [sic], 224 feet long, and 100 feet wide. Leaving Bukohola, accompanied by some natives, I visited Mairikini, another heiau, a few hundred yards nearer the shore. It was nearly equal in size, but inferior in every other respect. It appeared to have been literally crowded with idols, but no human sacrifices were offered to any of its gods.

Journal of William Ellis, 1823

On the shoreline immediately below Pu'ukoholā Heiau, a famous temple built by Kamehameha I, is Spencer Beach Park. The park was named in honor of Samuel Mahuka Spencer, who served as the Big Island's county chairman, the equivalent of the present position of mayor, for twenty years from 1924 to 1944. Born in Waimea in 1875, Spencer was named after Samuel

Mahuka, an uncle who raised him. After graduating from the The Kamehameha Schools for Boys in 1893, he held a number of government positions until his election as county chairman in 1924. Spencer died in Honoka'a Hospital on February 28, 1960.

Spencer Beach Park centers on 'Ōhai'ula Beach, a large flat pocket of white sand with a very gentle underwater slope. A long shallow reef directly offshore and the extensive harbor landfill to the north provide good protection from the prevailing winds and offshore waves. Swimming, snorkeling, and skin diving opportunities are excellent. Hazardous conditions ordinarily occur only during severe storms.

The protected beach and the facilities provided at the park have made it a very popular site, especially for families with little children. Facilities include restrooms, picnic tables, showers, tennis courts, a roofed pavilion, parking lots, a camping area, and a lifeguard tower. In the park are open grassy lawns, many large shade trees, and large population of birds, mostly mynahs and sparrows.

Immediately *mauka* of Spencer Beach Park, Pu'ukoholā Heiau stands atop the most prominent hill in the area, overlooking Kawaihae Bay. On orders from Kamehameha, Hawaiian laborers completed the imposing temple in the summer of 1791. The great chief was acting on the advice of Kapoukahi, a famous *kahuna* on Kaua'i, who had predicted that Kamehameha would successfully unify all of the Hawaiian Islands if he built a *heiau* to his war god, Kūkā'ilimoku, on a hill called Pu'ukoholā at Kawaihae. Four years after the temple's dedication, at which human sacrifices were offered, Kamehameha had established the Kingdom of Hawai'i by conquering all of the major islands except Kaua'i and Ni'ihau. In 1810, these two remaining islands also came under his control through an agreement with their king, thereby fulfilling Kapoukahi's prophecy. Pu'ukoholā Heiau National Historic Site, a unit of the National Park Service, consists of 77 acres administered by the superintendent of Pu'uhonua o Hōnaunau National Historical Park in South Kona. The Kohala historic site was authorized by Congress on August 17, 1972.

A short distance to the north of Spencer Beach Park, a dirt road leads to Mailekini Heiau, which was restored by Kamehameha at the time of the construction of Pu'ukoholā. Mailekini had served as the principal temple of the ruling district chief. It was apparently converted into a fort about 1812 by John Young, an Englishman who was Kamehameha's most important foreign advisor. Young built a house in Kawaihae in 1798 and lived there until his death at about age 90 in 1835. From his home he acted as Kamehameha's business agent. He also governed the island of Hawai'i from 1802 to 1812, during which time he apparently decided that a fort was necessary to protect the harbor and the king's arsenal. Today, *kiawe* trees surround the ruins of the *heiau*.

The section of shoreline fronting Mailekini Heiau is known as Pelekane. It consists of a short stretch of white sand and coral rubble abutting the harbor landfill and a small brackish-water estuary. No sunbathing, swimming, picnicking, or camping are permitted at Pelekane because the beach is part of the Pu'ukoholā Heiau National Historic Site complex and is considered a sacred area. Fishing, however, a traditional activity, is allowed at this beach, which is noted for its large schools of mullet.

The ocean bottom at Pelekane, once several feet deeper, is now very shallow due to the deposition of coral rubble and rocks from the harbor landfill and soil runoff from the shore. Poor circulation keeps the shallow nearshore waters continually dirty and murky. Perhaps 100 feet offshore of the beach is the now submerged site of Haleokapuni, a third *heiau* in the Pu'ukoholā complex, that is reputed to have been a *heiau* for the feeding of sharks. It is said that human remains were among the offerings placed in Haleokapuni for the sharks to consume. Remnants of the structure have been leveled by tsunami and severe storms and are being slowly covered by silting from the harbor landfill. However, a large shark population still patrols the waters surrounding it. Most of the sharks are small, ranging from 3 to 6 feet in length. Although they are always in the vicinity, they are seen more often during high tides. Pelekane is considered by many local residents of Kawaihae to be a traditional breeding grounds for sharks, particularly black tips and grays. Pelekane is also an important feeding and resting site for the numerous green sea turtles that frequent the extensive Kawaihae Reef.

Kawaihae

'Ike ia e makou a Kawaihae.
I ka kai nehe 'ōlelo me ka 'ili'ili

Kau aku ka mana'o no pua ka 'ilima
I ka nalu ha'i mai la o Ka'ewa.

Ho'ike Poliahu i ka kapa hau
Ho'i ana i ka piko o Mauna Kea

Ha'ina ia mai ana ka puana
I ke kai nehe 'ōlelo ma ka 'ili'ili

It was seen by us at Kawaihae
The rustling sea conversing with the beach pebbles

A thought about an *ilima* blossom settles
In the breaking surf of Ka'ewa.

Poliahu exhibits a snowy covering
Returning to the summit of Mauna Kea

Thus is the story told
Of the rustling sea conversing with the beach pebbles.
"Kawaihae Hula"
Traditional song

In 1823, the missionary William Ellis sailed to the Big Island aboard the brig *'Ainoa*, which stopped first at Kawaihae. After anchoring off Honokoa at the northern end of Kawaihae Bay, Ellis went ashore to visit John Young, a former advisor to Kamehameha I. He wrote: "At six a.m. the next day, I went on shore, and walked along the beach about a mile to the house of Mr. J. Young, an aged Englishman, who has resided thirty-six years on the island, and rendered the most important services to the late king; not only in his various civil wars, but in all his intercourse with those foreigners who have visited the islands." This information is of interest not only for its brief biographical sketch of Young, but also because Ellis had to walk over a long stretch of beach to reach Young's house, which was located immediately north of Pu'ukoholā Heiau. Although the beach no longer exists, many long-time Kohala residents remember it as a long, narrow, black sand beach that extended from Pelekane to the northern end of the present harbor. The beach fell victim to the complete alteration of the shoreline that accompanied the construction of Kawaihae Harbor. The harbor and its atten-

dant landfill also destroyed a substantial portion of the Kawaihae Reef, the most extensive coral reef on the island of Hawai'i.

Prior to the harbor development, interisland steamers tied up at a single pier that was erected in 1937 for their use. The pier offered a berthing space of 60 feet at a depth of 25 feet with support facilities including a wharf and storage area. In 1950 Congress authorized the dredging of a deep-water harbor, and by 1959, the construction of the entire harbor complex had been completed. Facilities include an interisland terminal barge wharf, an overseas terminal wharf, a military cargo ramp, storage areas, a small boat harbor, two small craft moorage areas, and a large harbor basin with a wide entrance channel, all protected from the open ocean by a breakwater and an extensive landfill. Most of the landfill remains completely bare and serves only as a stockpile for the coral spoil material that was dredged out of the reef during the harbor's construction. The material is used by various governmental agencies for public works projects and is also sold to private contractors.

Though it is primarily a commercial deep-water port, Kawaihae Harbor is used by many local residents, particularly on weekends and holidays, for a wide variety of shoreline recreational activities. These activities include all types of fishing, canoe paddling, sailing, windsurfing, swimming, and picnicking. The *makai* end of the landfill affords a spectacular view of Pu'ukoholā Heiau. During periods of calm seas, snorkelers, nearshore scuba divers, and spear fishermen frequent the reef beyond the breakwater. Board surfers and occasionally bodysurfers find some excellent waves in this area during periods of high surf. Although beachgoers are found from one end of the complex to the other, two areas are especially popular: the small sand beach at the northern end where the canoe paddlers and boaters congregate, and the small coral rubble beach near the military cargo ramp where the windsurfers gather to sail.

The 12 miles of shoreline north of Kawaihae Harbor to Lapakahi State Historical Park consists of low sea cliffs, prominent headlands, and numerous coves and small bays. Except for an occasional pocket of black pebbles or coral rubble, there are no beaches anywhere along this reach. Many places along the coast, such as

KAWAIHAE. The Big Island has two major deep-draft harbors, Hilo and Kawaihae. The southern border of the Kawaihae harbor consists of an extensive landfill that was created when the harbor basin was dredged. The landfill's artificial beaches, protected from the open ocean by a massive breakwater, attract many fishermen, swimmers, and windsurfers.

Honokoa, Waiaka'ilio and Keawe'ula, are visited by snorkelers, fishermen, nearshore scuba diving groups, and campers. Access by land is over foot or jeep trails from Akoni Pule Highway.

(79)
Lapakahi State Historical Park

Father Bond, a missionary of North Kohala, related the decrease in population of the southern and western areas (including Lapakahi) in the 1860s:

During the seven years preceeding the recent census, the decrease in the population of the District was nearly one hundred per annum. This decrease it scarcely need by said, was chiefly caused by removals and with few excep-

tions to Oahu. . . . The herds of cattle and horses belonging to the natives themselves, suffered to run at large through the most ruinous negligence, had well nigh annihilated all possibility of cultivation; and thus commenced the work of expulsion, ere foreigners with large herds of cattle came in to complete the process of depopulation.

Lapakahi, Hawaii
Tuggle and Griffin, 1973

The Lapakahi historical complex measures approximately one mile in length along the shoreline and extends 4 miles inland into the Kohala Mountains, to an elevation of 1,900 feet. This very large section of land is the Lapakahi *ahupua'a*, a fundamental Hawaiian land division stretching from the ocean to the uplands. A number of successive ecological zones comprise this area, including a narrow habitation zone along the shore, a barren zone of little vegetation, an upland agricultural zone, and a dense forest zone. For years, Lapakahi has attracted the attention of archaeologists and anthropologists. Intensive investigations were made during the summers of 1968, 1969, and 1970 by members of the Department of Anthropology of the University of Hawai'i. One of the purposes of the study was to collect information for the Divison of State Parks, to be used in shaping Lapakahi State Historical Park, which focuses on Koai'e, Lapakahi's fishing village.

Results of the study show that Hawaiians first settled in the Lapakahi area during the 1300s, probably forced there by the pressure of expanding populations in the wetter, more desirable lands and valleys of Kohala. With low, irregular rainfall and periodic droughts, Lapakahi was not a particularly hospitable place for an agricultural community, but people settled there anyway and managed to subsist successfully. The fishing village of Koai'e, with its brackish-water spring and one of the best canoe landings in the neighborhood, served as the center of population and cultural activity in the coastal Lapakahi area until the late 1800s. At this time Koai'e was abandoned as a permanent settlement, as Hawaiians in North Kohala and throughout the islands gave up their former subsistence lifestyle in response to the spreading influence of Western civilization.

The 265-acre Lapakahi State Historical Park encompasses a variety of partially restored sites, such as living units, animal pens, canoe sheds, salt pans, and outdoor working areas, that once comprised Koai'e village. A good trail system through the sites and a free trail brochure available at the information desk provide visitors with excellent means of visualizing the pre-contact way of life in this seemingly desolate, inhospitable place. The excavated and reconstructed ruins here are similar to many other sites around the Big Island's shoreline that are not marked or identified, so the park offers a good starting point for amateur students of archaeology.

The interpretive hiking trails skirt the water's edge, a good vantage point from which to observe several geo-

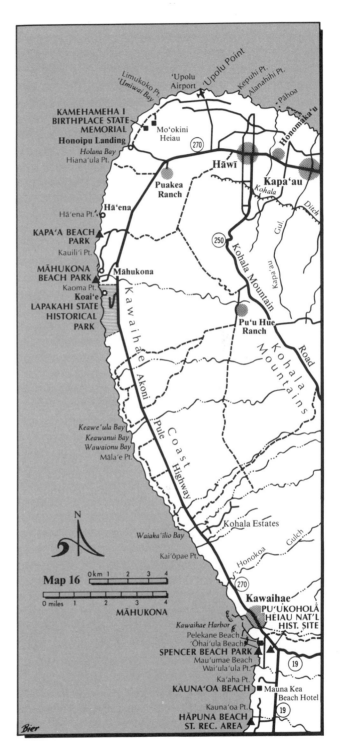

139

graphical features that contributed to the selection of Koai'e area as a village site. The *mauka* lands slope gently to the ocean over a wide section of this coastline. The sea cliffs that constitute the shoreline for miles on both sides of the village are markedly absent here, providing an excellent canoe landing site, a vital feature for any fishing village.

Within Koai'e Cove, two small coral rubble beaches across which the canoes were probably carried, and bordering fingers of *pāhoehoe* provide entry and exit points into the offshore waters for contemporary swimmers, snorkelers, and scuba divers. The lack of sand beaches and beach park facilities generally discourage most casual swimmers, but the very clear water in the cove, combined with a variety of fish and other marine life, attract snorkeling and scuba diving enthusiasts. Huge boulders cover the ocean bottom, which slopes gradually to a depth of 30 feet before it drops off steeply. Scuba divers report numerous caves along the sides of submarine cliffs at a depth of 80 feet. Swimmers and snorkelers should remain within the cove because of strong longshore currents and powerful winds in the open ocean beyond. During the winter months, seasonally heavy surf often precludes all in-water activities.

In February 1979 the State of Hawai'i created the Lapakahi Marine Life Conservation District at the shoreline of the historical park. The conservation district is divided into two subzones, in each of which certain activities are prohibited. Within Subzone A, the prohibited activities include all fishing; the removal, injuring, or possessing any finfish, crustacean, mollusk (including shells and 'opihi), live coral, *limu*, and other marine life, or their eggs; taking, altering, defacing, destroying, possessing, or removing any sand, coral, rock, or other geological objects or specimen; and having or possessing in the water any spear, trap, net, crowbar, or other device that may be used for the taking or altering of marine life, geological features, or specimens. In Subzone B, permitted activities include fishing by hook and line or throw-net for finfish and crustaceans, and fishing for 'ōpelu using bag or lift-nets. Further information and maps of the subzones may be obtained at the information desk in the park or from the Hilo office of the Division of Fish and Game. A sign on Akoni Pule Highway marks the entrance to the park.

Mahukona Beach Park

Thence the road passes through cane fields and pasture lands until, at a point between two mills, just after sight can be had of the ocean directly westwards, a fork is encountered. The southerly branch leads past the ancient sugar mill, which was the first built on this island, and on to Mahukona, which is the shipping point for the entire district, hence a railroad runs throughout the district, but it carries no regular passenger traffic.

The Island of Hawaii
Henry Kinney, 1913

Mahukona Beach Park borders a small open bay that once served as a port of the former Hawaii Consolidated Railway Company. The railway was the lifeline of the port, running around the northern base of the Kohala Mountains to Niuli'i. It existed primarily to haul sugar cane and bagged sugar, but it also transported freight to some of the villages and plantations along the way and carried passengers in tiny wooden cars.

When the Hawaii Consolidated Railway Company ceased operations in 1937, the port and railway were taken over by Mahukona Terminals, Ltd., a subsidiary of Kohala Sugar Company. Kohala Sugar Company, incorporated on February 3, 1863, originally covered 3,282 acres, but by 1937 it had expanded to 13,000 acres through consolidation with other mills and plantations. The railway linked all the components of the extensive plantation with its shipping port. Raw sugar manufactured in the mills was bagged, transported on railcars to a warehouse at Mahukona, and stored until the arrival of a freighter. Loading operations began after the bags were carried by conveyor to the edge of the landing, where stevedore crews then piled them onto rope slings. Landing One was equipped with a 20-ton-capacity steam crane, and Landing Two with a 15-ton-capacity electric crane, both of which were used to hoist the slings and deposit the bags into the lighters below. The lighters, shaped like open lifeboats, were then towed by motor launches to freighters, which were moored stern-to-shore about 900 feet from the landings in waters 40 to 50 fathoms deep. These loading operations continued until December 7, 1941.

During World War II, the United States Navy closed

MAHUKONA BEACH PARK. The harbor at Mahukona served the Kohala sugar plantations as a shipping point until it was closed in 1956. Many of the port structures are still standing on the shoreline. The ocean floor in the harbor is littered with discarded equipment and machine parts, providing snorkelers with some unique marine attractions. Boaters from Kohala launch their crafts at the old wharf with a winch-and-boom rig.

the port of Mahukona for security reasons, forcing Kohala Sugar Company to find an alternative shipping system. The plantation then sent its sugar by truck to Pa'auilo mill, the Hāmākua terminal of the Hawaii Consolidated Railway Company, and from there by rail to Hilo Harbor, the only open port on the Big Island. This system proved successful and continued until April 1, 1946.

On April Fool's Day in 1946, one of the most destructive tsunami ever to strike the Hawaiian Islands demo-

lished three of the great railroad bridges that linked the railway to Hāmākua. This catastrophe, which destroyed many other sections of the line, put the railway company out of business. The Kohala Sugar Company, once again faced with the problem of shipping its sugar, reopened the port of Mahukona, and trucks carried the bagged sugar to the warehouse on the shoreline.

In April 1949 a bulk sugar plant opened at Hilo Harbor with the capacity to receive and store the daily sugar production of all of the Big Island's eleven plantations.

Nevertheless, Kohala Sugar Company continued its operations at Mahukona. With the eventual improvement of the 90 miles of road between the mill and Hilo in 1956, however, the company began again to transport all of its sugar to Hilo Harbor in bulk sugar trucks. This move ended the commercial activity at Mahukona. Any possibility of the port reopening as a sugar shipping point terminated in October 1975, when the Kohala Sugar Company phased out all of its sugar operations.

Although Mahukona is no longer used as a commercial harbor, many of the port structures still stand at the shoreline. In the harbor itself, dredged and modified to accommodate the former shipping traffic, are found an abundance of railroad and industrial remnants, such as railroad wheels, cables, and large pieces of sheet metal. Snorkelers and nearshore scuba divers find these artifacts of interest and are also attracted by the wide variety of marine life in the reefs outside the harbor. Underwater visibility is usually excellent. Swimmers, fishermen, and boaters also utilize the area. A chain hoist with a winch is used for launching. During the winter months, the harbor and surrounding shoreline are subject to heavy surf, precluding all in-water activities.

Mahukona Beach Park consists of a small grassy lawn with picnic tables, a pavilion, restrooms, showers, a camping area, and a parking lot, all of which are adjacent to the harbor. It offers an excellent view of Maui for picnickers and a base of operations for shoreline hikers and water enthusiasts.

(81)
Kapa‘a Park

Haina School (1860–?). Haina School was a small one-room school that was located between Honoipu and Mahukona. It was the last boarding school built when Father Bond was superintendent of schools in Kohala.

"Kohala Keia"

Kapa‘a Park consists of a small section of shoreline improved with a pavilion, restrooms, showers, picnic tables, a camping area, and a parking lot. Picnickers and fishermen are the principal visitors to the park, although some swimmers, snorkelers, and nearshore scuba divers also visit the area. Entries and exits for in-water activities are made over the rocks and low sea cliffs that make up this rugged stretch of coast. During the winter months, heavy surf and powerful currents discourage almost all ocean-related activities. The park offers an isolated picnicking and camping site with an excellent view of Maui, in an otherwise undeveloped section of North Kohala.

In former times, this remote shoreline area was well populated, and many habitation ruins can be found on either side of the park. South of the park is the Kapa‘a Village complex, which includes platforms, yard walls, enclosures, and a well. North of the park behind Ha‘ena Point the Ha‘ena Village complex occupies a large area with numerous sites of archaeological interest. However, both the villages are largely overrun with thick growths of kiawe, lantana, and other nearshore vegetation.

(82)
Kamehameha I Birthsite Memorial to Kapanai‘a

He was a man of powerful physique, agile, supple, fearless, and skilled in all the warlike and peaceful exercises suitable for an Ali‘i. He had likewise a strong mind . . . well filled with the accumulated learning of his race and capable of thinking clearly and effectively. . . . Of the great chiefs he seems to have been the first to have an adequate appreciation of the advantages to be gained from friendly relations with foreigners, but he avoided the error of falling into their power; he had foreigners in his service, some of them being trusted confidential advisors, but they were always his servants, never his masters; his was the better mind and the stronger will.

The Hawaiian Kingdom, vol. I
Ralph Kuykendall

The 17 miles of Kohala shoreline from Kapa‘a Park to Kēōkea Beach Park wind around ‘Upolu Point, the northernmost tip of the Big Island. In this region the sea cliffs are indented by a number of small bays. This rugged and irregular reach of coast contains no sand beaches and very few protected places for swimming, diving, or other in-water activities. The ocean is dangerous throughout the year, with persistent alongshore currents, strong, gusty winds, and powerful waves surging across the rocky points and boulder beaches. During the winter months, huge surf generated by winter storms in the North Pacific commonly assaults most of this shoreline, compounding the dangers.

Despite the dangerous waters between Kapaʻa and Keōkea, this long stretch of shoreline was once inhabited. There is clear evidence of a number of Hawaiian villages, canoe landings, surfing sites, and fishing grounds of years gone by. Although the former habitation areas have long since been abandoned, many people, Kohala residents in particular, continue to visit various points and bays to harvest *limu* and *ʻopihi* and to picnic, fish, and camp. Much of the access is across private property. Several places along this coast have seen limited development: construction of a boat landing, a transmitting station, a landing strip, and a lighthouse.

In an article in "Kohala Keia," Thomas Kaiawe described the boat landing at Honoipu, a small bay approximately 4 miles southwest of ʻUpolu Point. The landing served the Hāwī Plantation, founded in 1881 by Robert Hind, in the same manner as that at Mahukona.

> The landing at Honoipu used similar methods of unloading supplies and loading sugar onto the ship. The warehouse was situated on a bluff, ninety-three feet above sea level. Slings were secured from the warehouse to the anchored ship offshore. This system continued at Honoipu until 1912, when Hawi Mill Company discontinued its use of the Honoipu landing and joined with the other sugar plantations in transporting their sugar by railroad to the port of Mahukona.

Ruins of the former landing still stand on the bluff above the bay, a popular destination for fishermen and other visitors to the area. The beauty of this shoreline was described in the traditional song "Paliakamoa" composed by an unknown poet as he sat atop Kehoni, a hill 667 feet above sea level.

> *I ka luna maua aʻo Kehoni*
> *ʻIke ʻia i ka nani aʻo Puakea,*
> *Kau aku ka manaʻo no Honoipu,*
> *I ka neʻeneʻe malie i ka ʻae kai.*
> *Lae kaulana o ʻUpolu i ka malie,*
> *He hōʻailona ʻai nō ke Kaleponi,*
> *O ke kū kilakila mai aʻo Paliakamoa,*
> *Ka uwea kila holu i ka ili kai.*

Two of us on top of Kehoni
The beauty of Puakea is seen,
Think about Honoipu
With the gentle movement at the water's edge.
Famous point of ʻUpolu in the calm,
Looks like California
Paliakamoa stands commanding,
The seaweed sways at the surface of the sea.

During World War II, the federal government installed a transmitting station near Honoipu for an electronic navigation system called Loran, an acronym for long-range aid to navigation. The system enables receiver-equipped vessels or aircraft to determine their position at sea or in the air from signals emitted from ground stations. In addition to this Loran station, the Coast Guard maintains two others in this system, a secondary transmitting station at Kure Atoll and a master transmitting station at Johnston Island.

ʻUpolu Airport, located a short distance from ʻUpolu Point, was built during the early 1930s and was originally maintained by the army as an auxiliary landing field called Suiter Field. Eventually converted to civilian use, the short landing strip is used only occasionally by small commuter aircraft, and not at all by larger interisland carriers. Facilities include a terminal building and waiting area, restrooms, and a parking lot.

The Coast Guard built the first lighthouse at Kauhola Point in 1912 with a light visible for 9 miles at sea. In 1917 the power was increased to provide visibility at 14 miles. The present structure, built in 1933, stands 85 feet high, contains a spiral stairway, and has a light visible for 17 miles. Beginning on June 30, 1951, the now automatic light has been unattended. No remains of the former dwelling or station buildings are evident.

Probably the single most important historical thread running from pre-contact to post-contact times in the Kohala area is the association with Kamehameha I, the great warrior-statesman king who has been called the Napoleon of the Pacific. According to tradition, Kamehameha was born about the year 1758 at Kapakai in Kokoiki, approximately midway between the Loran station and Moʻokini Heiau. At that time, Alapaʻi, the chief of the Big Island, was headquartered temporarily at Kokoiki, making plans for an invasion of Maui. His war fleet was distributed along the shoreline from Pu'uepa to Lapakahi. The leaders of Alapa'i's forces were two high chiefs of his court, half-brothers, Kalani'ōpu'u and Keoua. Keoua's wife, Kekuiapoiwa, had accompanied her husband to the chief's encampment at Kapakai, a common practice for Hawaiian women of chiefly rank, and it was there that she gave birth to Kamehameha.

Kamehameha eventually became Hawai'i's greatest king and successfully united all the island chiefdoms into a single kingdom. In *King Kamehameha I and Father Damien Memorial Statues* is this description of the great man and his achievements:

> Kamehameha the Great, is, beyond all others, the most revered and beloved of Hawaiian heroes. So far as is known, no other leader of his stature had appeared before his time; none has arisen since. At the time of this birth—somewhere between 1752 and 1761—the normal state of the islands was that of war, with single islands and parts of islands ruled by fiercely covetous chiefs. Kamehameha's great achievement was the conquest of these warring islands and their unification under one government. Establishing himself as king and surrounding himself with strong men, he ruled the people wisely. The Hawaiian Kingdom lasted for nearly a century, until, in 1900, it became a territory of the United States. Born before the islands were known to the outside world, Kamehameha saw the coming of the discovery ships under Captain James Cook in 1778. In his intercourse with foreigners Kamehameha adopted those things he felt would help his people and forbade those he believed would harm them. Kamehameha lived to see the monarchy he had created out of chaos become known and respected—even coveted by powers through Europe and America.

The Kamehameha I Birthsite Memorial occupies a half-acre parcel of land along an unpaved coastal road in Kokoiki. The boulders within the memorial are said to be the birthstones marking his birthplace.

A short distance from the birthsite in Pu'uepa stands one of the most famous *heiau* on the Big Island, Mo'okini Heiau, which tradition says was built or rebuilt in the twelfth century by the great priest Pa'ao. The massive, well-preserved structure offers a com-

manding view of Maui, and on particularly clear days, Kaho'olawe and even the West Maui Mountains can be seen. Two early accounts describe the *heiau*. One by William Ellis, was recorded in his journal in 1823:

> At noon we stopped at Kapaau, an inland village, where, with some difficulty, we collected a congregation of about fifty, principally women, to whom a short discourse was addressed. When we had remained some time for rest and conversation, we resumed our journey, and proceeded towards the north point of the island, near which we passed through the district of Pauepu, in which formerly stood a temple called Mokini, celebrated in the historical accounts of the Hawaiians, as built by Paao, a foreign priest, who resided in Pauepa, and officiated in this temple.

Another appeared in Henry Whitney's 1875 *Hawaiian Guide Book*: "The walls are partly in ruins. Tradition says the stones for the construction of these monstrous walls were passed from the valley of Pololu, twelve miles distant, by a file of workmen standing in battle array the whole distance."

Rounding 'Upolu Point in an eastward direction is a long section of high sea cliffs that preclude shoreline access for most people, although surfers occasionally find some rideable waves at Keawa'eli, a bay in the lee of Kauhola Point. To the east of Kauhola Point is Hāpu'u, another bay that is well known to the *kama'āina* of the area. From approximately 1950 to 1965, Pierre Bowman, a prominent Kohala resident, held an annual shark hunt at Hāpu'u. The event was one of the district's most popular social gatherings and also resulted in the deaths of a few sharks.

The former Hawaiian village of Hālawa once stood on the sea cliffs between the two bays of Hāpu'u and Kapanai'a. It was at this village that Kamehameha had lived as a child and to which, as a young man, he returned for a time at the advice of his uncle, Kalani'ōpu'u. In 1780 Kalani'ōpu'u, the aging ruler of the Big Island called council at Waipi'o. He named his son Kiwalaō as his successor and at the same time entrusted to his nephew Kamehameha the war god Kūkā'ilimoku, thus creating a rift between the two cousins. Later that year, in a *heiau* dedication ceremony in Ka'ū, Kiwalaō was about to sacrifice the body of a captured rival chief when Kamehameha boldly stepped in front of his cousin and completed the sacrificial ritual himself. This deliberate affront to the designated heir to the kingdom caused a great stir among the other chiefs, and Kalani'ōpu'u, fearing an attempt on Kamehameha's life, advised him to leave his court.

Kamehameha retreated to Kohala, to the village of Hālawa, taking with him his wife Kalola, his half-brother Kaleimāmahu, and the war god Kūkā'ilimoku, a carved image with a menacing, toothed, open mouth. During this period, Kamehameha busied himself with a variety of projects and leisure activities. One of this most famous projects was the construction of a road at Kapanai'a from the top of the sea cliffs to the pebble beach below. The road's gradual incline much facilitated the transportation of the village's canoes to and from the safety of the storage sheds on the cliff tops. Kamehameha and his companions also chipped out *kōnane papamū*, checker-board-like depressions, on flat shoreline boulders, providing places to play the game *kōnane* near the water's edge.

In *Fragments of Hawaiian History*, historian John Papa I'i reported that Kamehameha loved the sport of surfing and that as a young chief in his uncle's court in Ka'ū, he often disappeared for days to watch and ride the waves. One day in 1782, Kamehameha and his brother were at Kapanai'a sporting in the waves when they received the news from Kekuhaupi'o that Kalani-'ōpu'u had died. Kamehameha was urged to go to Hōnaunau to join with the others in mourning the loss of the high chief and to see how Kiwalaō would redistribute the lands of the kingdom. The redistribution displeased not only Kamehameha, but a number of the island's other powerful district chiefs as well. Under Kamehameha's leadership, they revolted and successfully otherthrew Kiwalaō and his army. This battle marked the beginning of the wars that ultimately resulted in Kamehameha's complete dominion over the entire island chain.

Nothing remains of Hālawa village, the site having been leveled, along with many others in North Kohala, in the interests of modern agricultural pursuits, but a few fishermen apparently lived on the beach at Kapanai'a well into the twentieth century. In *The Island of Hawaii*, written in 1913, Henry Kinney noted: "Further eastwards is Kapanaia, a beautiful bay, which is used as a steamer landing on the rare occasions when a southerly storm makes Mahukona too rough. On the land side is a fine beach, where stand a number of grass houses which are used by fishermen."

Except for an unpaved access road to the beach, the margins of Kapanai'a Bay are undevelped, but the area is popular among local residents for shoreline fishing, for netting *akule*, and particularly for surfing and body-surfing. Kapanai'a is one of the most protected and easily accessible of North Kohala's few surfing sites. The public's traditional right of access to the bay was reconfirmed in March 1982 in a legal settlement between Hui Māmalahoa and the Kohala Corporation, a subsidiary of Castle and Cooke which owns the uncultivated land surrounding the bay. Hui Māmalahoa, a group of Kohala citizens, felt that they were being denied access to Kapanai'a and filed suit requesting easements for public rights-of-way to the bay. Represented by Tim Lui-Kwan and Ben Gaddis, attorneys with the Legal Aid Society of Hilo (who also assisted the Ka'ū community in securing shoreline access to Kāwā Bay), Hui Māmalahoa won its case.

(83)
Keōkea Beach Park

The beach line from Niulii striking back westwards is very pretty and interesting, but the trails along the cliffs, with cane fields mauka and puhala trees makai, are not easy to ride over and cannot be found without a guide. They lead to several beautiful beaches. Nearest Niulii is the Keokea Beach, a favorite bathing and picnic ground, which was formerly a schooner landing.

The Island of Hawaii
Henry Kinney, 1913

Keōkea Beach Park consists of 7 sloping acres tucked into the leeward sea cliffs of Keōkea Bay, a large, open bay in the rocky North Kohala shoreline. The park was originally developed and landscaped by local residents as a community-service project before its official designation as a county beach park. The loose boulder

KĒŌKEA BEACH PARK. Many of North Kohala's beaches are found at the bases of the district's prominent sea cliffs. This boulder beach at Kēōkea is a typical example. Although swimming here is marginal at best, the scenic park is a favorite site for family picnics and other social gatherings.

breakwater at the foot of the park was also constructed as a community-service project, but in this case as a joint venture between the people of Niuli'i and the Kohala Corporation. Shortly before the Kohala Corporation phased out its sugar operations in October 1975, the plantation loaned some heavy equipment to the park project, and several heavy equipment operators volunteered their time to the effort. The numerous boulders scattered at the water's edge were shaped into a small breakwater to form a shallow protected cove for beginning swimmers.

Kēōkea Beach Park is usually crowded with North Kohala picnickers and swimmers, particularly on weekends and holidays. During the summer months, under normal tradewind conditions, swimming is safe offshore of the boulder beach, but because the bay is exposed to the open ocean there is an almost continuous inshore surge. During the winter and spring months, severe storms in the North Pacific generate heavy surf that sweeps unchecked into Kēōkea Bay, causing hazardous nearshore water conditions. Occasionally, the waves are good enough for surfing and bodysurfing, but the rocky shoreline deters most wave-riding enthusiasts. Facilities in the park include picnic pavilions, restrooms, showers, drinking water, electricity, a camping site, and parking.

Beyond Kēōkea Bay the sea cliffs continue on to 'Ako'ako'a Point where Neue, a beautiful little bay, lies in the lee of the point. Many Kohala residents know Neue Bay as Navy Bay, a popular mispronunciation of Neue. The bay and the lands surrounding it are undeveloped and have no convenient public access, but are still often used by fishermen and picnickers.

(84)
Pololū

Pololu is a pleasant village, situated in a small cultivated valley, having a fine stream of water flowing down its centre, while lofty mountains rise on either side.

The houses stand principally on the beach, but as we did not see many of the inhabitants, we passed on, ascended the steep mountain on the north side, and kept on our way.

Journal of William Ellis, 1823

The idyllic scene observed by Ellis and his group, who were making their way to Hālawa from Honokāne Nui, remained undisturbed until shortly after the turn of the century. In 1904, John Hind of the Hāwī Plantation launched the enormous and ambitious project of building a ditch to carry water from deep in the Kohala Mountains to the fields of sugar cane of North Kohala, from Niuli'i to Puakea. The Kohala Ditch was dedicated on Kamehameha Day, June 11, 1906—16 miles of tunnels and 6 miles of open waterways. Unfortunately, however, it drastically reduced the once copious water of Pololū's stream, causing serious problems for the farming community in the valley. Eventually most of the residents had to abandon their taro lands and move. Rice replaced taro for a short time, but by 1926 the paddies had also been abandoned. From observations made in the 1930s, Handy, Handy, and Pukui in *Native Planters in Old Hawaii* recorded the following:

As a wet-taro valley, Pololu on the northeastern coast of Kohala ranked first in that section, having a flatland area, about one mile long and about a third of a mile at its widest point; this area used to be entirely covered by terraces except for the section immediately inland from the seashore which is under very high sand dunes and another portion in the lower valley on the west side which is made up of fishponds and swamp. The upper terraces are now all under kukui and guava. Hau and guava cover

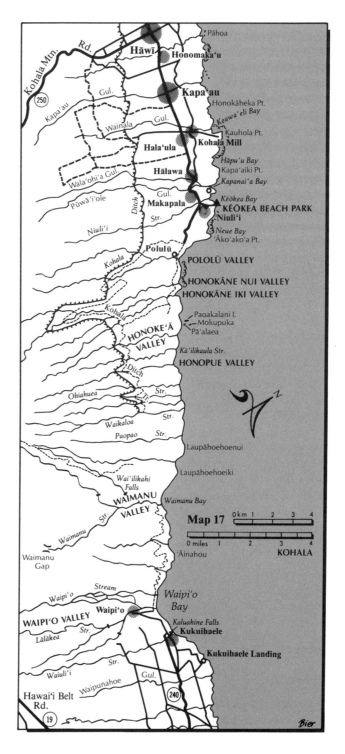

POLOLŪ. Pololū is one of seven amphitheater-shaped valleys located along a remote, isolated stretch of shoreline. Taro was grown at one time in all of these wet valleys, but today, with the exception of Waipiʻo, they are uninhabited, the taro patches overrun with introduced vegetation. The three islands visible in the distance front Honokeʻā, the centermost of the seven valleys.

some of the old terraces along the side of the valley, and the central area of the lower valley is now used for pasturing horses. Water formerly used for irrigation has been taken by the Kohala Ditch for sugar plantation purposes.

The Pololū Valley Lookout at the end of the highway is as close as most visitors get to Pololū. To reach the floor of the deep, flat-bottomed valley one must hike down an unimproved switchback trail, the same one that William Ellis ascended in 1823. Heavy rains leave the trail muddy and slippery, and long periods of continuous sunshine heat the rocky sections unpleasantly, and so protective footwear is a necessity for the hike no matter what the weather. Because both horses and cattle are pastured in Pololū, the heavy iron gate across the bottom of the trail must be kept closed at all times.

The backshore area of the beach is mostly sand dunes covered with ironwoods and grass and a scattering of *hau, pōhuehue,* and *naupaka*. The high dunes wall off the mouth of the valley from the ocean. Cobblestones and boulders comprise the southeastern margin of the beach in front of the dunes, whereas black sand surrounds the stream mouth at the northwestern margin of the beach. A shallow sand bar extends offshore along most of the beach, which creates a continuous shorebreak during the summer months, attracting swimmers, bodysurfers, and surfers. The surf also generates rip currents, however, which have caused many drownings and near-drownings at this remote, unguarded site. North Kohala residents, who are familiar with the area, try to avoid a particularly powerful rip current, the *wiliau*, that forms frequently in the center of the beach. *Wiliau*, the word commonly used by many of the older residents for rip current, literally means a circular current, and most Hawaiians who use the term point out that the *wiliau* begins nearshore, moves through the surfline, and then dissipates outside the surf. From that point the swimmer can circle back to the beach by allowing the waves to carry him in to shore.

During the winter months, the powerful high surf that strikes Pololū Beach intensifies the hazardous water conditions and erodes parts of the sandbar and the beach. These periods are best for shoreline fishing, sunbathing, picnicking, and beachcombing—not for swimming or surfing.

(85)
Honokāne Nui to Honopuʻe

Along the 12-mile reach of steep, high sea cliffs between the Pololū Valley Lookout and the Waipiʻo Valley Lookout are seven beautiful valleys opening into the ocean. The best known of the seven are Pololū, Waimanu, and Waipiʻo. The remaining four—Honokāne Nui (often called simply Honokāne), Honokāne Iki, Honokeʻā, and Honopuʻe—are rarely visited because access is difficult. Both Honokāne Nui and Honokāne Iki are leased and controlled by a North Kohala family, and Honokeʻā and Honopuʻe are accessible only by water. The original *mauka* trails into the latter two valleys are now practically nonexistent and are extremely precipitous and dangerous.

All four valleys at one time supported self-sufficient fishing and farming communities, but by the turn of the twentieth century most of the inhabitants had moved to more urban areas. No longer able—or content—to keep up with the physically demanding subsistence lifestyle, many Hawaiians found work outside the valleys in the larger towns and port cities where the activity and economic opportunities seemed more attractive.

In an article for the Spring 1982 inaugural issue of *Native Planters: Hoʻokupu Kalo*, Thomas Riley observed:

> The valleys of Pololu and Honokane Nui have both undergone intensive study by archaeologists from the University of Hawaiʻi. They discovered that intensive use of these valleys for taro agriculture did not begin until about A.D. 1500. The reason for this late development became clear with excavation in some of the now abandoned systems in these two valleys. At Honokane Nui a number of taro complexes are quickly buried by alluviation from flooding and had to be reconstructed at regular intervals. In Pololu, the flood hazard was great as well, and the taro systems that withstood these natural catastrophes were the ones protected by thick, free standing drystone masonry walls and terrace frontings. The amount of labor that went into the construction of these small complexes was immense, and at the same time the people of these two valleys always suffered the possibility of losing their hard won crops to the winter rains.

The labor demands Riley describes would have severely taxed the physical resources of the few valley residents who chose to remain behind in the absence of a community support group. As the populations decreased, the amount of land under cultivation did, too. The final discouraging blow to those who still practiced the traditional ways of life was not the attraction of Western civilization itself, however, but rather the effects of its exploitation of the Kohala Mountains. In 1906 the Kohala Ditch had been completed, successfully tapping the abundant water supply in the wet mountainous regions to irrigate the sugar cane fields in the distant drier areas. The ditch severely reduced the stream flows in all of the valleys from Pololū to Honopuʻe. Unable to irrigate effectively their taro and other crops, all but a very few of the remaining residents finally abandoned their homes and moved away. By the mid-1930s, only a few individuals and individual families were left in various remote locations. Today no one resides permanently in the region from Pololū to Honopuʻe.

HONOKĀNE NUI
We landed at Honokane, and went through the village to the house of Ihikaina, chief woman of the place, and sister of Arapai, the chief of Waimanu, from which this

district is distant about twenty miles. Ihikaina received us kindly, and for our refreshment provided a duck, some vegetables, and a small quantity of excellent goat's milk, large flocks of which are reared by some of the natives for the supply of ships touching at the islands for refreshments.

The valley contained fifty houses. A number of the people collected round the door of the house, and listened to a short address.

Journal of William Ellis, 1823

Honokāne Nui, once cultivated to a distance of 1½ miles inland by Hawaiians and later by Hawaiians and Chinese, is now completely overgrown with introduced vegetation. The construction of the Kohala Ditch cut off the stream waters, and the once lush valley has become an arid entanglement of guava, grasses, Christmasberry, and ironwoods. The stream bed meets the ocean on the eastern side of the valley mouth.

A long boulder beach, extending all the way to Pololū, fronts the valley. It was over this rocky shoreline that William Ellis and his group walked on their way to Hālawa in 1823. Behind the boulder beach, near the Honokāne Nui stream mouth, a grove of ironwoods stands in a small pocket of black sand, the only semblance of a beach in the area. Much larger deposits of black sand cover the ocean floor directly offshore. The primary shoreline activity is fishing.

HONOKĀNE IKI

From Honokane Nui the trail leads up to the Awini Plateau. A climb over a 500-foot hogsback brings the visitor into Honokane Iki, where Bill Sproat has his home.

Honolulu Star Bulletin, 1936

The small, narrow valley of Honokāne Iki is probably best known to Big Island residents as the home of Bill Sproat, the superintendent of the Kohala Ditch Trail for 40 years. William Kaneakala Sproat was born at Mahiki on February 12, 1903, to a Spanish-Hawaiian mother and a Dutch father. His parents had met and married in Honolulu in 1900 and then moved to the Big Island, where they eventually took up homesteading on the ʻĀwini Plateau *mauka* of Honokāne Iki. During the late

1800s the Hawaiian government had set aside about 1,000 acres of land for homesteaders at ʻĀwini, but had not restricted the parcels to Hawaiians only. Many families had taken advantage of the opportunity, the Sproats among them, and the community started the ʻĀwini Fruit and Coffee Company. Supplies, building materials, and farming equipment were shipped to Honokāne Iki on steamers and then brought into the small bay on lighters. A boom rig at the base of the eastern cliffs assisted the ship-to-shore transfer operations.

After the completion of the Kohala Ditch in 1906 the Kohala Sugar Company bought out the ʻĀwini homesteaders and allowed the natural vegetation to overrun the plateau. The Sproats had a beach house in Honokāne Iki, where the family often visited and spent their summers; so they built a bigger home at the site and moved into it in 1917, two years before Bill's graduation from Kamehameha School.

About 1915 Bill's father assumed the position of superintendent of the Kohala Ditch Trail. His responsibilities included the monumental tasks of maintaining the intakes and flumes and keeping open the nearly 40 miles of mule and foot trails that led to every part of the ditch, however remote. To accomplish this work, crews established a series of line camps along the main mule trail, and the Sproat home in Honokāne Iki became the base of operations.

Bill Sproat took over the superintendent's job from his father in 1928, remaining in the position until his retirement in 1968. He raised his own family in the Honokāne Iki home from 1928 until 1938, when he and his wife decided they should maintain a second home outside the valley for the sake of their children's education. In June of each year when school let out, the family returned to the valley.

When Bill retired in 1968, his son Dale took over as superintendent of the trail. Dale, who had already been working for the Kohala Sugar Company in various capacities for many years, stayed on until his own retirement in 1977, bringing to an end over 60 years of continuous service from three generations of Sproats on the Kohala Ditch Trail. After Dale's retirement, the family's visits to the homestead in Honokāne Iki became less frequent, a situation which unfortunately did not go unnoticed by transients familiar with the area. The Sproat home was looted and vandalized, and today stands empty and in partial disrepair. Because of these problems and others caused by thoughtless and malicious passersby, the Sproats are now very protective of the Honokāne Iki and Honokāne Nui valley lands under their control.

Honokāne Iki, like its neighbor Honokāne Nui, is choked with vegetation through the entire length of the valley. A small clearing in a grove of ironwood, *kamani*, and coconut trees between the Sproat home and the beach is the only open space near the shoreline. Below the clearing a short, black detrital sand beach approximately 350 feet long heads the narrow bay at Honokāne Iki. During the summer months, a shallow sand bar extends seaward from the beach, where the shorebreak is occasionally good enough for bodysurfing. During the winter months, heavy surf funnels into the bay unchecked, creating hazardous water conditions and also partially eroding the sand beach. At the southeastern end of the beach, above the stream bed, a short section of the narrow road that led to the old loading boom can be seen, almost completely covered with vegetation and slide material from the steep valley walls. The small landing provided a drop-off site for materials, originally for the farming community on the ʻĀwini Plateau and later for construction and maintenance crews working on the Kohala Ditch and the Kohala Ditch Trail system.

HONOKEʻĀ

About noon we passed Honokea, a narrow valley which separates the divisions of Hamakua and Kohala, and shortly after reached Honokane, the second village in the latter.

Journal of William Ellis, 1823

Honokeʻā, the centermost of the seven valleys from Pololū to Waipiʻo, marks the eastern, seaward border of the district of Kohala. The lands beyond Honokeʻā, traveling from northwest to southeast, fall in the district of Hāmākua. Very few visitors ever find their way into Honokeʻā because the valley walls are extremely precipitous, and a steep boulder beach lines the water's edge. The 450-foot-long boulder beach faces directly into the prevailing currents. An almost continuous surge of surf makes landing difficult, on even the calmest days. Extensive deposits of black detrital sand cover the ocean floor directly offshore of the beach, but very little of it accumulates on shore.

The former Hawaiian village in Honokeʻā was tucked against the *makai* base of the southeastern valley wall in a now dense grove of coconut and *hala.* Here, the community was protected from the constantly blowing tradewinds, but was still near the shore. The dry stream bed on the opposite side of the vally is unusually wide, occupying nearly one-third of the valley mouth. This was a result of an enormous flash flood that swept down the valley in 1980. The Kohala Ditch has diverted the normal stream flow since 1906, leaving the bed dry except after especially heavy *mauka* rains. Generally, what little water falls at the head of the valley disappears underground long before it reaches sea level.

Three islands lie directly offshore from Honokeʻā: Paʻalaea, Paoakalani, and Mokupuka. Mokupuka ("Hole Island"), often misspelled Mokupuku, was apparently named for the large *puka*, or tunnel that passes through the center of the island. Although the islands themselves are easily visible from both the Pololū and Waipiʻo Lookouts, the hole through Mokupuka can be seen only from Honokeʻā or from a vantage point at sea. Both Mokupuka and Paoakalani provide nesting sites for a variety of seabirds and are part of the Hawaiʻi State Seabird Sanctuary.

In the November 10, 1849, issue of the newspaper *The Polynesian,* an unnamed sailor recorded this incident near the islands offshore Honokeʻā while making a trip by canoe from Waipiʻo to Neue:

In the morning, dividing our company, we embarked with two canoes, got through the surf—a proceeding which nearly filled one of them—and found ourselves afloat again on the bosom of a calm, quiet sea. Our course lay along the shore. We passed several beautiful valleys—high, rich looking cliffs—dark, rugged valleys and had in sight at one time 26 waterfalls pouring their treasures into the sea. Each varied in respect to height of fall and volume of water and course; but beautiful as the eyelids of the morning.

We had scarcely completed half our journey when the

outrigger of one canoe came off, and our companions were in peril. Fortunately, they reached the lee of an island, where they secured it, for a time, and were able to go on.

HONOPUʻE

The valley of Honopue which has flatland in its lower part—about a quarter of a mile wide and three quarters of a mile long—was developed in terraces. Beyond this the terraces continued wherever practicable for about a half a mile up the narrower portion of the valley. Just east of Honopue Valley, on flats below the cliffs, were terraces on land named Makakiloia.

Native Planters in Old Hawaii

Honopuʻe is a beautiful, deep, and symmetrically shaped valley with very high, steep sides. Although the Kohala Ditch has robbed the Honopuʻe stream of its water since 1906, a small trickle continues to reach the ocean. Boulders comprise the entire 900-foot length of beach that fronts the valley mouth. Large shallow deposits of black sand cover the ocean floor directly offshore, but very little of it accumulates onshore. The southeastern valley wall projects beyond the boulder beach as a point of land into the ocean, forming a small bay and giving some protection from the prevailing tradewinds and usual surge. Landings over the boulder beach therefore can be made fairly uneventfully. During the winter and spring months, however, heavy surf inundates the bay. Water conditions are then so hazardous as to preclude all access to the valley from the ocean. Occasionally, the waves that form at the southeastern point of the bay are good enough for surfing. Surfers have also located rideable winter surf outside Laupāhoehoe Nui, a large flat between Honopuʻe and Waimanu that was once inhabited and terraced for agriculture.

The Hawaiian village in Honopuʻe was located directly behind the boulder beach. Like all the other valleys whose stream waters were captured by the Kohala Ditch, Honopuʻe was almost completely deserted soon after the turn of the twentieth century. A Hawaiian man who lived on the bluff above the southeastern point of the bay was probably the last permanent resident of Honopuʻe. However, even he, along with a few other people who still lived scattered along the coast, finally

moved away after the tsunami of April 1, 1946, totally devastated the shoreline from Pololū to Waipiʻo.

(86)
Waimanu

The Waimanu Valley lay 2500 feet (it is said) below us, and the trail struck off into space. In a second the eye took in the twenty grass lodges of its inhabitants, the five cascades which dive into the dense forests of its upper end, its river like a silver ribbon, and its meadows of living green.

Six Months in the Sandwich Islands
Isabella Bird

The lovely valley of Waimanu described by Isabella Bird has changed little since her visit during the late 1800s, although it is now uninhabited and uncultivated. In *Native Planters in Old Hawaii*, Handy, Handy, and Pukui record that in pre-contact times Waimanu was second only to Waipiʻo as a wetland-taro producing valley and that the entire flatland of the main valley floor was completely covered with taro patches. By the turn of the twentieth century, most of the valley had been abandoned, although a handful of Hawaiians and Chinese still maintained homes near the shoreline from which they tended their rice and taro fields. The harvested produce was carried out of the valley over the steep and difficult trail by mule train. Some of the residents also raised pigs, breeding their domestic stock with the wild varieties from the mountains. The progeny of the cross breeding, the "hapas," still roam the backlands of Waimanu and are said to be among the biggest wild pigs in the Hawaiian Islands. In addition to producing pork, rice, and taro, the valley residents supplemented their diet and their income by fishing for the once abundant *moi, ʻoʻio,* and *ulua.*

The tsunami of April 1, 1946, destroyed all of the remaining homes and all the fields under cultivation and marked the end of permanent habitation in the valley. Today, the lower half of the valley floor is a vast marsh in which grow mostly California grass and bulrushes. A guava forest covers most of the upper valley. A seasonally shifting beach of black sand fronts a portion of the seaward edge of the marsh. Sand accumulates to the west, making it larger, during the summer months, then erodes and drifts toward the east during the winter months. Boulders cover the rest of the shoreline, particularly around the river mouth. A shallow sand bar fronts the black sand beach, often providing excellent waves for bodysurfing and surfing. During the winter months, high surf makes swimming extremely hazardous, with rip currents and undertows, but these same waves are fine for experienced surfers.

Waimanu Valley is a popular destination for backcountry hikers, particularly during the drier summer months which the ocean is comparatively calm. Reaching Waimanu involves back-packing along the famous 11-mile Z Trail, which zigzags 1,100 vertical feet out of Waipiʻo Valley, passes through nine small valleys, and then drops 1,100 feet to the beach. In a traditional chant, "He Huakaʻi Kaʻapuni ma Hawaiʻi," a Hawaiian hiker offered the following description:

> ʻO Hāmākua:
> ʻO Hāmākua ia o ka pali Koʻolau
> Ke kuʻukuʻu la i ke kaula
> Ke ʻaki la ka niho i ka ipu
> I ka pali ʻo Kohalalele
> ʻO Waipiʻo, ʻo Waimanu e.

> Hamakua:
> It is Hamakua at the windward side,
> Lowering the rope
> He grips the calabash [net] with his teeth
> At the cliff of Kohalalele,
> Waipiʻo, and Waimanu.

Campsites abound in the backshore area among the *naupaka* and *pōhuehue*. Because of the danger of leptospirosis contamination of the stream waters, drinking water should be obtained only from spring-fed sources, such as the small falls *mauka* of the northwestern end of the beach. Leptospirosis is a disease caused by a virus that is transmitted when the urine of infected wild animals is passed into moist soil, vegetation, or water. The symptoms include fever, headache, chills, vomiting, muscular aches, and other complaints. The wild pigs and rats in Waimanu are considered to be potential carriers of the virus, and so campers are advised against swimming in the rivers or drinking the stream waters without first boiling or purifying it with tablets. Campers hiking into the *mauka* regions of Waimanu should also be cautious of the very large and sometimes aggressive pigs that tend to congregate at the upstream end of the marsh.

In 1980 Waimanu Valley was designated by the State of Hawaiʻi as an estuarine sanctuary to be preserved as a wilderness and as an example of an Hawaiian stream ecosystem.

(87)

Waipiʻo

> *Kaulana kuʻu home puni Waipiʻo*
> *Me na peʻa nani o ka ʻāina.*
> *Kakela he hale aliʻi*
>
> *E ola māua me aʻu kini*
> *Me aʻu lei e nei ʻāina*
> *Pulupē i ka hunakai*
> *Ka iʻa mili i ka lima*
> *Heha Waipiʻo i ka noe.*

> Famous is my home, beloved Waipiʻo,
> And the beautiful fringes of the land.
> My house is a castle, a royal residence
>
> He and I, my relatives,
> And my children stay in this land
> Drenched with sea spray
> Where fish are caught in the hands.
> Waipiʻo is drowsy in the mist.

"Waipiʻo"
Traditional song

Waipiʻo Valley is one of the most famous and beloved places in the Hawaiian Islands. Its natural beauty, its historical importance, its place in Hawaiian tradition, and its mythological associations, all have rendered it a source of inspiration for writers, poets, and songwriters, in whose works the name Waipiʻo has been extolled and perpetuated. One of the earliest descriptions of the valley while it was still occupied by a thriving fishing and farming community was recorded in 1823 by William Ellis:

> Viewed from the great elevation at which we stood, the charming valley, spread out beneath us like a map, with

153

its numerous inhabitants, cottages, plantations, fish-ponds, and meandering streams (on the surface of which the light canoe was moving to and fro), appeared in beautiful miniature.

The next morning unveiled to view the extent and beauty of the romantic valley. Its entrance from the sea, which was blocked up with sand hills, fifty or sixty feet high, appeared to be a mile or a mile and half wide.

The bottom of the valley was one continued garden, cultivated with taro, bananas, sugar-cane, and other productions of the islands, all growing luxuriantly. Several large ponds were also seen in different directions, well stocked with excellent fish.

A number of small villages, containing from twenty to fifty houses each, stood along the foot of the mountains, at unequal distances on each side, and extended up the valley till the projecting cliffs obstructed the view.

From this eloquent description of Waipi'o's beauty and productivity it is easy to understand why the valley was well populated and a favored home of some of the Big Island's important chiefs. In *Native Planters of Old Hawaii*, Handy, Handy, and Pukui describe Waipi'o as the greatest wetland taro valley on the island of Hawai'i and one of the largest planting areas of the entire island chain. An area of the vast valley floor 3 miles long and one mile wide was cultivated and productive.

Today, only a few people live permanently in Waipi'o, and only a small fraction of the land is still cultivated, primarily by taro farmers who commute from their homes outside the valley. During the twentieth century, out-migration, transportation problems, severe flooding, and inundations from tsunami all have played a part in severely reducing the once intense production of taro. Dense growth of guava and other introduced vegetation have now overrun much of the valley floor, although from the Waipi'o Valley Lookout many of the formerly productive walled terraces are still visible.

During the 1960s, the Peace Corps maintained a training station in Waipi'o to prepare volunteers for primitive conditions they could expect to encounter in tropical, undeveloped countries in Latin America, Africa, and Southeast Asia.

The extensive expanse of high sand dunes described by Ellis, Isabella Bird, and other nineteenth-century travelers, has been considerably reduced in height and

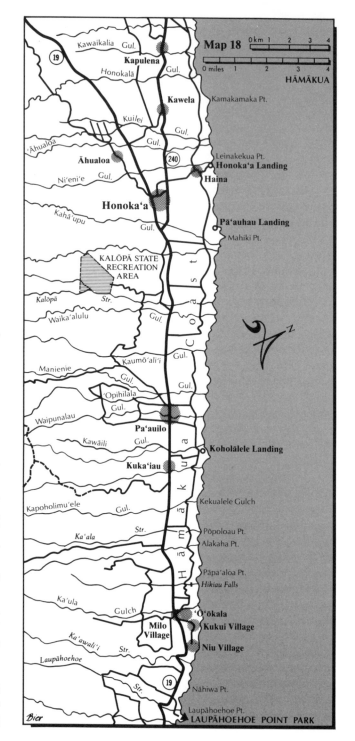

154

volume during the twentieth century by the erosive forces of the ocean. In particular, the tsunami of 1946 scoured the shoreline and redeposited much of the sand in nearshore sand reservoirs on the ocean bottom.

A black sand beach lines almost the entire extent of the valley mouth. During the summer months the sand tends to accumulate to the northwest, whereas during the winter months, it is carried by wave action to the southeast. A long, broad sand bar fronts the beach, generating an almost continuous, moderately-sized shorebreak. Often the waves are good enough for surfing and bodysurfing, but are rarely taken advantage of because access to the beach is difficult. The constantly breaking waves also generate many rip currents, a potential hazard for water enthusiasts unfamiliar with the area. Most Big Island residents consider the remote beach at Waipiʻo a very dangerous one. During the winter months, frequent high surf causes extremely treacherous conditions, but at the same time brings some good waves for experienced surfers.

The only road into Waipiʻo, and therefore to the beach, begins at the Waipiʻo Valley Lookout. Although paved, it is long, narrow, and extremely steep, hugging the cliff as it descends to the valley floor. Only vehicles with four-wheel drive are allowed over it, and downhill traffic must yield to uphill traffic. A commercial shuttle service based at the top of the access road offers rides and tours into the valley for visitors. No public facilities exist at the beach.

Water Safety

Dangerous Water Conditions

Most of the Big Island's beaches are not well protected by coral reefs, points of land, or other barriers. For this reason strong currents and other potentially hazardous water conditions occur in many nearshore locations. Visitors not familiar with the ocean should be aware of such hazards as dangerous shorebreak waves and fast-flowing rip currents that are not encountered in lakes and streams or at other protected ocean sites.

Although a few of the popular county beach parks are served by lifeguards, most of the island's beaches are not. If you if get into trouble in the ocean, help will be a long time coming unless someone happens to be nearby who is capable of assisting you. You must be prepared to be your own lifeguard and rescue service. If you are unfamiliar with a beach you'd like to visit, learn as much as you can about it by reading available literature and/or by consulting a lifeguard, a beach attendant, or a local resident who knows the area.

All beach users, especially those unfamiliar with island waters, should be able to recognize and avoid dangerous water conditions. The following are some of the potential water hazards any beachgoer may encounter.

Shorebreaks

Shorebreaks are beach sites where waves break close to or directly on shore. Shorebreak waves from 1 to 3 feet generally pose little threat to adults and usually provide good surfing for novice bodysurfers and bodyboarders. Shorebreak waves of 4 feet or higher, however, present some major hazards. These larger waves break with considerable downward force and often slam inexperienced swimmers onto the ocean bottom. Swimmers may suffer loss of breath, or disorientation, or various minor to serious injuries. Any person temporarily incapacitated in the surf may come close to drowning. It is at shorebreak sites during periods of high surf that most of the near-drownings, drownings, ocean rescues, and ocean-related injuries occur every year on the Big Island. Swimmers, bodysurfers, and bodyboarders should approach with a great deal of caution such popular sites as Hapuna Beach, Kauna'oa Beach, and White Sands Beach during periods of high surf.

Although shorebreak waves from 1 to 3 feet are generally safe for teenagers and adults, they may be dangerous to young children. As a general rule, any wave that is waist high or higher on any individual, either a child or an adult, should be considered dangerous.

Rip Currents

Rip currents are narrow, fast-flowing currents of water that travel from shallow, nearshore areas out to sea. These riverlike movements of water are called rip currents because they can quickly tow or "rip" an unsuspecting swimmer away from the beach. Rip currents are generated chiefly by surf and are commonly found anywhere that waves are breaking. Incoming sets of waves transport large volumes of water into nearshore areas. As this water builds up, it begins to flow along the shore in an effort to level itself. When the moving water finds a suitable place to escape, it rushes seaward into the open ocean. The rushing water, moving at a much faster speed than the water surrounding it, constitutes a rip current.

Rip currents are short-lived and die out usually within 50 to 100 yards of the beach. Anyone caught in a rip current should simple ride along with it until it loses its power, or swim slowly out of it to either side as the current begins to dissipate. Swimmers should never attempt to swim against the rip to their original point of departure from the beach. The effort may soon tire them to the point of exhaustion—a real danger to life. Rip currents are a leading cause of many of the drownings and near-drownings that occur annually on Hawaiian beaches.

Rip currents can be recognized from the beach by watching their effect on incoming waves. Strong rips flowing through the surf zone tend to override and flatten incoming surf. At sandy beaches, rip currents carry sand and other beach matter seaward, and can be recognized as small discolored rivers of foam and debris. The location of rip currents in a given area, however, is not constant and often shifts with changes in the intensity and size of the surf. Rip currents also develop frequently where rivers flow into the ocean, as on the Big Island's Hilo, Hāmākua, and Kohala coastlines.

Undertows

To most swimmers the terms undertow and rip current are synonymous and are used interchangeably. The undertow phenomenon, however, occurs only when a strong rip current travels directly into large, incoming surf. In this situation, the rip current continues to flow beneath the surface water. A swimmer caught in the rip and then dragged into the turmoil of a set of waves will feel that he is being pulled underwater. Undertows are common also at the edge of steeply sloped beaches. Here, backwash from a wave can pick up considerable speed at it flows back into the ocean, like a small, localized rip current. A swimmer caught in the backwash will feel that he is being pulled underwater if the backwash meets a large breaking wave at the water's edge.

For a struggling swimmer, an undertow complicates his other problems, and he usually becomes panic stricken. The best way to handle the situation is to go with the rip current and remain as much as possible above water while still in the surf zone. Once a swimmer is beyond the waves, he can relax and regain his strength for the swim back to shore.

Tsunami or "Tidal Waves"

Tsunami, or seismic sea waves, are frequently called tidal waves because, as they move up a river or over the land, they resemble the bore tidal floods that occur daily in the mouth of the Amazon River, the Bay of Fundy, and other such funnel-like configurations. Tsunami, though, have nothing to do with tides. They are set in motion by great disturbances of the earth, such as earthquakes, volcanic eruptions, landslides, and other similar occurrences. Most tsunami that strike the Hawaiian Islands are generated in the oceanic trenches around the borders of the Pacific Ocean. The most unstable of these areas are along the Pacific coast of Japan, the Kurile-Kamchatka chain, the Aleutian Island arc, and the Pacific coasts of Central and South America.

Tsunami have been more destructive on the Big Island than on any other island in the Hawaiian chain. Major portions of the city of Hilo have been totally destroyed twice in the twentieth century, once in 1946 and then again in 1961. Visitors to the Big Island should understand that these catastrophic waves, set in motion by distant events, do occur, but because there are now world-wide warning systems, they are usually heralded by the sounding of civil defense sirens.

Local tsunami, however, may be generated by local earthquakes. Any violent earthquake, one that causes you to fall to the ground, should be considered a natural tsunami warning. If you are in a low-lying area, move immediately to higher ground. In 1975 two campers at Halapē were killed by a locally-generated tsunami before they had a chance to escape. That tsunami followed immediately an extremely violent volcanic earthquake centered only a few miles away.

Dangerous Marine Animals

The tropical waters of the Hawaiian Islands abound with fish and other marine life to the delight of beachcombers, tidepoolers, snorkelers, skin divers, and scuba divers. Some marine animals, however, have pincers, teeth, or poisonous stingers, and others are protected by built-in defenses such as spines, thorns, or bristles.

While none of Hawaii's marine animals are normally aggressive toward people, chance encounters with them may lead to injury. The following are some of the animals potentially dangerous to anyone in the marine environment.

Cone Shells

As their name implies, these are conically shaped shells, usually with brown or black patterns on the shell. The snails that inhabit them have a poisonous "dart" which is used to inject venom to paralyze or kill their prey. To be on the safe side, it is best simply not to handle any live cone shell.

In case of a wound, soak and clean the puncture in hot, but not scalding, water for 15 to 90 minutes. The hot water will increase the flow of blood and move the venom away from the wound. Reducing the venom concentration will reduce the pain. Then consult a physician. In the event of any unusual symptoms, indicating allergic reaction, take the victim immediately to the nearest emergency medical facility.

Corals

Coral reefs and rocks, common in most Hawaiian waters, account for many of the abrasions and lacerations suffered by swimmers, divers, and surfers. Some of the common stony corals have sharp, crumbling edges that are covered with slime. Cuts from such corals are unusually susceptible to infection and often slow to heal. Contrary to popular belief, there is no evidence that coral lodged in a cut will grow, but it must be removed because of the high risk of infection.

Coral cuts should be cleaned thoroughly with soap and water and hydrogen peroxide to remove all foreign material. Apply antiseptic as soon as possible. Check frequently for infection and consult a physician if necessary.

Portuguese Man-o'-War

The Portuguese man-o'-war is a floating marine jellyfish that resembles a translucent, crested, blue bubble, usually 1–4 inches long. The man-o'-war propelled by wind and currents, has retractable thread-thin tentacles that are trailed underwater to snare its food. Each tentacle, usually several feet long, contains thousands of minute poison-filled stinging cells that paralyze tiny fish and other prey it encounters. The tentacles need only to brush against a swimmer's skin to cause a burning pain; if they remain in contact with any part of the body, such as the neck or an arm or leg, they usually deliver severe, extremely painful, stings. Because the stinging tentacles retain their toxin for many hours after the organism itself is dead, even a dried up man-o'-war on the beach should be handled carefully.

The most effective way to remove man-o'-war tentacles that stick to a victim's skin is to rub them off gently with a soft cloth soaked with undiluted vinegar—except, of course, for sensitive areas such as the eyes. Vinegar retards the further discharge of venom by the stinging cells. Then the affected area should be sprinkled with unseasoned meat tenderizer, a substance that helps neutralize the venom. Some island residents simply make a paste of the vinegar and unseasoned meat tenderizer and keep a jar of the mixture in the car for first-aid use.

The traditional island method of removing the tentacles is to rub them gently with wet sand while immersing the affected area in the ocean. The sand quickly breaks up the tentacles and prevents the helping hand from being stung. Most physicians do not advocate this method because rubbing the tentacles with sand seems to stimulate them to discharge more toxin. Also, because sand is abrasive, excessive scrubbing of the skin in an effort to reduce the stinging may cause increased inflammation. However, if the wet sand method is done properly—that is, gently in the water—it provides immediate first aid and may be preferable to leaving the tentacles on the skin when vinegar and unseasoned meat tenderizer are unavailable.

Man-o'-war stings, like those of certain insects, can cause acute reactions in people who are allergic to venom; so if any unusual symptoms are observed, take the victim immediately to the nearest emergency medical center.

Eels

Eels are snakelike fish found in reefs and among underwater rocks. They live in crevices and under coral heads, where they feed on fish, crabs, and other similar forms of marine life. Eels have powerful jaws and many sharp teeth that can inflict serious wounds or even amputate fingers. Tidepool enthusiasts and divers should never reach into holes or cracks where these animals may be living. Fingers may be mistaken for food.

Eels are not usually aggressive unless they are confronted or threatened. They may be observed without fear—but leave them alone. Eel bites may become infected from the bacteria on the animal's teeth or in the surrounding sea water. In case of a severe wound, apply direct pressure to stop the bleeding, and take the victim to the nearest emergency medical center.

Sharks

Sharks are common in Hawaiian waters but usually do not pose a threat to swimmers. Sharks living around the islands are well fed by the natural abundance of reef and pelagic fish and do not need to hunt for other kinds of food, as is the case in other parts of the world.

Sharks are generally found in the open ocean and only rarely come into shallow, nearshore waters. However, they frequent bays and harbors such as Hilo Bay and are sometimes observed close to shore in certain areas, such as Pelekane Beach in South Kohala. They also commonly appear around river and stream mouths after periods of heavy rains. Flooding in the *mauka* regions washes fish and crustaceans that inhabit the rivers and streams into the ocean, and sharks and other predators, such as *ulua*, often patrol the flood waters to feed on this abundance. Danger to swimmers and surfers from shark attack at these times is compounded by extremely poor underwater visibility caused by increased soil runoff.

If you should meet a shark face-to-face, do not panic. Try to keep the shark in view at all times and swim smoothly and steadily to safety. Do not make any erratic or thrashing motions that might be interpreted as signs of panic. In case of a severe wound, apply direct pressure to stop the bleeding, and get quickly to the nearest emergency medical center.

Spiny Sea Urchins

Spiny sea urchins, also commonly known by their Hawaiian name, *wana*, are found in all Hawaiian waters. They are covered with sharp, brittle, needle-like spines that protect the animals from predators. Even the slightest contact with the spines often cause them to break off and embed themselves in the skin. Extensive puncturing from the spines will cause an immediate, intense, throbbing pain and swelling that may last for several hours. Immediate relief for pain may be obtained by soaking the affected area in hot water. Watch the victim carefully for signs of shock.

The slender, brittle spines are not easily removed, even with a needle. Most will dissolve and disappear, however, if left alone for one to two weeks, but longer, thicker spines may have to be removed surgically by a physician. Keep the puncture wounds clean and watch for infection, especially while the spine tips are still embedded in the skin.

Ocean Recreation Activities

Swimming

Swimming is the most popular water activity in the Hawaiian Islands. Good swimming opportunities exist at almost any shoreline site that offers protection from the prevailing currents and winds. Most people prefer to swim at sandy beaches where sunbathing is most comfortable and where it is easy to walk in and out of the water with bare feet. Although many people believe the Big Island's shoreline is made up almost entirely of sea cliffs and rocky coasts, many sand beaches exist that are excellent for swimming during calm seas.

Snorkeling and Nearshore Scuba Diving

The nearshore waters that surround the Big Island, particularly in the districts of Kona and Kohala, offer a wide variety of marine life and spectacular underwater terrain. The Kona area, especially in the wind-shadow of the Big Island's great volcanoes, is protected from the prevailing winds. Here the water is calm and clear, with excellent underwater visibility throughout the year. Some of the world's most exciting snorkeling and scuba diving sites are found in Kona. In addition, island waters are warm the year 'round, and most scuba divers are comfortable with only a wetsuit jacket.

Novice snorkelers and scuba divers can arrange for lessons and equipment rentals through beach concessions, tour desks, and dive shops. Although some of the best diving sites can be reached only by boat, just as many are easily accessible from shore. The Big Island's most popular snorkeling and nearshore scuba diving sites are noted in the chart on page 2.

Surfing

Most of the surfing sites on the Big Island are appropriate for surfers of intermediate, advanced, or expert caliber, but there are a few breaks suitable for novice surfers. Surfers unfamiliar with the Big Island should first inquire at a beach service desk or a local surf shop for information on suitable sites, instruction, and equipment. All of the major surfing sites on the island can be easily located by consulting the chart on page 2.

Bodysurfing and Bodyboarding

Bodysurfing and bodyboarding are very similar wave-riding sports and often practiced at the same location. A bodysurfer uses only his body to ride and manuever on the wave. In bodyboarding the rider lies prone on a small, foam bodyboard that supports his entire upper body weight. For both sports a pair of swimming fins gives added propulsion in the water.

Bodysurfing and bodyboarding are very popular because good rides can be obtained in almost any size of surf, and only a minimum of inexpensive, easily portable equipment is needed. Fins and bodyboards may be rented at beach concessions or purchased at many retail shops and department stores. All of the major bodysurfing and bodyboarding sites on the island can be easily located by consulting the chart on page 2.

Windsurfing

Windsurfing, the sport of riding a surfboard powered by a sail, was developed in Southern California in the late 1960s and has became an internationally popular form of water recreation. The sport was first introduced to the Hawaiian Islands in 1970, but did not really catch on here until 1972. Since 1972 windsurfing has become tremendously popular in Hawaii and is firmly established on all of the major islands.

The Hawaiian Islands are considered one of the best windsurfing sites in the world. The always-warm waters, the ever-present trade winds, and the fine Hawaiian surf bring enthusiasts from all over to try Hawai'i's exciting and challenging open ocean conditions. On the Big Island, 'Anaeho'omalu is one of the beaches most frequented by the windsurfing community. The beach has favorable wind conditions, good public facilities, and easy access to the shoreline. The major windsurfing sites on the island can be easily located by consulting the chart on page 2.

References

AECOS, Inc. "Field Reconnaissance of the Ruddle Property and Adjacent Marine Areas South of Puako, Hawai'i." AECOS, Inc., Kaneohe, October 17, 1980.

Ahuimanu Productions. An Ornithological Survey of Hawaiian Wetlands. Vol. Two. Honolulu: Ahuimanu Productions, 1977.

Allen, Gwenfread. *Hawaii's War Years*. Honolulu: University of Hawaii Press, 1950.

Apple, Russell. "Report on the Hawaiian Wall Job and Archaeological Matters in the Vicinity of Kaunaoa Beach, Hawaii." Report for Haas and Haynie, Inc. Honolulu 1964.

———. *Trails*. Bishop Museum Special Publication 53. Honolulu, 1965.

Apple, Russ, and Apple, Peg. Tales of Old Hawaii, in *Honolulu Star-Bulletin:* "Kamehameha's First Victory," A-9, March 15, 1969; "Place of Refuge at Honaunau," A-23, December 3, 1982.

———. *Tales of Old Hawaii*. Norfolk Island, Australia: Island Heritage Press, 1977.

Ayres, William S. "Preliminary Report on the Archaeological Survey of Coastal Areas of Honuapo, Hionaa, and Hokukano, Ka'u, Hawaii." Department of Anthropology, MS Report 060170, Bishop Museum, Honolulu, June 1970.

Barrera, William, Jr. "Archaeological Excavations and Survey at Keauhou, North Kona, Hawaii." Department of Anthropology Report 71-10, Bishop Museum, Honolulu, October 1971.

Barrera, William, and Hommon, Robert. "Salvage Archaeology at Wailau, Ka'u, Island of Hawaii." Department of Anthropology Report 72-1, Bishop Museum, Honolulu, February 1972.

Barrère, Dorothy. *Kamehameha in Kona: Two Documentary Studies*. Pacific Anthropology Records, no. 23, Bishop Museum, Honolulu, 1975.

Beckwith, Martha. *Hawaiian Mythology*. Honolulu: University of Hawaii Press, 1970.

Best, Gerald. *Railroads of Hawaii*. San Marino, Ca.: Golden West Books, 1978.

Bevacqua, Robert. "Archaeological Survey of Portions of Waikoloa, South Kohala District, Island of Hawaii." Department of Anthropology Report 72-4, Bishop Museum, Honolulu, July 1972.

Bevacqua, Robert, and Dye, Thomas S. "Archaeological Reconnaissance of Proposed Kapoho-Kalapana Highway, District of Puna, Island of Hawaii." Department of Anthropology Report 72-3, Bishop Museum, Honolulu, June 1972.

Bird, Isabella. *Six Months in the Sandwich Islands*. Honolulu: University of Hawaii Press, 1966.

Bowman, Pierre. "Sunday Afternoon in a Hilo Bar and a Talk with a Legend." *Honolulu Star-Bulletin,* B-1, September 13, 1973.

Brennan, Joseph. *The Parker Ranch of Hawaii*. New York: Harper and Row, 1979.

Bushnell, O.A. *The Return of Lono*. Boston: Little, Brown, 1956. Reprint. Honolulu: University of Hawaii Press, 1971.

Ching, Francis; Stauder, Catherine; and Palama, Stephen. "The Archaeology of Puna, Hawaii." *Hawaiian Archaeological Journal* 74-2. Lawai, Kauai, July 1974.

Cluff, Deborah. "An Archaeological Survey of the Seaward Portion of Honokohau #1 and #2, North Kona, Hawaii Island." Department of Anthropology Report 69-5, Bishop Museum, Honolulu, 1971.

Conde, Jesse, and Best, Gerald. *Sugar Trains.* Felton, Ca.: Big Trees Press and Pacific Bookbinding, Glenwood Publishers, 1973.

Cooke, Mary. "Iolani at Napoopoo." *Honolulu Advertiser,* C-1, May 23, 1971.

Crozier, S. Neal. "Archaeological Survey of Kam III Road, North Kona, Island of Hawaii." Department of Anthropology Report 71-11, Bishop Museum, Honolulu, July 1971.

Davies, Theophilus H. *Personal Recollections of Hawaii.* Honolulu, 1885.

Doyle, Emma Lyons. *Makua Laiana: The Story of Lorenzo Lyons.* Honolulu: Privately printed, 1945.

Edwards, Sally, and Curl, Jim. *How to Organize a Triathlon.* Sacramento, Ca.: Fleet Feet Press, 1983.

Elbert, Samuel. *Selections from Fornander's Hawaiian Antiquities and Folk-lore.* Honolulu: University of Hawaii Press, 1959.

Elbert, Samuel, and Mahoe, Noelani. *Nā Mele o Hawai'i Nei.* Honolulu: University of Hawaii Press, 1970.

Ellis, William. *Journal of William Ellis.* Advertiser Publishing Co. Honolulu, 1963.

Emerson, Nathaniel. *Pele and Hiiaka, a Myth of Hawaii.* Honolulu: Honolulu Star-Bulletin, 1915.

_____. *Unwritten Literature of Hawaii.* Rutland, Vt: Charles E. Tuttle Co., 1965.

Emory, Kenneth, and Soehren, Lloyd. "Archaeological and Historical Survey, Honokohau Area, North Kona, Hawaii." Department of Anthropology Report 61-1, Bishop Museum, Honolulu, 1971.

Frear, Walter F. *Mark Twain and Hawaii.* Chicago, 1947. Reprint. Golden, Co.: Outbooks, 1981.

Gutmanis, June; Monden, Susan; and Kelsey, Theodore. *Kahuna La'au Lapa'au.* Honolulu: Island Heritage Press, 1979.

Handy, E. S. Craighill; Handy, Elizabeth G.; and Pukui, Mary Kawena. *Native Planters in Old Hawaii.* Bishop Museum Bulletin 233. Honolulu, 1972.

Handy, E. S. Craighill, et al. *Ancient Hawaiian Civilization.* Rutland, Vt.: Charles E. Tuttle, 1965.

Hansen, Violet, and Kelly, Marion. "Cultural and Historical Survey of Kaalualu, District of Ka'u, Island of Hawaii." Department of Anthropology, MS Report 082972, Bishop Museum, Honolulu , September 1972.

Hapai, Charlotte. *Hilo Legends.* Hilo: Petroglyph Press, 1966.

Haraguchi, Paul. *Weather in Hawaiian Waters.* Honolulu: Hawaii Reprographics, 1979.

Hawaii County. "Inventory of Public Shoreline Access." Report prepared for County of Hawaii Planning Department, Hilo, September 1979.

Hawaii Redevelopment Agency. "Project Kaikoo." Final Report, Hilo, 1971.

Hawaii State, Department of Land and Natural Resources. "North Kohala: Preservation Master Plan for Historical Resources." Honolulu, DLNP, 1972.

Hawaii State, Department of Land and Natural Resource and Department of Planning and Economic Department. "Na Ala Hele." Honolulu, DLNP and DPED, 1973.

Hawaii State Statuary Hall Commission. "The King Kamehameha I and Father Damien Memorial Statues." Senate Document No. 91-54, Washington, D.C., 1970.

Hawaiian Mission Children's Society. *Missionary Album.* Sesquicentennial Edition. Honolulu: HMCS, 1969.

Hill, S.S. *Travels in the Sandwich and Society Islands.* London: Chapman and Hall, 1856.

Hobbs, Jean. *Hawaii, a Pageant of the Soil.* Palo Alto: Stanford University Press, 1935.

Holmes, Tommy. *The Hawaiian Canoe.* Hanalei, Kauai: Editions Limited, 1981.

Hosaka, Edward. *Sport Fishing in Hawaii.* Honolulu: Watkins Printing, 1944.

Hungerford, John. *Hawaiian Railroads.* Reseda, Ca.: Hungerford Press, 1963.

Judd, Walter F. *Palaces and Forts of the Hawaiian Kingdom.* Palo Alto: Pacific Book, 1975.

Kaaiakamanu, D.M. *Hawaiian Herbs of Medicinal Value.* Rutland, Vt.: Charles E. Tuttle, 1972.

Kahele, Mona K. "Recollection of Some of the Events of Kapu'a." Unpublished manuscript in private collection, n.d.

Kalakaua, David. *The Legends and Myths of Hawaii.* Rutland, Vt.: Charles E. Tuttle, 1972.

Kamakau, Samuel. *Ruling Chiefs of Hawaii.* Honolulu: Kamehameha Schools Press, 1961.

Kamehameha Investment Co. "Keauhou-Kona, Sites in History." Honolulu: Kamehameha Investment Co., n.d.

Kelly, John, Jr. *Folk Songs Hawaii Sings.* Rutland, Vt.: Charles E. Tuttle, 1962.

Kelly, Marion. "Kekaha: 'Āina Malo'o." Department of Anthropology Report 71-2, Bishop Museum, Honolulu, March 1971.

_____. "Majestic Ka'u: Mo'olelo of Nine Ahupua'a." Department of Anthropology Report 80-2, Bishop Museum, Honolulu, May 1980.

Kelly, Marion; Nakamura, Barry; and Barrère, Dorothy. "Hilo Bay: A Chronological History." Report prepared for the U.S. Army Engineer District, Honolulu, March 1981.

Kelsey, Theodore. "Ocean Fish-farming in Ancient Hawaii." Unpublished manuscript, Kelsey Collection, Hawaii State Archives, n.d.

Kennedy, Joseph. "Native Planters, Ho'okupu Kalo." *Native Planters,* 1(1), no. 1 (spring 1982). Honolulu.

Kimura, Larry. "Old Time Parker Ranch Cowboys." *Hawaii Historical Review,* October 1964.

Kinney, Henry W. *The Island of Hawaii.* Hilo, Hawaii: Hilo Board of Trade, 1913.

Kirch, Patrick. *Marine Explorations in Prehistoric Hawaii: Archaeological Inventory at Kalahuipuaa, Hawaii Island.* Pacific Anthropology Record, no. 29, Bishop Museum, Honolulu, 1979.

Krauss, Beatrice. "Ethnobotany of Hawaii." Department of Botany, University of Hawaii—Manoa, Honolulu, n.d. Manuscript.

Krauss, Bob. *Travel Guide to the Hawaiian Islands.* New York: Van Rees Press, 1963.

Kuykendall, Ralph. *The Hawaiian Kingdom.* Vol 1. *1778– 1854.* Honolulu: University of Hawaii Press, 1957.

Macy, William, and Hussey, Roland. *The Nantucket Scrap Bucket.* Boston: The Inquirer and Mirror Press, 1916.

Maguire, Eliza D. *Kona Legends.* Hilo, Hawaii: Petroglyph Press, 1966.

Makemson, Maud. "The Legend of Kokoiki and the Birthday of Kamehameha I." Annual Report of the Hawaiian Historical Society, Honolulu, 1935.

Macdonald, Gordon, and Abbott, Agatin. *Volcanoes in the Sea.* Honolulu: University of Hawaii Press, 1970.

McBryde, L.R. *Petroglyphs of Hawaii.* Hilo, Hawaii: The Petroglyph Press, 1969.

McClellan, Edwin. "The Inter-Island Merchantship Navy." *Paradise of the Pacific,* August 1939.

McEldowney, Holly. "Archaeological Reconnaissance Survey of Bernice Pauahi Bishop Estate Land at Ke'ei Beach, South Kona, Hawaii Island." Department of Anthropology, MS Report 120679, Bishop Museum, Honolulu, December 1979.

McGaw, Sister Martha M., C.S.J. *Stevenson in Hawaii.* Honolulu: University of Hawaii Press, 1950.

McPherson, Michael. "Malama." *Hawaii Review,* no. 14, 1981.

_____. *Singing With the Owls.* Honolulu: Petronium Press, 1982.

Menzies, Archibald. *Hawaii Nei 128 Years Ago.* Honolulu, 1920.

Mitchell, Donald D. Kilolani. *Hawaiian Games for Today.* Honolulu: Kamehameha Schools Press, 1975.

_____. *Resource Units in Hawaiian Culture.* Honolulu: Kamehameha Schools Press, 1982.

Morrison, Boone. *Journal of a Pioneer Builder.* Kilauea, Hawaii: Hawaii Natural History Association, 1977.

ORCA, Ltd./D. P. Cheney. *West Hawaii Coral Reef Atlas.* Honolulu: U.S. Army Corps of Engineers, 1981.

_____. *West Hawaii Coral Reef Inventory.* Honolulu: U.S. Army Corps of Engineers, 1981.

Paris, John D. "Fragments of Real Missionary Life." *The Friend* (Honolulu), 1926.

Powell, J. W. Fourth Annual Report of the U.S. Geological Survey of the Secretary of the Interior, 1882–1883. Washington, D.C., 1884.

Preston, C. *Captain James Cook, R.N., F.R.S., and Whitby.* Whitby, England: Whitby Literary and Philosophical Society, 1965.

Propellor Club of the United States, Port of Honolulu. *Ports of Hawaii.* Honolulu: Red Dot Publishing Co., 1967.

Pukui, Mary Kawena. "Games of My Childhood." *California Folklore Quarterly* 2 (3), July 1943.

Pukui, Mary Kawena; Elbert, Samuel H.; and Mookini, Esther T. *Place Names of Hawaii.* Honolulu: University of Hawaii Press, 1974.

Pukui, Mary Kawena, and Korn, Alfons. *The Echo of Our Song.* Honolulu: University of Hawaii Press, 1973.

Readers Digest. *Guide to the Australian Coast.* NSW, Australia: Readers Digest Services Pty. Ltd., 1983.

Renger, Robert C. "Archaeological Reconnaissance of Coastal Kaloko and Kukio I, North Kona, Hawaii." Department of Anthropology, Bishop Museum, Honolulu, November 1970.

Resource Planning Inc. "Fisheries Accessment for First Spring Season Environmental Studies, Hilo Bay, Hawaii." Honolulu, 1977.

Science Management, Inc. "Mauna Lani Resort: An Interpretive and Management Plan for its Historical Resources at Kalahuipuaa." Honolulu, January 1982.

Shimoda, Jerry. "Pu'uhonua-o-Honaunau: Place of Refuge." *National Parks Conservation Magazine.* National Parks Conservation Assn., February 1975.

Soehren, Lloyd. "An Archaeological Survey of the Shores of Ouli and Kawaihae, South Kohala, Hawaii." Department of Anthropology, Bishop Musem, July 1964.

_____. "The Royal Slide at Keauhou, Kona, Hawaii." *Hawaii Historical Review,* January 1966.

Sinoto, Aki. Archaeological Reconnaissance Survey of Kamoa Point, Holualoa Ahupuaa, Hawaii Island.

Department of Anthropology Report 69-5, Bishop Museum, Honolulu, 1971.

Sinoto, Yosihiko, and Kelly, Marion. "Archaeological and Historical Survey of Pakini-Nui and Pakini-Iki Coastal Sites; Waiahukini, Kailikii, and Hawea, Ka'u, Hawaii." Department of Anthropology Report 75-1, Bishop Museum, Honolulu, January 1975.

Sox, David. "Rycroft's Pohoiki: A 19th Century Boat Landing." *Historic Hawaii News.* Honolulu, September 1981.

Stephenson, Larry. *Kohala Keia.* December 1977.

Stevenson, Robert L. *Travels in Hawaii.* Honolulu: University of Hawaii Press, 1973.

Surfing Education Association. "1971 Statewide Surfing Site Survey." Honolulu, 1971.

13 letters to the editor signed "Sailor." *The Polynesian,* October 20, 1849–January 12, 1850.

Thomas, Mifflin. *Schooner from Windward.* Honolulu: University of Hawaii Press, 1983.

Thrum, Thomas G. *Hawaiian Folk Tales.* New York: AMS Press, 1907.

Tilling, Robert, et al. "Earthquake and Related Catastrophic Events, Island of Hawaii, November 29, 1975: A Preliminary Report." Geological Survey Circular 740, U.S. Geological Survey, 1976.

Tinker, Spencer. *Pacific Sea Shells.* Rutland, Vt.: Charles E. Tuttle Co., 1952.

Tuggle, H. David and Griffin, P. Bion. "Lapakahi, Hawaii: Archaeological Studies." Asian and Pacific Archaeological Series No. 5, Social Science Research Institute, University of Hawaii, Honolulu, 1973.

U.S. Army Engineer District, Honolulu. "Pohoiki Bay Navigation Improvement." February 1978.

Walters, Kimura, and Associates, Inc. "Keaukaha Shoreline Plan." N.d.

Westervelt, William. *Hawaiian Historical Legends.* New York: Revell, 1926.

_____. *Hawaiian Legends of Volcanoes.* Rutland, Vt.: Charles E. Tuttle, 1963.

Whitney, Henry M. *The Hawaiian Guide Book, 1875.* Republished by Charles E. Tuttle Co., Rutland, Vt., 1970.

Wilkes, Lt. Charles. *Narrative of the United States Exploring Expedition during the Years 1838–1842.* Philadelphia, 1845.

Wood, Amos L. *Beachcombing for Japanese Fish Floats.* Portland, Oregon: Binford and Mort Publishers, 1967.

Wright, Bank. *Surfing Hawaii.* Los Angeles: Tivoli Printing Co., 1972.

Index

168

About the Author

John R. Kukeakalani Clark, author of *The Beaches of O'ahu* and *The Beaches of Maui County,* is a former lifeguard who excels in a wide variety of ocean sports. He is also actively involved in many sporting competitions, both as an organizer and as a participant. A graduate of the University of Hawaii in Hawaiian Studies, he has worked for the Honolulu Fire Department since 1972. He is also a private consultant on ocean recreation and water safety.